Benjamin William Mkapa

My Life, My Purpose

A Tanzanian President Remembers

Mkuki na Nyota
DAR—ES—SALAAM

PUBLISHED BY
Mkuki na Nyota Publishers Ltd
P. O. Box 4246
Dar es Salaam, Tanzania
www.mkukinanyota.com
© Benjamin William Mkapa 2019
ISBN 978-9987-084-00-5 (Hardback)
ISBN 978-9987-083-03-9 (Paperback)
ISBN 978-9987-083-01-5 (eBook)
Design & Layout: Mkuki Bgoya

Publication of these memoirs was made possible by financial support of UONGOZI Institute.

All rights reserved. No part of this publication may be reproduced, stored in a retrieval system or transmitted in any form or by any means, electronic, mechanical, photocopying, recording, or otherwise, without the prior written permission of Mkuki na Nyota Publishers Ltd.

Visit www.mkukinanyota.com to read more about and to purchase any of Mkuki na Nyota books. You will also find featured authors interviews and news about other publisher/author events. Sign up for our e-newsletters for updates on new releases and other announcements.

Distributed worldwide outside Africa by African Books Collective.
www.africanbookscollective.com

*To my parents, William and Stephania,
The Father of our Nation, Julius Kambarage Nyerere,
and those others who know they have inspired me.*

A Brief Description of Tanzania

The United Republic of Tanzania had an estimated population of 10.4 million people at independence in 1961. The population had grown to 27.4 million when I took office in 1995, and there were 36.1 million citizens at the end of my term in 2005.

Tanzania has a total area of 947,300 square kilometres, which makes it the 32nd largest country in the world, about four times larger than the United Kingdom.

It borders eight countries: Republic of Mozambique, Republic of Malawi, Republic of Zambia, Democratic Republic of the Congo, Republic of Burundi, Republic of Rwanda, Republic of Uganda and Republic of Kenya.

Contents

Foreword by His Excellency Joaquim Chissano . . . . *vii*
Preface . . . . *xi*

Chapter 1
A Test of Our Faith *1*

Chapter 2
Ora et Labora Pray and Work *7*

Chapter 3
Seeds of Awakening *17*

Chapter 4
Facing a Volcano *28*

Chapter 5
Observer of the Struggle *46*

Chapter 6
Writing to Serve Our Nation *55*

Chapter 7
First Steps on My Political Journey *70*

Chapter 8
War With Idi Amin *87*

Chapter 9
We Must Change Ourselves or We Will Be Changed *96*

Chapter 10
Mzee Ukapa and the *Askari wa Miavuli* (Paratroopers) *114*

Chapter 11
Reforms and Yet More Reforms *129*

Chapter 12
Struggling with The Dependency Syndrome *154*

Chapter 13
Internal and Foreign Relations *168*

Chapter 14
"There's no art to find the mind's construction in the face." *195*

Chapter 15
Pseudo Retirement *219*

Chapter 16
The Second *Chimurenga*: Africa's Struggle Continues. *241*

Appendix I
The Arusha Declaration:Part One, The TANU Creed *289*

Appendix II
Socio-economic Achievements of the Third Phase Government
of the United Republic of Tanzania. *291*

Photograph Credits *309*
Index *311*

FOREWORD BY

His Excellency Joaquim Chissano

It is a great pleasure and privilege to write this foreword to the memoirs of a long-standing friend, comrade and colleague, the third president of the United Republic of Tanzania, H.E. Benjamin W. Mkapa. I have known Ben from way back in the 1960s when I was in Tanzania as a member of the Front for Liberation of Mozambique (FRELIMO) and as its chief representative. In those difficult days of our struggle, besides our own resolve to liberate our country, the most important source of our strength was the unwavering support we received from the Tanzanian government and its people, as well as TANU and Afro–Shirazi, the ruling parties that would merge in 1977 to become *Chama Cha Mapinduzi* (CCM).

The solid foundation of solidarity between Tanzania and FRELIMO was laid by Presidents Mwalimu Julius Kambarage Nyerere of Tanzania and Eduardo Chivambo Mondlane of FRELIMO. Their friendship was based on a common vision of, and commitment to, African liberation; a vision and commitment that was in turn carried on by Tanzanians from all walks of life through their parties, TANU and Afro-Shirazi. It was shown by the brotherly way in which they treated us as freedom fighters; by the Tanzanian people's selfless support to our cause, including shedding their blood. On FRELIMO's side, despite setbacks in the early years, we were determined to end the centuries-old Portuguese colonialism whatever price we had to pay.

President Mkapa occupied many important posts in government, but it was from 1966 when he was editor of the TANU newspapers — 'The Nationalist' and 'Uhuru' — that I came to work with him closely. FRELIMO had the full support of these party newspapers. They were in the forefront of mobilising the people to support us in every way possible. His team of journalists never wavered in championing the cause of African liberation; indeed the liberation of all downtrodden people everywhere. Looking back, the level of journalism of the two newspapers under his editorship was, by any standards, very high.

In his memoirs, Ben explains in plain language his long journey from his village, his quest for education and ultimately to his graduation from the University of Makerere. He traces the various positions he held in government, and the challenges and lessons each had in store for him. His closeness to Mwalimu Nyerere, effectively his mentor, inevitably led him to the decision to run for parliament and ultimately to run for the highest office in the land. It is a fascinating story, told with humility but also with wit and language that is peppered every now and then with literary allusions.

He explains the challenges of different posts he held in the government and the satisfaction from achievements as: editor of the party newspapers, 'The Nationalist', 'Uhuru' and later the government newspaper, 'Daily News'; press secretary to Mwalimu Nyerere; head of the Tanzania News Agency (SHIHATA); high commissioner to Canada; ambassador to the United States, high commissioner to Nigeria and finally as foreign minister. In all these positions, one learns of his guiding principles, faith in his religion and interests of his country. With appreciation, he names individuals he worked with, a good number of whom became lasting friends.

The main body of these memoirs is understandably about his ten years as the third president of Tanzania. This will also be the part that most readers will be interested in. It is in this respect that I wish to raise a few points that may be necessary for the reader to fully appreciate the perspectives from which President Mkapa's policies and actions stemmed.

Memories are not about justifying past actions – for that history is the best judge – they are not about settling scores either or seeking vindication for controversial policies undertaken or actions initiated that succeeded or failed. Memoirs are the writer's recollections of time and events, in this case of a political leader, and his or her responses to internal and external events and pressures about which he had to take positions and to provide leadership.

In this foreword, I shall not attempt to list his policy initiatives, particularly in the economic field, coming to power as he did when the Tanzanian economy was in dire situation, and having to initiate negotiations with the World Bank and IMF with their stringent conditionalities. He explains in detail the economic and public service reforms he initiated that brought these two institutions to engage positively with his government, as well as other donors who had withdrawn aid to Tanzania. Other policies, some of them very controversial, are explained in the context of the time, the knowledge and the wisdom that existed then.

He is humble enough to accept in retrospect, mistakes he made politically, and about which he wishes he had acted differently. All in all, President Mkapa's memoirs tell his story as best as his memory serves him, without exaggerations and without rancour or attempt to settle scores with his critics. It is the story of a president of a progressive African country doing his best to deal with the myriad problems that confront it and its people and, by all considerations, it is the story of success against great odds. His successor found the country in a relatively better situation than Ben found it. Evidence of this is that his leadership is still sought at home and even more so abroad among international organisations and think tanks. The Benjamin William Mkapa Foundation is providing greatly needed support in the health sector, proving, if proof were required, that his commitment to improving the lives of ordinary Tanzanians is a lifelong preoccupation. That should be his legacy.

I have always appreciated the role played by my friend Ben, as minister of foreign affairs and as president of the republic, in the building up of the relations between Tanzania and Mozambique, and in the realisation of the noble objectives of the Frontline States, SADCC and SADC. I have enjoyed his deep analysis of the many situations confronting Africa in the context of OAU and later AU, as well as of the global issues in multilateral bodies such as the UN and the Movement of the Non-Aligned Countries.

We Mozambicans were inspired by Tanzanians to promote the development of our country and in the diplomatic front. Yet Ben Mkapa never ceased to encourage us by showing his admiration of whatever he regarded as great achievements of Mozambique. He would not hesitate to learn from us even when we did not give ourselves enough recognition for our country's successes. I would not end without underlining his role in the construction of the unity bridge between Tanzania and Mozambique over the Ruvuma river, which was the joint dream of Mwalimu Julius Kambarage Nyerere and Samora Moisés Machel.

I congratulate *Ndugu* Ben Mkapa for all that he has done for Tanzania, Southern Africa and Africa as a whole and for offering us these excellent memoirs which give us and generations to come a good source of inspiration in our endeavours to build a better future.

Joaquim Alberto Chissano

Preface

Everybody's memories are different, and this book contains my personal account of my unique memories. To spare the reader from a voluminous tome I have chosen to only briefly mention some, not all the key issues throughout my life. Also, I cannot recall everything during my nearly eighty years on this earth! Hence I ask for exculpation if I have omitted some event or person you think I should have included. All errors in recollection are mine and I request your forgiveness if you detect an error. The quotes are my paraphrasing, they are not the actual word by word record of what was said that time. Also, I have been hampered by the scarcity of archival records, especially those relating to matters which occurred during the last century.

This book arose due to encouragement from Joseph Semboja of the UONGOZI Institute in Tanzania. It is not my style to speak about what I encountered and achieved during my life, but he persuaded me of the importance of leaving a record of my career which coincided with a time of great change in my beloved country. I appreciate the opportunity to pay tribute to those who contributed to my personal growth, to the liberation of African States and to leadership in Africa. I am especially grateful that I can provide another perspective of Julius Kambarage Nyerere as a person and as a leader. I am pleased that these memoirs will contribute to Tanzania's political, economic, social and cultural history, for more has been written about our nation by foreigners than by Tanzanians.

As UONGOZI Institute[1] is concerned with leadership in Africa, I have commented on aspects of leadership which I hope may help aspiring leaders. I have also provided some context for those who do not know Tanzania and Africa well, or are too young to know about the formative years of our nation. There is an appendix which provides several indicators for those who like statistics. I thank my personal assistant, Macocha Tembele, and Sonja Tiscenko, for accompanying me on my quest to produce this book.

I hope that this book will inform and inspire a new generation of African leaders, as well as those who want to know more about Tanzania's development. I hope that my memoirs will enrich the history of our beloved country. I hope my book matters to you.

Benjamin William Mkapa
September 2019

---

[1] UONGOZI Institute works with leaders in Africa to promote recognition of the importance of sound leadership and sustainable development. www.uongozi.or.tz

Chapter 1

A Test of Our Faith

How do I start my life's story? I will begin simply. I was born in the Catholic mission hospital at Ndanda. My home was in a village called Lupaso in southern Tanganyika, in the district of Masasi, of the region of Mtwara, which is near the border with Mozambique. My tribe is the Makua, a Bantu ethnic group in South East Africa. Most of the Makua live in Mozambique, where they are the largest tribe. My grandfather said he had crossed the Ruvuma river, which forms the border between Mozambique and Tanzania, looking for new land to farm. The Makua are a matriarchal society; my surname, Mkapa, is my mother's clan name, not my father's.

Lupaso had a church, a primary school and a dispensary, all run by the Roman Catholic missionaries. The Christian missionaries provided much for the welfare of the people throughout the country, establishing a church, school and health facility wherever they settled. In those days there were much fewer government schools and health dispensaries than those provided by missionaries. The housing in the village was basic, mud huts with thatched roofs; only the church and the priest's house had corrugated iron for the roof.

My father, William Matwani, was a catechist in the Roman Catholic Church, as well as a bush school teacher. In the large geographical parishes in Africa, priests could only visit different parts of their parish periodically due to the difficulty of travelling in those days and the substantial distances to be covered. Thus, the parish catechist took on the role of a teacher of the Faith in the parish, aiding the missionaries to spread the Word amongst the people. My father must have been one of the earliest converts in my part of the country. He had been working as an assistant cook for the missionaries at Ndanda and would accompany a priest as he travelled from station to station around the extensive parish. The missionaries saw his potential, so taught him to read and write and about the Catechism. He was then formally appointed as a catechist and sent to Lupaso. The missionaries sought to address the absence of schools for us natives as there were so few government schools throughout the country and it was difficult to spread the faith when people cannot read or write. Hence they innovated 'bush schools', which taught rudimentary reading, writing and arithmetic. Thus my father led an itinerant life, travelling from village to village to convert people to Catholicism and to teach basic literacy. From time to time we would join my father at a missionary station where he was working.

My mother, Stephania Nambanga, was illiterate; she had no opportunity to go to school when she was a child. In adulthood she was so hard-pressed with her major concern of providing food for our family that she could not take the time to learn to read and write. Stephanie was the foundation stone of our family, a woman of fortitude. Our mother was stricter with us children than my father. She was a tough person, though to be fair maybe she had to be that way with my father so often away. Stephanie was a great listener and thoughtful in her conclusions, while my father was more extrovert, though also good at listening to others. They lived together in conditions of tremendous integrity and mutual respect, sharing a common love for their children.

The missionary influence was very great on us; obviously we all were raised with the Catholic faith. My father's strong desire was that I would become a priest, failing that a doctor or teacher; but his heartfelt wish was for me to become a priest. A great deal of emphasis was placed on education by both our parents. Despite my mother not having received any formal education, she valued it and encouraged us to study diligently. She was a far-sighted woman who made sacrifices for our future.

I am the last born, with three siblings. There is a three-year age gap between us children, which was notable for that time when there was no birth control. My sister, Marcella, was born in late 1928, my oldest brother Blasius was born in 1932, followed by Bernard in 1935, and on 12 November 1938, I was born. Marcella became a primary school teacher. Blasius went to primary school, but it was quite a tough regime at the boarding school, and he couldn't bear it beyond grade six, so he absconded from school and came back home. Subsequently, he would seek clerical jobs in various places in South East Tanzania. Blasius was the one who helped to kindle my interest in politics, he was a fervent nationalist. My immediate elder brother, Bernard, went to school up to the tenth grade, which was quite remarkable at the time. He passed what was called the Standard Ten Territorial Examination, which qualified one to work for the government. We were a close-knit family and Bernard was especially caring of me.

Marcella got married quite quickly after completing her teaching course and left home with her teacher husband. They were sent to teach at a school quite far away from home. With Marcella and Blasius away, it fell to Bernard and me to help our mother work on the land and keep house. There were too many womanly chores around the household to be undertaken by my mother without my sister's help, especially as she had to carry the extra burden of the duties my father couldn't undertake as he was often working away from home. Hence Stephanie taught us boys to do traditional girls' work' such as fetching water and firewood, which was unusual in a traditional society such as ours where the roles of males and females were clearly defined. In addition to working on the little plots of land where we grew maize, legumes and other vegetables, we helped our mother with all the daily chores. I believe this experience of shared labour taught me a tolerant approach to relationships between brothers and sisters, men and women. It also helped me not to have a discriminating attitude to others, as whatever work had to be done was done, no matter who you were.

Our staple food at that time was maize flour and beans, which is the main food for my tribe. Most of this we grew ourselves, but after a while the land around the village lost fertility so we had to go further and further away from the village to find new land to cultivate. The plot we had was about ten kilometres away; quite a distance to walk to and from home every day, so when it was a busy period of planting or harvesting we would camp there. We would build a small mud hut with a thatched grass roof and live there with our mother. The hut would be partitioned in two, with one part for our mother and the other side for us boys.

Traditionally the Makuas shared a cooperative or collective attitude towards each other. For example, if someone had a big plot of land which he couldn't clear in time before planting, he would prepare some food and brew some beer and call in everyone to help weed the land on a certain day. We would weed until about two in the afternoon then go to the landowner's home and to eat and drink what he had made for us. Or you might be rewarded with part of the harvest if it was that work which we had done. This meant that those workers could also call upon others there to help them when they needed it.

The only source of cash income for most people in the village was their agricultural produce, such as cashew nuts, groundnuts and simsim (sesame seed), which they sold to the local Indian traders. It was a buyer's market, with little if any competition at all. Worse still, the native clerks working for the Indian merchants would often conspire with them to short-change the peasant farmer by tampering with the weights. Those clerks would then be rewarded by a share of what had been fleeced from the farmer's dues. There was quite a bit of agitation about this unfairness, so eventually the colonial government intervened by introducing a system of regulated weights and measures, thereby creating a significant improvement in the payments to the peasant farmers. Then, in the early 1950s the colonial government established and supervised proper trading centres, called the Native Authority Centres, which introduced competition amongst the buyers, thus helping to reduce exploitation of the peasants, as well as improve their incomes.

My mother, Stephania, was one of four children; she was the third in a family of three girls and one boy: Cyriaca, Benjamin (from whom I have my name), Stephanie and Agnes. Attending school was rare in those days, as there weren't enough schools for the population. Those who did have the opportunity to go to school tended to be boys, as people viewed girls as destined to help their mothers at home and then become mothers themselves, therefore education for them was regarded as unnecessary. My uncle, Benjamin, attended primary school, the only one from my mother's family to do so. Although all my mother's siblings were married in church, my mother's marriage was the only one which lasted. Her sisters had children as well, though not by one father, there was an element of instability in her family. Stephanie's family and siblings looked upon her lifestyle as better than their own. This caused a certain aloofness and occasional tension amongst the extended family, which was not in keeping with the tradition of ones' family not being your immediate mother, father and siblings, but the entire extended family.

Another aspect which set my family apart from the Mkapa clan and other clans of the area, such as the Milanzis and Mropes, and created a bit of tension was that we were perceived as being privileged. As a catechist and unqualified teacher, my father had an assured monthly income, however small it was; a rarity in a community where the majority did not earn a regular paid income. It was also rare that all four of us children were educated, including my sister. This meant we had better prospects, but it also set us apart from others in our village.

This envy and tension culminated in a horrific event which affected us all and is still painful for me to recall now. I think I was in grade two or three, so I would have been around eight or nine years old. Our father was away working, so it was just us two boys and mother at home. There was a serious drought during 1947, which meant that people were suffering with not enough food as crops were failing. The men of our clan had left the village to seek jobs on the coast. This included my uncle, Benjamin, who would had been a formidable opponent if he had been there, but he was away working on a sisal estate in Lindi. Despite there being Christians and a few Muslims in our community; most still believed in witchcraft and many thought that someone had 'killed the rains' with witchcraft. A witch doctor looked around and settled on my grandmother and great grandmother, who were aged widows, as the ones who had stopped the rains and caused this severe drought. It was common for old women to be accused of being witches. To my regret accusations of witchcraft occasionally still happen today, not just in Tanzania, but in other African countries as well. Many blameless old women have suffered or died due to this.

A big assembly of people from several villages came to us and dragged out my great grandmother, grandmother and mother who were interrogated and beaten; tortured to confess that they practiced witchcraft and had caused the rains to fail. There was nothing we two boys could do to defend our mother and grandmothers. I remember my older brother Bernard, who would have been around twelve, trying to pull away my mother and grandmothers to prevent the crowd from assaulting them; but he was kicked away by the adults. Bernard still gets worked up about this, saying, "If I was bigger I would have killed nine of them before they managed to subdue me".

It was dreadful, I will never forget what happened. They tortured my grandmother and great grandmother; my great grandmother did not live very long after that torture. My mother was not tortured as much, though as they were together she had to watch her mother and grandmother suffering horribly. One of the torture contraptions they used consisted of two pieces of wood bound together like pincers, which were put on their heads and pressed from either side. The torture went on and on, with Bernard and I forced to watch.

Eventually, the parish priest learnt of what was happening and rushed to remonstrate against the villagers, who would not listen to him at first. Even though he was white and therefore expected respect and obedience, the villagers did not fear him as they were so worked up with the frenzy of what they were doing. Finally, the priest succeeded in getting the torturers to stop and get these three poor women to his mission station. The villagers followed him to the station, scolding and cursing him; it was a very tense situation. Thankfully, the district commissioner learnt about this and sent the police who arrested some of the torturers and calmed down the villagers.

It was a shock that our neighbours could turn on us. However, our family's faith remained strong, despite this being an extreme and horrifying test of our faith. This deeply traumatic incident showed me that sometimes one's faith can only be skin deep. Many of those torturers were Christians by name, but when it came to a severe difficulty in their life they were ready to fall back to their old beliefs; they failed their test of faith.

Over time the enmity amongst the villagers evaporated and despite what had happened our sense of belonging to the community was unbroken; we remained in the village and continued to cooperate with our neighbours. My father followed the commandment that you must love your neighbour and I imagine our parents' distress would have been assuaged somewhat by the torturers being tried and imprisoned for around eighteen months to two years. My bond to Lupaso village persists until today; I have a home there to which I return as often as I can.

Chapter 2

Ora et Labora
Pray and Work

There were two Catholic dioceses in our region then, Ndanda and Peramiho, which had predominantly German and Swiss missionaries and offered secondary school education. To get into fifth grade, which was secondary school, you had to sit an examination which was set by the diocese, as there was no government secondary school in the whole Southern Region at that time, which stretched from Mbamba Bay on Lake Nyasa, Songea, all the way up to Mtwara and Lindi on the Indian Ocean, a large area of 143,026 square kilometres, which is approximately 60% of United Kingdom's land area today. The missionary teachers and parish priest judged whether you could progress to secondary school based on the results of this examination, though the diocese didn't publish the results. If you were Catholic, you would go to Ndanda secondary school; while if you were Anglican you went to the Anglican missionary secondary school at nearby Chidya. There was a healthy rivalry in sports and the like between these two schools. I sat this fifth-grade examination in 1948 and the teachers at the mission school in Lupaso and the parish priest determined that I should progress to the secondary school in Ndanda, where my brothers Blasius and Bernard had progressed before me.

In later years, when I returned to Lupaso I would look at my fellow classmates from primary school and wonder how it was that I, out of a group of about twenty-five to thirty pupils, was selected with just one other to progress to secondary school. I am sure that there were other pupils in our class who were as good as we were, yet they did not receive this opportunity to advance their education. In those days there were so few opportunities for education, it was almost like a kind of lottery of who would 'win' and progress to secondary school. Many of us from my age group are really winners in the grand lottery for rare secondary education scholarships. How much more prepared would our country have been at independence if the colonialists had provided sufficient education opportunities to Tanganyikans? Furthermore, where would we have been without these dedicated missionaries providing education?

Ndanda is about sixty kilometres from my village of Lupaso, and for us there was no transport except your own two feet; so we walked all the way to our secondary school at Ndanda. It was tough going to walk this far and at ten years old I was the youngest of the group of school students going from the mission station at Lupaso to Ndanda. To make it worse, as the smallest my strides were shorter than those of the other students walking, some of whom were six years older than me. No adult accompanied us; the older children led the way and as there weren't many dangerous wild animals about, we didn't feel threatened. Nevertheless, it was still only a group of six to eight children walking alone all that distance of around sixty kilometres. We walked barefoot as no-one owned shoes at that time; it was particularly hard going during the hot dry season.

We couldn't make that journey in one day, so would spend the night at an Anglican missionary station at Mpindimbi. We would arrive unannounced and ask if we could spend the night at the Anglican school. I have the fondest respect for the missionary teachers there; they were very hospitable, regardless of the difference in our religious denomination. They would provide us with bed nets, as well as pots and pans to prepare our food. We carried food with us from home and sometimes these kind teachers would give us some additional food. We would gather firewood, cook our food and then sleep in a classroom. We would start walking very early the next morning because we didn't want the sun's full heat to hit us, wearily arriving at Ndanda by mid-afternoon on the second day of our trek.

Our baggage was simple during the first years I went to Ndanda secondary school. Bernard and I rolled our possessions inside the woven mat our father made for each of us and carried the mats on our heads. It was not until our third year of walking to school that we were able to obtain metal boxes and carry our belongings in these boxes, though still on our heads. I see some children use similar metal boxes going to boarding school even today.

Later during my time at school, when the term ended my fellow students from the village, who were more grown up, wanted to walk home in one day. We tried to walk the sixty kilometres in one day, but I couldn't keep up as I was still the youngest and smallest. Eventually, they felt sorry for me and left me behind to stay the night at the Anglican school, and Bernard stayed with me for he would not leave me alone. The others proceeded on to Lupaso; Bernard had asked them to tell our father where we were, and to find someone who had a bicycle to come to collect me and our luggage, while Bernard would walk the last stretch home alone. Being taken by bicycle for this last stretch was great, my first time taking 'public transport'!

At that time, the main means of transport for everyone was on foot. Vehicles were rarely seen; only the district officer and district commissioner had vehicles, also the Indian traders who came to buy crops from the peasantry. A vehicle was such a rare incident that when you heard that there was one coming you would go to the road and put your ear to the ground to listen for the rumble of its approach; we were so excited that we were going to see a vehicle. When the bishop came to conduct a church service we would stand along the roadside with palms to wave to greet him. During the early 1950s government took over the responsibility to pay the salary of those teachers at missionary schools and their newfound prosperity manifested itself by the fact that they could afford to buy bicycles. You looked up to someone who owned a bicycle as being advanced indeed, this was development! There were four brands of bicycles you could buy: Rajah, Raleigh, Aruj and Gazelle, all heavy and made in India. It was a proud moment for my family when my father had saved enough money to buy his first bicycle. I was happy when father finally could buy his own bicycle and could meet us on the way home from school to give me a lift.

The missionaries at Ndanda were of the Order of St Benedict – the Monks of St Ottilien. They have a very strict code of life which is encapsulated in their phrase '*Ora et Labora*' – 'Pray and Work'. It's not surprising that I was demanding of myself and others in my adult life, as much was demanded of me by the missionaries who educated me and brought me up, coupled with my father's high expectations of me.

These were Benedictine priests from Germany and Switzerland; except for an English priest who taught English and an American priest who taught physics, chemistry and biology. Our teachers, especially the German ones, could be quite demanding. There were also some Tanganyikan teachers who had completed their grade ten, followed by two years of teacher training. They dressed in black shoes, long white socks, white shorts and white shirts, and usually taught the junior grades. I recall my mathematics teacher, Aloyce Chungu from Iringa; we liked him immensely, he was a fine gentleman who undoubtedly influenced me to like maths. Another of our indigenous teachers, Vincent Mponji, would later enter politics and eventually became a deputy minister in the prime minister's office. There were Benedictine sisters who taught maths, geography and history. They were very conscientious in their work, though sometimes a bit shy. This was the first time I had a female teacher and some boys found it strange at first to be taught by a woman.

The secondary school had an average of around twenty-five students in each class, with around 250 students in the whole school. The small class size meant that our teachers got to know us very well. While there had been both boys and girls, though fewer girls, at primary school, only a few girls went on to secondary school. They had a different syllabus to us boys and were taught by the Benedictine sisters in a convent school.

Although most of the priests, monks and nuns were German, they did not teach the German language and all classes were held in English. Those of the staff who had been in Tanganyika during World War II had been sequestered by the British, along with German farmers and tradespeople. The teachers had to be careful not to be seen to be subverting the British, so their syllabus reflected the British perspective. The textbooks were the standard territorial textbooks; the Benedictines only used their textbooks for religious instruction. Our teaching did incorporate our local environment to some degree; for instance, our studies of geography began with the geography of Tanganyika, then we moved on to Africa. When we studied the geography of the world; it was predominantly the British Empire, for Tanganyika was administered by the United Kingdom as a trust territory of the United Nations. History lessons concerned

British colonial history; so we learned about countries such as Nigeria, Australia and Canada. For our country's history we only learnt about the First and Second World Wars. However, for sciences there was an effort to produce local textbooks. I liked the English classes because we had the opportunity to read additional books which were not part of the curriculum; my favourite authors were Shakespeare and Dickens.

My favourite textbook was called '*Kwa nini na kwa namna gani?*' – 'Why and how?'. This book addressed issues analytically – focussing on why something happened and how, rather than merely addressing what happened. My tendency to think analytically was showing at this young age. This is my biggest complaint about today's media; journalism's '5 Ws' of who, what, where, when, why and how is not followed by the media. They do not conduct analysis these days, rather just repeat what someone has said. Another favourite book during my time at school was '*Aesop's Fables*'.

My best and favourite subjects were maths and English, all the way up to university. I liked science, particularly physics, but struggled with biology and chemistry and didn't qualify to study this at university. In maths I liked geometry and algebra very much; I liked the logic of equal angles; I think this reinforced my inquisitiveness. The teachers at Ndanda taught us to read out loud and we were required to read clearly. When I listen to the newsreaders nowadays I am horrified, as they have not been taught how to read out loud. At Ndanda we were introduced to the phenomenon of films; we looked with such wonder at those films which showed such a different world to ours.

The Benedictine teaching not only influenced my faith, it helped build my character. Their attitude towards work and self-discipline was fantastic and influences me to this day. The rules in the school were clear and we all obeyed them, regardless of what we thought of them. A whistle at 5 a.m. woke us; we then lined up bare chested in the school square and said our morning prayers. Then we would greet the priest in unison "Good morning Father". After a cold-water wash we would line up and march to the church for morning mass. After mass we would clean our dormitory, while someone amongst us would prepare our maize gruel *uji* for breakfast, for we pupils cooked our own food. Then we lined up and marched to class. There was an enforced rest time of one hour from 12.30 p.m. when we had to lie on our beds and were not allowed to read or talk. If we were caught doing either then we were punished by being made to sit in the glare of the full midday sun. Classes resumed at 1.30 until 4 p.m., followed by recreation such as football or working in the school's gardens. We had a swimming pool at the school, which was extraordinary for those times. Prayer followed the evening meal, then a period of study before bed.

On Saturdays we only had a few hours of study for we had to prepare our food for the next week, collect firewood, wash and iron our clothes and clean the school's rooms and grounds. Of course we still went to church in the evening. On Sundays there was no school, though we had Compline prayers during the afternoon. Late afternoon we were allowed out of the school compound to go to the village. The route we were allowed to take was determined by the priests and we had to be back on time or we would get into a lot of trouble. We had two holidays during the school year. One coincided with the early days of preparing the land for planting, this was before Christmas; which meant that we could spend Christmas at home. Then we would come home for the harvest, which was around May–June. It was a very strict regime at school, almost military, which conditioned our bodies to accept rules and time keeping. I am grateful to the Benedictines for this discipline as it has had a great positive influence on me throughout my life

The buildings of the secondary school at Ndanda were mud huts with grass thatch; even the priests' residence was grass thatched, though during my time at school these roofs were tiled. The food at Ndanda improved during the last years I was there. At first our breakfast was plain gruel without sugar or salt. Then we were given sugar (*sukari guru*), a brownish semi-processed sugar; eventually this was upgraded to white sugar. At first we received sugar once a week, then twice a week, then every day; what a treat! We had meat to eat on average twice a month, as well as the local small sardines, *dagaa*, twice a month. I cannot recall ever having eggs or bread to eat while at school. Our lunch was maize meal which we prepared ourselves accompanied by beans, which were prepared in the school's kitchen. Because we cooked most of our food we also had to gather our own firewood and lay the fires. As I was the youngest in my class there were only a few chores I was good at, one being washing the cooking pans. After every meal I would put the cooking pans on my head and carry them that way to where I washed them. This method of carrying pans on my head is the reason I give now for my baldness!

During our first two years at secondary school our uniform was a piece of white cloth called a *shuka*, which is a kind of sarong, along with a white shift which had no sleeves or buttons. I used to wear this occasionally at university to tease my teachers as part of the anti-colonial struggle. Later we received shorts, though still no shoes; all pupils were barefoot. We had to wash and iron our own clothes.

Secondary school is where I encountered other tribes for the first time; for at my primary school the students were all fellow Makuas. Ndanda secondary school took in students from the whole Southern Region; the large intake area meant that I now encountered all the tribes of southern Tanganyika. We were permitted to speak in Kiswahili or English outside of class, but not our local language as this would have set the tribes apart from each other. There was good camaraderie between us students; despite that we came from different tribes our shared Faith brought us together.

My elder brother, Bernard, was strong and good at physical chores, but he wasn't a fast learner; he was required to repeat sixth grade which meant we were in the same class. Bernard was protective of me, but I had to learn to be my own man at secondary school. One or two of my classmates were born the same year as me, but I was always the youngest and smallest in any class, all the way through my schooling. I felt inadequate at times, especially because I could not manage some of the physical chores we had to do around the school. Another effect of my size and age was that I was not a sportsman of any kind and I couldn't qualify for anything. No wonder when I became president many said, "This is a president who has no time for sports".

Many of us were classmates from the fifth grade through to university. Three have remained lifelong friends: Philip Magani became an agricultural officer, rising to become the head of National Agricultural and Food Corporation (NAFCO) and the National Ranching Company (NARCO). He was also the first African head of the CRDB bank in Tanzania and a member of parliament when I was president. John Kambona did a general science degree, began as a fisheries officer and ended up working for the Food and Agricultural Organisation in Rome. Benno Nkane became a teacher.

The most contact we had with non-Tanganyikans was with the missionaries. There was an underlying feeling that the missionaries were not necessarily superior to us, but certainly better. One or two of the teachers would show sentiments of superiority to us Africans calling us 'black man', but that seldom happened at our school, and in that sense our school was very egalitarian indeed. Mind you, the missionaries picked who they thought were the best to come to secondary school; so perhaps it was easier for them to consider that we were ok. You saw that the missionaries were obviously materially better-off than you were of course; they dressed better and ate better food; we students only ate maize flour and beans. Seeing what the missionaries possessed subliminally drove me to study hard as I wanted a better life for myself.

There were no European settlers in our area, other than the few British administrators. The district officer would occasionally visit the school and talk to the headmaster, but not to us students. If the district commissioner was travelling in the district while you were home on holiday then you would go to watch the public meetings. There was also the district agricultural officer who would come to inspect the farms. We had more contact with the Indian community, as there were Indian shopkeepers around every ten kilometres or so, as well as a few Arab traders. The Indians were also the clerks for the British administration and there were also the Seychellois who usually worked for the public works department as mechanics and supervisors.

It wasn't a question of blatant discrimination, but you did notice you were being made to feel different, especially with the Indians, though to be fair they were the foreigners we encountered most. If you were in a shop and a European came into the shop then the Indian shopkeeper would leave serving you to attend to the European. There was this subtle differentiation, which may have started the drive within me to join the anti-colonial struggle later.

Usually by the time you join secondary school you will have undergone the traditional rite of passage for a boy or girl. I was at a disadvantage because I had not gone through this rite of passage; everyone at secondary school would look at me with a little contempt. I was already the youngest in the entire school and physically small, but the fact that I was not circumcised meant I was regarded as a little boy, yet I was eleven. So, during my first long vacation from secondary school, my father arranged for a special rite of passage for me and two other boys from our village of Lupaso. Usually not less than thirty boys from the area would attend this rite of passage, but a special one was organised to ensure I could return to school with some male dignity.

The rites of passage to manhood or womanhood are regarded with great importance by the Makua. For boys there are six weeks of intense exclusion, when you are taught the manners of the tribe, how to greet elders, how to deal with one another, attitude towards women, and of course you were circumcised. We experienced the adventure of being taught how to hunt and how to provide for the family. Girls went through a shorter rite and the Makua tribe did not circumcise girls unlike some other tribes in Tanzania. In my time the circumcision was done in the bush, nowadays circumcision is done in a clinical way, many go to the dispensary to have their circumcision. There is still the six-week exclusion in an encampment though.

During this period of exclusion you have a mentor, (*namku*), who is supposed to be in charge of your education and food during the time you are in camp for this rite. If you are not obedient your *namku* has every right to beat you; their punishments could be quite harsh. This rite teaches you about social mores and traditions, the dos and don'ts, as well as a little bit about the history of your tribe. You are taught that you must now start to be self-reliant; you are on your path to becoming a man. It is a valuable way for a young person to ground himself and gain a sense of belonging; while also prompting you to start thinking about your personal moral code. The shared experience of this initiation rite forges a sense of community amongst those attending; we boys from the 'class of 48' formed a strong bond.

When you have completed this rite and return home you are not supposed to spend a night under the same roof where you lived with your parents ever again. Ideally, once you return to your village the first thing you do is build a hut of your own; building your home is a sign of your newfound maturity after completing this rite of passage. However, I couldn't build one then because I was returning to secondary school.

How you would do such a rite of passage now I don't know. Certainly, present day upbringing is not conducive to the kind of wholesome self-growth that I was taught during my rite of passage; particularly with regards to relations with colleagues, elders and those in authority. I think there is a strong deficiency in the way young people treat such persons nowadays. For example, it surprises me today how during sessions in the Tanzanian parliament members of parliament sometimes address the prime minister, for example, with disdain and disrespect. A person can be wrong, but there is a way of telling him he is wrong in a dignified manner; their position in authority means that they should be treated with respect. I don't know how this lost aspect of respect for and courtesy towards others can be recaptured nowadays. I hope there is a way in which a rite of passage for young people could be brought into their lives. If they don't like religion, well fine, but this way of imparting to the young people the do's and don'ts, and their place in society should take place during a critical time of their development. I feel they are missing this important element of self-awareness and personal growth.

Another aspect of my personal growth was my Catholic faith. I received the Holy Communion when I was between seven and eight years old; Confirmation when I was around nine or ten. It was a matter of fervently learning by rote and an act of faith; at that time there was very little reasoning. Religious instruction was the imparting of known fact and history: the existence of God, His mercy and His anger. God was always 'He', though in Kiswahili it is not very clear whether God is a he or she. At secondary school they tried to teach you about religion by rationalising the tenets you had learnt by rote when you were younger. I remember a terrific book we read at the senior secondary school I attended after Ndanda: *'Apologetics and Catholic Doctrine'* by Archbishop Michael Sheehan covered rationalising the Faith, assimilating it, internalising it, making it part of your life.

This combination of experiencing a traditional rite of passage, being received into the Catholic Church with Holy Communion and then Confirmation, as well as living under the disciplinarian missionaries strongly influenced my lifestyle and attitude to work as an adult: *Ora et Labora*.

Chapter 3

Seeds of Awakening

My father said "I want any one of these futures for you: first as a priest. If this is impossible I hope that you will become a doctor, but if those two are impossible then at least become a teacher". After being persuaded to become a priest by my father and my headmaster at Ndanda secondary school I decided that I should attend a seminary. Thus, when I completed seventh grade after three years at Ndanda, I joined the junior Benedictine seminary at Kigonsera, in the Ruvuma region, Southern Tanganyika. Founded in 1897, it was one of the largest Catholic missions and abbeys in Africa. This major seminary later became known as Peramiho seminary.

I was nearly 15 years old in 1952 when I began eighth grade at the Catholic seminary. My father was very happy indeed, saying to many "He's on his way to becoming a priest". But I felt restless there, for while my faith remained strong, I was not sure if I was destined to become a priest. A factor was the relationship that existed between the predominantly German white Benedictines and the African priests, who were beginning to be ordained then. The Germans tended to be rather aloof to the Africans, though to be fair it was their cultural background to be somewhat aloof and formal. I don't know if there was a distinction between the Benedictines at Kigonsera and the ones at Ndanda; perhaps those at Ndanda were more enlightened in their attitude to Africans. Although this was the same Catholic Church, I felt uneasy within this atmosphere.

My disquiet was highlighted by a visit to the seminary by the Catholic Dutch bishop of Mwanza, Joseph Blomjous; his visit made a big impression on me. The morning of his departure there was a difficulty with his car; Bishop Blomjous removed his cassock, put on overalls and went under the car to sort out the problem with the African driver. I noted his attitude towards his driver – they were equals, the bishop was not condescending towards him at all. Bishop Blomjous was extremely liberal; while the predominantly German Catholic priests expected you to be very respectful of the bishop. I could not accept that inequality, as the Bible says: we were all one under the eyes of God. I went to the rector and told him that I was quite certain that I was not called to the priesthood. He was shocked and gave me three weeks to ponder about it, advising "I am sure that if you pray you will be enlightened". Despite praying hard, I couldn't persuade myself to stay, so after three weeks I returned to the rector, apologised and declared I wanted to leave the seminary. The rector asked me to dedicate myself to pray for one more week to be absolutely sure and after that week I was even more resolute to leave. The rector wished me well and arranged for me to rejoin my classmates at Ndanda for the tenth grade. When I returned to Ndanda secondary school friends laughed at me and said that they had been quite sure that I would not become a priest! My father was naturally disappointed, though not angry; hoping that I would study to become a doctor, his second choice of career for me.

I was happy to be back at Ndanda secondary school; there were some events which I fondly remember to this day. My fellow students from the upper classes took part in two musicals: Gilbert and Sullivan's *'The Mikado'* and Rodgers and Hammerstein's *'The King and I'*. After the Second World War the British had started a scheme to grow groundnuts for peanut butter, hence there was quite a large community of British expatriates in Nachingwea who came to see our school's productions. I became very interested in drama and when I progressed to St Francis College Pugu I always was involved in the school's theatre productions. Another event I have happy memories of was a treat during our tenth grade when we were taken by lorry to Mtwara to see the sea for the first time. This outing was intended to relax our mind and ease pre-exam tension. Such a memorable occasion; the sea was an incredible sight and it was the first time I was in a lorry, we pupils sat in the deck on the back.

The final year at the Ndanda secondary school, the tenth grade, was the critical year of your schooling, culminating in the national exams. I passed the Territorial Standard Ten National Exams well, being first in my class at Ndanda and given a First by the Ministry of Education. In those days education was the only path to an improved way of life, of being able to gain a job where you could earn enough to enjoy some of the luxuries experienced by the missionaries and British administrators. The government would send forms to all the grade ten graduating students listing jobs available; you submitted your form applying for a government position and then waited for the government's response advising that you had been selected to be a veterinary, policeman or to proceed to teacher training, for example. I applied to become a sub-inspector of police, which was the rank you went straight into. When the headmaster Father Gereon Schramm saw my application form he called me in and said "What is this? You don't want to study more?"

"This is what I want to be", I replied, then asked, "What more is there to study?"

He told me about grades eleven and twelve and university; none of my siblings or acquaintances had progressed beyond grade ten. After completing their grade ten my sister had gone to teacher training and my brother Bernard into the civil service. I simply didn't know that there was more education to be gained beyond grade ten. "Oh, well then I am ready for grade eleven," I replied. My headmaster was strict and dedicated; he really adhered to *Ora et Labora*. It was his timely intervention that resulted in me progressing to grade 11 and I am thankful that he encouraged me to study further. My father was very proud as I was advancing the farthest of his children; he still desired me to become a doctor and this was a step in the right direction.

I was selected for St Francis College, Pugu, which was near to Dar es Salaam, the capital of Tanganyika. Dar es Salaam was the largest town in Tanganyika then, recording a population of around 128,000 in 1957. The city amazed me, it was my first time in a city, there were so many Indians, so many Europeans, so many buildings. It was an eye-opener, I had never seen anything like this before.

St Francis College was the first national Catholic senior secondary school established in Tanganyika; it was attended by the most promising pupils selected from all the Catholic secondary schools in Tanganyika. The first president of Tanganyika, Julius Nyerere taught history, English and Kiswahili there from 1953–1955. I was a student there during 1955–1956. The school commenced at grade eleven and you would sit the Cambridge School Certificate Examination at the end of grade twelve, which determined whether you could enter Makerere University College in Uganda; there being no university in Tanganyika at that time.

I didn't feel that I was being deliberately groomed for the future of my country, but I was conscious of the privileged education I was receiving, because so few were able to go to senior secondary school. It is difficult to obtain verified data from this period, though *'The Colonial Office List 1957'*[1] states that in 1955 there were 1,813 African students at secondary school, 30,845 at middle school, and 310,089 at primary school. Indian, non-Asian and European students were counted separately. However, only not all of these secondary schools offered the opportunity to sit for the Cambridge School Certificate Examination. In 1951 only three of the nineteen secondary schools offered the opportunity to sit the Cambridge School Certificate Examination, St Francis College Pugu being one of those three secondary schools. Passing this examination was a prerequisite to gaining entrance to Makerere University College, Uganda. I have been told that by 1960 a cumulative total of only 480 Tanganyikans from all the senior secondary schools in Tanganyika had completed twelve years of schooling and sat the Cambridge School Certificate examination during all the preceding years. There were some government schools, though few; the equivalent government school to St Francis was Tabora Boys' Senior Secondary School, which Julius Nyerere had attended as a pupil. The Anglican equivalent of St Francis was St Andrew's College, Minaki, which we had sporting fixtures with.

I am thankful for the contribution the Catholic and Anglican missionaries made to the education of us Tanganyikans. They helped to produce

---

[1] *'The Colonial Office List 1957'*. London: Her Majesty's Stationery Office. Information provided by the Foreign and Commonwealth Office and made available under the Open Government Licence for public sector information, version 3.

a cadre of immediate post-independence workers in the government and private sector, much larger in number than those the British administration had educated. The colonial administration failed us indigenous Tanganyikans in that sense. *'The Colonial Office List of 1951'*[2] states that there were eight government and Native Authority secondary schools for 'Africans'. We were classified as distinct from the Colonial Office's categories of 'Europeans', 'Asians' and 'other non-Native'; while there were nineteen secondary schools run by 'voluntary agencies', such as the missionaries. This failure by the British administration also contributed to reduced opportunities for people of other faiths, particularly Muslim students. While the missionary schools were not discriminatory, and at Ndanda secondary school there were at least three Muslim students during my time there, generally Muslim students preferred to attend government schools, as they were secular. As there were few government secondary schools this meant that Muslim students were at a disadvantage because they had fewer opportunities for secondary education. What's more, the government secondary schools were in the cities, such as the schools in Tabora and Dar es Salaam. This meant that despite the large number of Muslims in our nation, they were under-represented in the higher ranks of the post-independence civil service.

There was a diverse representation of the Tanganyikan population at St Francis College; the chief tribes represented were from Moshi, Bukoba, Mwanza, Mbeya and Iringa, tribes quite culturally different to my own. We were also exposed for the first time to the racial differentiation in education; there were African schools, Indian schools and a few European schools. We would come into Dar es Salaam for elocution competitions with the Indian secondary schools; which St Francis usually won. I think that by enrolling us in these competitions the Fathers were trying to show us that race did not matter and to instil confidence in our future ability to contribute to our nation.

The Fathers were Holy Ghost Fathers, all from Ireland. I expect that

---

2   *'The Colonial Office List 1951'.* Colonial No. 265. London: Her Majesty's Stationery Office. Information provided by the Foreign and Commonwealth Office and made available under the Open Government Licence for public sector information, version 3.

coming from Ireland at that time it was likely that they also came from rural and perhaps impoverished backgrounds, though not as simple a background as most of us pupils. They also would have had an appreciation of what it was like to be ruled by others, due to their own country's history, though the Fathers were very careful not to speak against our colonial rulers. The Fathers hoped that our religious instruction would help us to be morally and ethically upright; they strived to instil a lifelong core of integrity within us. For the sake of acknowledging the important contribution to the development of Tanganyikans by these worthy men from St Francis College, I would like to record their names: our headmaster was called Father James (Jamie) Lynch; Father Liam O'Sullivan taught mathematics; Father Liam (William) O'Connor taught history and geography, and from him we learnt for the first time about countries gaining independence, such as United States of America and India. Father Michael McTiernan was my English teacher; other Fathers I recall were Cyril Byrne, Bartholomew (Bertie) Lyons and Cornelius (Con) Foley. The positive effect of the missionaries on the education of Tanganyikans in those days should never be forgotten. There were a few indigenous teachers, Julius Nyerere was among them during my first year there; a banner hangs in my home at Dar es Salaam showing an old photo of some teachers from St Francis College, Nyerere included.

The teachers were very good, and our lessons were held in English. The conditions were similar to Ndanda secondary school, though the classes were larger; with fifty-one of us sitting the Cambridge Certificate of Education in my final year. We read intensely, everyone had a favourite tree to sit under where we would read. There was a lot of essay writing; this required you to think and have a good vocabulary. We had a lot of debates within the school, which helped us to focus and to reason. The learning style was not rote, we were expected to think and reflect and rationalise, especially about religion. The approach of Q.E.D.[3] which I learnt there has proved useful throughout my working life.

I continued to enjoy mathematics and English, especially debating and drama, acting as Lady Macbeth in Shakespeare's *'Macbeth'* and

---

3   Q.E.D. *quod erat demostrandum.*

Mark Antony in his *'Julius Caesar'*. The skills I learnt from debating and drama later proved useful during my working life, particularly in the public arena and at parliament. Alas in the sporting arena I continued to be only a cheerleader, as once again I was the youngest and smallest pupil in my class. Though I was a vociferous and partisan cheerleader, sometimes this resulted in Father McTiernan shouting "Shut up Benjamin"! during competitions. I didn't start getting interested in girls until Makerere University College, and even then it was on the periphery. I was diffident and shy; maybe that is why Father McTiernan chose me to act as Lady Macbeth.

The independence movement was emerging as a force around that time. There was the Tanganyika African Association (TAA), which Julius Nyerere, commonly known as *Mwalimu*, which means teacher, transformed into the Tanganyika African National Union (TANU) in July 1954. I received only a few lessons from Nyerere before he resigned in March 1955 to devote himself fully to TANU, to which he had been elected as the party's first president. His resignation caused a great deal of conversation amongst us, we wondered if he had been intimidated by the priests. This was not the case, Nyerere decided that he could not teach full-time and lead this new political party. He saw it as his religious duty to serve his country first.

The senior class in 1955, which was one year ahead of us, was fairly political in agitation; endeavouring to establish a kind of political society called '*Pukka*' from the Hindi word meaning ripe or substantial. I was very active in this society, despite my friend John Kambona's cynicism about the society which he translated as an acronym of 'Political Union for Keen Africans'. The Fathers were very upset as the students had been so involved in this society that their GCE results were rather poor. So the following year they warned us to study hard for these exams, to stop this nonsense of following politics and wait until we finished our studies, then we would have plenty of time for politicking.

My eyes were being opened to the fact that we Africans were not receiving enough opportunities, certainly we were receiving unequal opportunities compared to the Asian community. That was beginning to really get me; you couldn't lose sight of that; for example, when you went to a major public office it was mainly staffed by Indians and Europeans, with only a few indigenous Tanganyikans. You sensed a certain class consciousness, especially with the Goans of the Indian community, who believed that they were a higher class and were closer to the Europeans than the other Indians. Indian society is very structured; it followed that they also felt that they were a cut above us Africans. I must emphasise that there was no real racial hostility, though of course there was quite a bit of racial discrimination in Dar es Salaam, with places where no Africans were allowed, such as a club or hotel. This question of inequality bothered me; you can't receive sermons every Sunday about all being equal before God but then you see Indians doing better than ourselves as they were favoured by the Whites over us indigenous citizens.

I did not feel oppressed, I conceded that the Europeans and Indians had knowledge of a world we didn't know about, of activities we didn't know how to undertake. Yet we were dismayed to read in newspapers that the British, Indians and others didn't think much of us Tanganyikans. They thought we could not lead our own country, that we were not ready for the responsibility. I wrote my first letter to the editor of the '*Tanganyika Standard*', now called the '*Daily News*', arguing the case for self-determination and independence; under a pseudonym of course. My letter, which was published, said that no-one can be ready without trying, so we must have the opportunity to have a go; there must be a conscious effort to open up to us Africans. Though this letter was a minor matter it does show my emerging interest in politics and rights, I was around 17 years old when I wrote this.

"I am Patrick George Kunambi. As the member of the Legislative Council for the Eastern Province I represent the people of Eastern Province, I represent Father Headmaster and I represent all of you". This shocking statement has stuck in my mind till today, over sixty years later. This was the first time I saw an African leader, other than a traditional chief, who was acknowledged by the colonialists. There was the added impact of Chief Kunambi having the nerve to say that he represented Father Headmaster together with us Tanganyikans, and what's more he said this seated next to the headmaster! My fellow pupils and I were so impressed, this was really something. This visit to our school by two Tanganyikans who had been nominated to the Legislative Council of Tanganyika had such a strong impact on my fellow students and me.

In 1945 the first African Chiefs were selected to the Legislative Council of Tanganyika, Chief David Kidaha Makwaia and Chief Abdiel Shangali. It wasn't until the elections which were conducted in two stages during 1958 and 1959 when Tanganyikans were allowed to vote for their representatives on this council, which served as the ruling body for Tanganyika from 1926 until Independence. Chief Kunambi of the Uluguru people was appointed to the Legislative Council in 1955 and was one of the founders of TANU. He was accompanied by Mary Josephine (Jo) Kasindi, the youngest member of the Tanganyikan Legislative Council and the second Tanganyikan woman to gain a university degree. They were visiting the area and our headmaster had decided it would be a good idea to get these African leaders to talk to us; I believe this was another subtle message by the Fathers, to instil confidence in our ability to contribute to the future of our country.

Meanwhile my eldest brother Blasius, who is six years older than me, was beginning to get really interested in politics; he was a nationalist, though not an activist as such. He was a strong influence on my political awakening because I spent at least three holidays with him during my time at St Francis College. We read newspapers, listened to the radio and talked politics. He wanted to start his own political party at the district level called 'Masasi African Democratic Union', but his employer, an Indian businessman, told him, "Please do not disturb our business relations, keep your political opinions to yourself".

My father wasn't political at all; he was very respectful, especially of the missionaries, which was to be expected as they made him what he was. He was also from a generation which had a much different attitude to the colonialists than my generation. My other brother, Bernard, was not really interested in politics. He was a civil service career person, a stickler for professionalism, ethics and integrity. Though, as the civil service became more and more Africanised after independence, he became frustrated as he couldn't stand the people who were taking forever to decide things or to serve people in need. He is retired now, but still interested in the civil service, and he's rather critical of the current performance of the civil service and some politicians.

A government warrant paid for our transport home and back to school at each holiday. During the dry season we travelled by bus, though sometimes this required an overnight stop at the Rufiji river, as there was no bridge and the ferry ceased at six each evening, so we would have to sleep in the bus, tormented by mosquitos. During the rainy season these dirt roads could be impassable, so we would take a boat called the MV Mombasa from Lindi to Dar es Salaam, where the school would arrange for a lorry to pick us up and take us to St Francis College.

Once the boat was not working and the road impassable, so the students from my region along with some army fellows going on home leave ended up travelling in a hired bus of the Tanganyika Transport Company from Dar es Salaam to Morogoro, Iringa, Njombe, Songea, Tunduru, finally to Masasi, ending up in Lindi. This roundabout route of about 1,500 kilometres on dirt roads to my home in Masasi was the toughest journey I undertook, it lasted nearly a week. When we reached Songea the regional manager of the bus company was so impressed by this new bus from the Dar es Salaam branch that he decided to delay its departure from Songea so he could show it off. Naturally all of us passengers were unhappy about this, we just wanted to get home. Despite there being adults on the bus it fell to me, a seventeen-year-old, to go the manager to complain. I went and gave him a piece of my mind, whereupon he allowed the bus to carry on. My unwillingness to accept poor service and willingness to speak up against it displayed itself early in me. When I finally reached home I was only able to stay three days there before we had to return to school. Fortunately the boat at Lindi was available for the return journey.

I would return to my home in Masasi almost every six months; I enjoyed seeing my friends from my school days at Ndanda and I, of course, knew the names of everyone in our small village. I didn't want to show-off about what I had seen or done, though usually they had many questions: What is it like there? What are the people like? What kind of food do they eat? What is their language like? How does it compare with us? Despite that I liked just fitting back in when I was home, though I did feel that I had changed much more than they had changed during my time away.

My father was still hopeful that I would become a doctor, so I had studied all the subjects necessary for medical school entrance at university. I did well in the Cambridge School Certificate Examination, I was in the top three of the fifty-one students in our class who sat the exam in 1956. We all passed that year and thirty-two students gained First Class which shows how well the Fathers had taught us and how hard we had studied. The Fathers would proudly draw attention to these excellent results to those students who followed us. I was unable to find out how many Tanganyikan students overall passed in my year. 1954 is the closest year reported in 'The Colonial Office List'[4]; it states that 98 'Africans' as we indigenous Tanganyikans were termed, passed the Cambridge School Certificate Examination.

During our long wait for the exam results and to know if we had been selected to go to Makerere University College in Uganda, we four school friends went to our old secondary school at Ndanda. We helped our former teachers with teaching and religious instruction to earn a little money before hopefully we would progress on to Makerere University College. The Fathers and Sisters there were respectful of us now that we had grown up and were waiting to go to Makerere.

St Francis College was the shaping of a young man and the beginning of my awareness of political issues. Now I will go on to the next stage of my personal development, which was Makerere University College and the real blooming of my interest in politics.

---

4   'The Colonial Office List 1956'. London: Her Majesty's Stationery Office. Information provided by the Foreign and Commonwealth Office and made available under the Open Government Licence for public sector information, version 3.

CHAPTER 4

Facing a Volcano

When I commenced my tertiary studies in 1957 there was no university in Tanganyika or Kenya. Makerere University College in Kampala, Uganda was the centre for higher learning in East Africa; drawing students from Uganda, Kenya, Tanganyika and Zanzibar. There were even some students from Nyasaland[5] and Rhodesia[6]. Despite there being a university in their area, they preferred to come to Makerere due to its good reputation and being affiliated to the University of London. '*The Colonial Office List 1957*'[7] states that in 1957 there were 166 students, not just first-year, from Tanganyika at Makerere. There were 26 students at the Royal Technical College in Nairobi, (which opened in 1957); and around 200 receiving post-secondary education in the UK. Your first two years of study at Makerere were devoted to the then equivalent of what is now called the A Levels, preparing one for the present-day entry examination to university. Altogether I spent five years at Makerere, up to April 1962.

---

5   Nyasaland was renamed as Republic of Malawi on 6 July 1964.
6   Renamed as Republic of Zimbabwe 18 April 1980.
7   '*The Colonial Office List 1957*'. London: Her Majesty's Stationery Office. Information provided by the Foreign and Commonwealth Office and made available under the Open Government Licence for public sector information, version 3.

Though I had received a first in my Cambridge School Certificate Examination, it was clear when I joined Makerere that I couldn't study science subjects, as I hadn't scored sufficiently high in them. Also, by that time my inclination was towards politics rather than medicine; so I chose to study history, economics and English. It was hard telling my father; he was obviously disappointed that I would not become a doctor as he had hoped but fell back to his third career choice for me: a teacher.

Most of my classmates from St Francis College went on to Makerere, only a few went to England on a privately financed arrangement to study further. My three friends since Ndanda secondary school: Philip Magani, John Kambona and Benno Nkane also came to Makerere. We travelled second class by train from Dar es Salaam to Mwanza from where we caught a boat to travel the length of Lake Victoria, the largest lake in Africa, to Port Bell, Kampala in Uganda. It was a beautiful scenic journey, we especially enjoyed the boat trip. We four attended the Makerere Freshman's Ball during the first week. You could easily see we were freshmen as our suits were new and we had trouble fixing our ties. I enjoyed my first time at a formal dance; beforehand I had only gone to traditional dances at my village.

Makerere was the first place I was in a multi-racial class, another new experience for me. Since we were all undergoing the learning experience, our differing skin colour didn't make any difference; though some could have a slight edge on the English language. This taught me that differing races could learn together; my experience beforehand had been that a differing race, whether Indian or White, always had greater knowledge and experience than us indigenous people.

The Colonial Office Lists[8] state that "African students from Tanganyika who qualify for entrance to Makerere at present are required to pay fees of only GBP 40 towards the cost of tuition and residence at the College, the balance being met from Government funds; provision exists for the remission of these fees in cases of need." Note the use of the word

---

8   The Colonial Office List, 1953, 1954 and 1955. London: Her Majesty's Stationery Office. Information provided by the Foreign and Commonwealth Office and made available under the Open Government Licence for public sector information, version 3.

'only'! This was an unattainable amount for most of us in those days, with the majority living in rural areas and surviving on subsistence farming. Despite my father's unusual status of receiving a monthly wage, there was no possibility of my parents being able to raise this substantial sum. I was interviewed by the district officer, who determined that I qualified for remission of these fees. As with my fellow Tanganyikan students, I received a small bursary from the Tanganyikan government to help with living costs while at Makerere, so for the first time in my life I received a personal allowance and could dress reasonably well. During the first two years, I shared a room in student accommodation with a fellow student from St Francis College, which was the first time when I had to share my sleeping area with only one other person. I had my own clothes and more personal space, a novel experience of luxurious living for me. For the last three years at university I was even more spoilt, having my own room; at around 21 years old this was my first experience of a private living space.

After the strict discipline and rigid regime of Ndanda and St Francis, suddenly at Makerere you were the manager of your time. It was a big jump in maturity, a different method of studying, something that some university students experience difficulty with to this day. Yet despite this drastic change I found it fairly easy to adjust to the more relaxed regimen than I was accustomed to at school, self-discipline having been well-grounded in me by the Fathers. Studying English meant that there was a lot of reading, something I still enjoy, and Makerere had an extensive library to draw from. For leisure reading, I liked detective stories such as those by Agatha Christie and for humour particularly P.G. Wodehouse's *'Jeeves and Wooster'*, while I read the *'Uganda Argus'*, an English language newspaper and a Kenyan Kiswahili newspaper *'Baraza'*, which could be very political. If I had a little spare money I would go to a dance hall during my leisure time.

An Indian Ugandan called Rajat Neogy founded and edited a journal called *'Transition'*. This literary magazine commenced in 1961 and grew to become recognised around the world as a platform for emerging African writers. The content covered African political, literary and cultural matters, including short stories by African writers. I was on the editorial board and also contributed several articles, particularly book reviews. Other contributors during my time were the Kenyan writer James Ngugi, now known as James Ngũgĩ wa Thiong'o, who was two years behind me at university. Another budding and soon to be famous writer associated with *'Transition'* was Chinua Achebe. His writing is steeped in his cultural environment, an African story in style and construction; I still appreciate his books. I was also involved in the English department's student literary magazine called *'Penpoint'* which commenced in 1958. There were also the annual inter-hall competitions in elocution, public speaking, creative writing and drama which I took part in.

Makerere was the centre in East Africa for the nurturing of young Africans; we were an elite as very few had access to this level of education in those times. We students could be reasonably expected to become future leaders; particularly during the 50s and 60s when independence was in the forefront of the minds of many Africans. Many political leaders would visit the university to give lectures on the progress of the struggle and of our nations shared political agitations for independence. Among those who came were Jaramogi Odinga – who later became Kenya's first vice-president, Tom Mboya – a nationalist and prominent leader in Kenya's independence struggle, Milton Obote – second president of Uganda, and Benedicto Kiwanuka – first prime minister of Uganda. I remember particularly Mboya and Obote, especially Tom Mboya, because he was very articulate; though they were all impressive characters to listen to. Although Tanganyika was a trust territory, Uganda a protectorate and Kenya a colony, there was a lot of shared sympathy with the causes which were being espoused by each because we were all under the yoke of the British government.

The environment at Makerere was conducive to political engagement and discussions about what we could do to help the process forward to independence in our various countries. There was generally freedom to discuss what you liked, though of course with the Kenyans we had to be more careful because of the fear of the effect of the *Mau Mau* rebellion. You were careful in what you said and who you met. The Political Science Department had not been established; it was the late Professor Ali Mazrui who taught political science at the new department from 1963 to 1973 who really stimulated politics at Makerere.

There were two student associations for the Tanganyikans. I was very active in the TANU student group, becoming secretary and later chairman. Notable Tanganyikans who preceded me as chairman were Dr. Wilbert Chagula, who became the first Tanzanian vice-chancellor of the University of Dar es Salaam and Dr Ambrose Chanji of the Aga Khan hospital in Dar es Salaam. I wrote a couple of letters to the TANU headquarters as a secretary first and then as a chairman, giving our views about the evolution process and the process of obtaining more power. I suspect that this is when I first came to Nyerere's attention.

This was the first time I was actively involved in politics and I found politicking for student government fun. There was an election every year for the president of the Students' Guild, the collective association of the student body. When I ran for president, my principal opponent was a Kenyan, Simeon Gor. Despite that this was the first time I ran for an election, I put up a good fight. It is funny that I won the votes from the women's hall of residence; not because I had a girlfriend there, but because I was more articulate than my competitor. Tom Mboya and the other politicians I had listened to had shown me the importance of being articulate. Simeon won the election, but he was smart and made me vice-president. He later rose into senior positions in the Kenyan government.

The year after that I was elected chairman of the Student Representative Council, to which the Students Guild was accountable, this was my most influential position up to that point, since I spoke as the representative of all students. The president of the Student Guild was Francis Nyalali, who later became chief justice of Tanzania[9]. There was good solidarity amongst us Tanganyikans then; we mobilised the vote for our man to be elected president of the Students Guild.

The other association, the Tanganyika Students' Body, was concerned with student matters such as bursaries and travel conditions and tended to be apolitical, although it was difficult to keep politics out of it. We sought an increase in the size of the bursary, which was refused by the Tanganyikan government. Naturally us students protested vigorously to Dr Jones, Director of Education, and Chief John Maruma, Assistant Minister for Education, who had come from Dar es Salaam to speak to us. I confess that we students shouted them down so they could not be

---

9   Chief Justice 1977–2000.

heard. We wound up with one of us describing the ministry of education as "rotten from top to bottom" which so infuriated Dr Jones that he walked out. Subsequently the government sent Randal Sadleir to talk to us[10] and those students who came from a poor background received a special extra living allowance.

It is a tradition amongst students all over the world to complain and protest; much later I would find myself at the receiving end of such protests when I was minister of science, technology and higher education. I recall an uproarious meeting in 1995 with students from the University of Dar es Salaam concerning allowances. The students were expecting me to be different from my predecessor and agree to an increase; I refused an increase in their allowances, quoting from Ecclesiastes 3:1 "To everything there is a season, and a time for every purpose under heaven", upon which many students responded by leaving the hall in noisy protest, though many lingered outside to hear the rest of what I had to say. Afterwards, I was amused recalling our protests for increased allowances when I was a student at Makerere, and how furious the director of education had been when we shouted him down as he tried to speak to us. Now it had been my turn to receive the rowdy complaints of students, the roles had been reversed!

I did very well in English in the equivalent A levels at the completion of my first two years there, so I decided to study for a three-year honours course in English literature, language and phonetics. The class in the honours course comprised of only four students: two Ugandans, a Zanzibari and me. John Nagenda was one of those Ugandans and we have remained friends. John has had a positive influence on my international life, often acting as a go-between with Yoweri Museveni, from when he was fighting in the bush to his time now as Uganda's president. John is a talented columnist, as well as a media advisor to President Museveni.

During 1959, the first year of my honours course, the United States Information Agency selected three students from Makerere to visit the

---

10   Randal Sadleir was a pre-independence colonial servant who became a friend of Nyerere and worked in the Tanganyikan/Tanzanian government as the last British official until the early 1970s. In 1999 he published his memoirs *'Tanzania, Journey to Republic'*, New York: Radcliffe Press.

USA for two weeks. My companions were Philip Ndegwa – who later became Governor of the Central Bank of Kenya, and Mutibwa Phares, a Ugandan who became an author and historian, including being professor of history at Makerere. My first exposure to a Western country was such an eye-opener. I was overwhelmed by the scale of material progress; all those neon lights, the highways, the lifts – it was amazing. We were so impressed at how well-equipped the universities were, such an impressive array of teaching materials and the libraries were fantastic. Tutorials in the United States were much more informal than we were accustomed to; we were somewhat reverential towards our tutors at Makerere.

Beyond this deluge of new sights and experiences in USA I learnt how to reach out to people who were not African and converse with them. I described Tanganyika to those I met as multi-ethnic and multi-racial and that progress in development was slowly being made. We tried to explain the differences between Tanganyika, which was not a colony, as compared to Kenya, which was. We also explained the active roles that the kingdoms in Uganda had at that time. We spoke of the open and blatant racial discrimination in Kenya. We didn't encounter any racial discrimination in USA ourselves; that unpleasant experience would come during my next trip there.

Students from Thailand, Japan, India and a few European countries were also on this tour, which meant that my experience was broader than learning about the way of life in USA There was the added benefit of opening my eyes to the world out there; to try to understand it as well as make some friends. I became infatuated with a young Japanese student on the tour, I had never seen a Japanese before. We kept in touch after the tour, though after a while our contact dropped off as we continued our studies. It was a pure relationship, just friendly. I wrote a poem *'Facing A Volcano'*[11] recounting when we visited a volcano in Hawaii. When I later became a well-known political figure someone researched my background and tried to put a political interpretation to this poem, not knowing that it was this young Japanese woman I was writing about!

---

11   *'Facing A Volcano'* was published in the book *'Origin East Africa–a Makerere Anthology'*, (pg. 51–52, London: Heinemann Educational Books. 1965.

Facing A Volcano

Like an angry lion of the tropical jungle
The red lava shoots up.
A red arrow piercing a canopy of the clouds,
It threatens the endless stretch of sky.
A circling garb of hot air,
And a circling garb of humans.

A red cross on a green jeep,
A red cross on a wood shack,
A red cross on a white breast.
They stand by, grim, unshaken,
To guard this circling garb of humans.

They are all here.
Men, women; young and old,
Mystified, terrified.
They gape it in, their cameras click;
Later, removed in space and time,
They will vent an endless chime:
'Is it not wonderful?'
A boy and a girl, but a few hours met,
Their backs to the volcano, they face the camera;
He wants a souvenir.
'Is it not wonderful?'
A beautiful girl, and behind – a beautiful monster.

A big truck unloads its cargo.
Majestic, springy, the cargo swells the circling garb of humans.
These are guards, of men against men.
The army of course! They too missed the red lion.
No, no, this is no enemy; just a 'glorious sight'.
And the red tongue lashes out.
But it won't lick the sky:
It won't lick the men – there are other tongues!

What thoughts do they all have? What feelings?
As the eruption's bowel of lost time hurls
The granitic deluge of suppressed earth which
Apace invades forlorn man and crop, and
Imposes a reign of barrenness;
What thoughts do they all have? What stirs them?
Fear, awe,
Man helpless in contest with nature.
He cannot harness this; he cannot explore it.

What a fire! It surpasses hell.
But the clergyman is not here;
He has known a hell fire; he doesn't have to see it.
It is better imaged in the cloister, in the pulpit
Better described.
Nothing real, this heat, and dust and fire.
It makes no souls repent.

They work at calculations,
Scientists and seismographs.
It defies them all, this tongue of fire, this fierce fiasco of rock and dust;
It defies time, this fiery testimony of nature.
Ruthless, devastating, defiant,
An angry arrow of fire.

From this trip I learnt what a long way Tanganyika had to go, how behind my country was. I keenly felt the deficiency in Tanganyika, knowing how advanced Kampala was and now seeing the huge difference in USA to my home country. There was more African development around Kampala and Uganda, certainly in the Buganda Kingdom. Uganda had a small African middle class, small, but nevertheless there, while there was no indigenous middle class in Tanganyika at that time. These Bugandans were more confident and self-assertive than Tanganyikans, saying "We have our kingdom, our own parliament", they were proud of the kingdom, their history and identity. While I was all too aware of how backward Tanganyika was, it also was an impetus for me to wonder: can we embark on a road of our own modernisation? I could see from what the Bugandans had achieved that we Tanganyikans could also develop.

My second visit to USA was organised by the International Union of Students, with a student each from the countries of the Federation of Malaya[12], the Kingdom of Norway and Tanganyika taken on a study tour to learn the role of higher education and student organisations in universities of the United States of America during 1961. This is where I encountered blatant discrimination for the first time. Part of the tour included Atlanta; where we arrived very early in the morning. We had been very busy the previous day in Texas and hadn't eaten a proper meal, so we were all very hungry and wanted to have breakfast as soon as we left the airport. Driving into town we stopped by a motel with a restaurant attached, not realising that the restaurant was segregated. The staff said they were sorry, but they couldn't serve us. I was obviously dark-skinned, and the Malayan was even darker than me, while the Norwegian was as white as can be, as was our host escorting us. The restaurant staff said: "If you want these people can stay outside and we will serve you white people". Our white companions declared "No, no way" and ordered takeaway meals for us all, which we all ate sitting in our car.

The second racist incident occurred when we reached Montgomery, Alabama, where we were met at the train station by African-American women from a women activist group who had arranged for our accommodation and would introduce us to the university's student body. We were no more than two hundred metres from the train station in the car driven by one of the African-American women when the car was stopped by a white police officer. Our host driver was polite, lowering the car window and greeting the police officer who looked inside the car and said, *'Don't you know that it is illegal to travel mixed?"* Our driver explained that she was taking us three to the university hall of residence, whereupon the policeman looked closely at us and realised that we were not Americans; our host then explained that we came from Tanganyika, Malaya and Norway. The policeman said "Ok, take them

---

12   The Federation of Malaya existed from 1948 until 1963, when it was replaced by the countries of Malaysia and Singapore, and the Crown Colonies North Borneo and Sarawak.

straight to where you are taking them and remember that it is illegal to travel mixed". Of course our hostesses ignored this ruling and we travelled around together during our visit there.

Our tour took place during 1961 when the civil rights activists, called Freedom Riders, were protesting against segregated public buses in the southern states. The way people looked at you, you could see that they thought it was odd to see this trio of two dark students and one white student together. I wasn't angry or embarrassed at this discrimination against me, rather it amused me; I was self-confident and thought these incidents absolutely ludicrous. I felt sorry for our African-American hosts though; African-Americans have suffered greatly over the centuries.

I had decided that when I graduated I would join the civil service to help advance the independence process, but not to be an active politician, or to make politics my profession; that thought had not yet entered my head. My desire to attain a senior position in government was reinforced when I got involved in educating voters for the Tanganyika Legislative Council elections of September 1958 and February 1959. These elections were very important as it was the first time indigenous Tanganyikans could vote for a representative; prior to this the indigenous Tanganyikan representatives were selected and appointed by the colonial British administration. Some African Tanganyikan males and females would be able to register to vote, provided they met certain qualifications for registration on the electoral roll which were determined by income level and asset ownership; such as whether you owned a home, cattle, a business and production from farming. One of my colleagues from St Francis College, Gisler Mapunda, had gone straight into politics with TANU when he had graduated from school. He was the assistant regional secretary of TANU in Kilosa, Eastern Province. TANU mounted a campaign to register as many Africans on the electoral roll as possible and during a holiday from university I joined Gisler in mobilising people to register to vote. We travelled around encouraging those who met the the colonial government's' mandated educational and income requirements to register, providing voter education and of course encouraging them to vote for a Tanganyikan. We moved from Kilosa to Kilombero to Ifakara to

Malinyi, which was the most south-western point in the Eastern Region, now called Morogoro Region. As to be expected, the colonial district commissioners and district officers watched our activities, but they didn't really intervene. However, we couldn't address public meetings as this would have required permission which would have taken too long to obtain. We received warm support from ordinary citizens, as well as the local party chairmen and party secretaries, who accommodated us in their homes, fed us and assisted with our work.

TANU, with Nyerere at the helm, won twenty-eight of the thirty elected seats of the sixty-four seat Legislative Council, winning 74% of the overall votes for elected seats. This election was an important landmark on Tanganyika's road to independence and in December 1959, Sir Richard Turnbull, the last British governor of Tanganyika, announced that Tanganyika would have some form of self-government during late 1960. This was my first experience of politicking in the field; it heightened my interest in politics as I realised there was something I could do to push the process to independence forward. Gisler later obtained his degree in Russia, returned to work for the government, then entered politics, rising to become the minister of labour.

I was president when I next visited Malinyi, where there was a bitter struggle for land between the pastoralists, who were from the Sukuma tribe and had migrated with their cattle, and those already farming there. The district commissioner had declared that the Sukuma should go back to where they came from due to the rising agitation. At the mass rally, I defended the right of everyone to live where they want, saying, "Look, I have heard all the complaints, I want to tell you that this is one country, we are one people, you are entitled to go any place you go. Just be sensible about how you compose yourselves; I don't want to hear anything about people being ejected out of here". As I was about to get into my vehicle a woman approached and said, "I want to say hello to the President". My bodyguards refused, but I instructed, "Let her come to me". She gave me a ten thousand shilling note, thanking me for arguing the case for her people to remain there. I kept this banknote in my briefcase for years as a reminder of how my words directly impact the lives of the people.

When independence came to Tanganyika on 9 December 1961[13], there was a feeling of overwhelming joy amongst us which lasted for the next six months. On Independence Day, I led a demonstration to the Kampala city council bus park, the public meeting place in those times, where we celebrated. We were free, free at last! Eventually, we came to ask, what now, now that we have got independence? How do we replace those administrators, and the governor who was the political head, who would leave at the end of one year? There were very few tertiary educated Tanzanians; Julius Nyerere was the first Tanganyikan to obtain a Masters degree, in 1952[14]. I have been told that at independence there were only 16 medical doctors, 12 accountants, 1 surveyor, 1 agricultural engineer, 427 government administrators, 158 professional nurses and 50 agricultural scientists who were Tanganyikans. This was an unbelievably small cadre of qualified and skilled citizens to lead our new nation. We had been neglected by the colonial power, who had not adequately prepared us. What is more there was an estimated adult literacy of 15% with only 23% of men and 7.5% of women having attended any kind of schooling at all. Tanganyika, (this excludes Zanzibar), had close to ten million people spread over a landmass of 883 thousand square kilometres, which is about four times the size of the United Kingdom from whence the colonial administrators came. What a starting point for our nascent nation!

Certainly as students we were not thinking about forming a republic and crafting a political ideology for this young nation. We students just considered what was happening now, who would take over being chief clerks in the government offices – because they were usually Indians, who would be district officers, would there be third class magistrates, where would they learn, how would they be educated? We considered little in the sense of ideology, except of course for far-sighted Nyerere; who had resigned as the country's first prime minister because he wanted to concentrate on the ideology and the shaping of our young nation.

---

13   You can watch the Independence Day Celebration at: https://youtube.com/watch?v=JxQ46KycJhg from British Pathé; as well as a recording by Adrian Roden (high court advocate 1950–1965) of three events at that time: https://www.youtube.com/watch?v=gkgD9TmTOOo

14   Nyerere obtained a Masters in Economics and History from the University of Edinburgh; he studied there under government scholarship, as he did at Makerere University College for his undergraduate degree.

Rashidi Kawawa became our nation's second prime minister and within a year he succeeded in Africanising the police service; he made promotions just like that. Naturally there were ups and downs here and there, but it worked overall. Kawawa worked hard to consolidate the notion that we were now independent. If we had kept having white policemen then the people would have asked, "What has changed?" If I had been the prime minister at that time I could not have done this, Nyerere said of Kawawa: "This fellow has got more courage than I have, I couldn't have done what he did". Our generation knew Kawawa as '*Simba wa Vita*' (the Lion of War) because he also mobilised support for the liberation movements.

It brought euphoria during those early days to see Africans becoming district officers and district commissioners. Then we began to fill these positions with political appointees. Political officers such as former TANU party secretaries were suddenly being appointed district commissioners or regional commissioners, without their having worked in the civil service and risen up the established ranks of administrators. The 'shiny' newness of society and structures after independence was giving a lot of satisfaction, but we hadn't really thought through what to do; it was much more the feeling that now we are somebody – so we can do this! The peasantry also did not have a concept of the challenges ahead of us all. They were proud that the positions of colonial officers would be taken over by Africans, and some expected that now the pace of transformation would speed up. There was a little cynicism, and perhaps apprehension as well, a question of let's wait and see, for they were wondering if we could manage.

During my last year at Makerere I became very fond of a white American student, Hilary Sims, who was studying sociology, social anthropology and women's issues under a student exchange arrangement. I was introduced to her by an elderly couple; the husband was an American lecturer at the university. Philip Ndegwa and I used to discuss literature, politics and life in America with Hilary at this couple's home. She and I empathised very much indeed; it was a meeting of minds, our relationship continued until she returned to USA to study for her final year at Stanford and I graduated. Our friendship continued for a while thereafter, we wrote to each other while I was working in Dodoma. We both thought our relationship could become serious, but it didn't develop further, largely because I was Catholic and she was Unitarian I believe, though not as strongly religious as I was. She knew the Catholics were very strict; so apart from colour I think my Catholic faith may have discouraged her. We did get in touch again later on in life, she had married and had two children, as had I. She was my sole girlfriend whilst I was at Makerere, I was so focused on my studies and my growing interest in politics.

I chose Thomas Hardy as my author to study in depth during my honours course as I liked his rural settings. Other authors I liked were Charlotte Brontë; as well as the poets Andrew Marvell, Alfred Tennyson, Lord Byron; I liked Percy Shelley's 'Ozymandias'. Shakespeare of course; oh I loved his sonnets. I liked poetry very much, I read a lot of poetry with my American girlfriend, especially that of Edna St Vincent Millay. We didn't study any American literature as the perspective at Makerere was mostly British, but since then I have come to like Emily Dickinson; her poetry is so pithy, fantastic, three lines holding so much wealth in it. I still like to read poetry from time to time, especially American and English poets; despite being down to earth, I am a bit of a romantic. I have no creative outlet now, despite being retired my reading continues to be technical material, politics and biographies. You need space to be creative, so I don't write poetry any longer, just draft speeches from time to time. Despite being 'retired' there are still many official demands on my time.

Independence had come on 9 December 1961 and early April 1962 I graduated. I look back at my time at Makerere with fondness. It was a very formative five years for my mind, my attitude to others and to strengthen my commitment to service. In those days the government would send out notices to those about to graduate advising them of positions on offer. I looked at the list and didn't like the jobs available; as I had decided I wanted to be a foreign service officer and there were no positions open. I asked about opportunities to work in foreign service, but the government official said, "No, the positions at the foreign service are all filled, there is no room, so why don't you go into the general service?", which I did not want to do.

My father had already given up on me, having learnt that I wasn't going to be a teacher. The reason, which some people may regard as arrogance on my part, was that I was told I must study further if I wanted to be a teacher; I must undergo an extra year of study to attain a diploma of education. I said "No please, I have been at university for five years, three of which I have spent doing nothing but learn every aspect of English. If in those three years I can't tell a bad teacher and how they teach badly – I don't want to come back here for another year of study". Meanwhile the Aga Khan was launching his newspaper 'The Nation' in Nairobi and having heard that I was finishing my studies and probably had a leaning towards journalism he sent someone to talk to me. Oxford University Press East Africa, who produced textbooks; also expressed an interest in me. Eventually, I decided I would try my hand at journalism with 'The Nation', so I told the Tanganyikan government official that I was not interested in working in the general public service area, but if they had any opening in the foreign service that would be ok. Just as I was about to sign my contract to work for 'The Nation' the government official came back to me and said, "Ok there is a position with the foreign service, but you will have to enter the civil service as a district officer cadet for four to five months, then you will go on a course at Columbia University, USA to gain in-depth knowledge of international diplomacy".

I started my working life as a district officer cadet, an administrative position in Dodoma in April 1962. As Tanganyika was only newly independent there were still many white officers, most of whom were prepared to share their experience and teach you about administration systems. Notably they tried to instil in you respect for the processes and to uphold governance, that you must do justice to your job and to your own code of conduct. There was no riding rough-shod on the populace, none. There were only a few Africans who had been promoted, so you wanted to learn from the Whites about how to do the things that they were doing. You felt honoured, a little over-awed to be with them and were anxious to learn from those who had been doing their job for some time. One event during my time working there that really brought me down to earth was the task of registering those people in the villages who were entitled to receive food relief; this really opened my eyes to how poor my country and its people were.

In August 1962, I reported to Dar es Salaam to make the preparations to go to Columbia University, then off I went to New York. There was a fellow student from Makerere, a Ugandan, Matias Lubega, who I knew, plus students from Sudan, Nigeria, Cyprus, Malaya and other countries. We were accommodated at International House, which is a long-established residence for predominantly non-American students, though a few American students resided there as well. The day after checking in to International House I began itching all over. It was terrible, so I went to the dispensary at International House and said, "There is something funny about my body, I am itching everywhere, what could it be?" I told them that over the last two to three weeks I had travelled quite a bit in Tanganyika. The medical staff suspected smallpox and were alarmed; they bundled me quickly to Bellevue Hospital, where I was promptly quarantined. All the students and staff at International House had to be vaccinated against smallpox and there was coverage in the newspapers and radio. This was how Hilary, my girlfriend from Makerere days who was now at Stanford University, learnt that I was in New York; she rang the hospital and we spoke, it was good to resume contact with her. The hospital diagnosed quite quickly that I didn't have smallpox, but measles. When I returned to International House they exclaimed, "So this is the fellow who made us go through hell, to be vaccinated against smallpox"! I was quite notorious for a couple of days, what a way to become known by my fellow students. At least this enabled me to resume contact with my ex-girlfriend.

During my time there Bernard Mkatte, a counsellor at the Tanganyikan Mission to the United Nations in New York, invited me to accompany him to Pittsburgh to witness the consecration of the first Catholic Bishop of the Diocese of Arusha, who was an American called Dennis Vincent Durning. I later met Bishop Durning[15] when president; when he recalled my attending his consecration. He is buried in Arusha, which is where he wanted; he had declared that Tanzania had become his country.

The year-long international diplomacy course was designed by the Carnegie Institute as at that time several countries were becoming independent or were newly independent. It was an excellent course. Towards the end of the course we visited foreign service offices in Washington

---

15   Ordained as Bishop of Arusha May 1963, resigned March 1989, died in February 2002.

DC, Ottawa, London, and Nicosia. We concluded our course in Cyprus with a very good session with President Makarios III and I was asked to give the concluding remarks on behalf of my colleagues, my debut in public speaking as a government representative.

I was still absorbed with the anti-colonial struggle during my time at Columbia; particularly the struggle against the racist regimes in the South – Mozambique, Angola, Rhodesia[16], Northern Rhodesia[17] and South Africa. The Cuban Missile Crisis occurred whilst I was there; I remember watching President John F. Kennedy on television, it was a scary time. We wondered what would happen next – would New York be hit, would we be able to return home? I learnt two things from this worrying experience: I realised that international relations can be about war. I also realised how scholarly politics and international affairs were in the United States, with authors and experts commenting on this crisis. This was a contrast to us Tanganyikans, who merely had commentary in the newspapers as sources of serious information; there were no books being produced, no think tanks producing reports.

This year of study confirmed to me that I had made the right decision to enter the foreign service; I would have more opportunity to work closely with my country's leader, as foreign affairs is always the concern of the president. Furthermore, this was a newly formed ministry, so the career path there would be better than in other ministries. I returned to Tanganyika eager to begin work.

---

16 Rhodesia would become Zimbabwe.
17 Northern Rhodesia would become Zambia.

CHAPTER 5

Observer of the Struggle

I entered the Foreign Service in 1963 as foreign service officer grade 3; where I worked on the Africa desk and from time to time as personal assistant to Oscar Kambona, the first minister of external affairs – now called foreign affairs. Africa was the busiest of all the desks at that time because the liberation of Southern Africa was uppermost in the mind of President Julius Nyerere in terms of foreign relations. As this is when I first started coming into contact with him, who from now on I will refer to as *Mwalimu* – teacher, a name he is commonly known as. He certainly was the person from whom I learnt the most throughout my working life. Mwalimu's foremost concerns were the unity of this country, followed closely by the liberation of the rest of Africa, including how to combine the influence and pressure of the independent African countries to bear upon the colonial powers. This was a tumultuous epoch in the history of Africa and it was an exciting time to be working in the ministry; I felt fortunate to be there.

In May 1963, the headquarters of the Organisation of African Unity's (OAU) Coordinating Committee for the Liberation of Africa were established in Dar es Salaam. When there were differences among the liberation movements, Mwalimu would get them together to unite in forging a liberation strategy to seek support within and outside of Africa. A main component of my job was to take notes when the minister of foreign affairs or the president met visitors, so sometimes I attended Mwalimu's meetings with leaders of liberation movements. Observing those exchanges was a learning process in itself; I learnt much about détente and forming cohesion; this was also how I grew to understand Mwalimu. I think this is also when Mwalimu noticed my ability to listen carefully and write an adequate report of meetings.

Issues which often featured in these discussions were: how to get Francophone Africa and Anglophone Africa to unite in supporting the liberation movements; how to minimise the rivalry between Russia and China when seeking their support, how to win international support at meetings of the United Nations or other international organisations; how to get more support from the Nordic countries – including declarations of support drawing attention to the evils of apartheid and the racist rule in Portuguese colonies, and mobilising Commonwealth support for the liberation struggle. Mwalimu was very adept at balancing different interests, advising, "You don't have to support one and hate the other". He also strove to persuade African countries to give financial support to the newly formed OAU Liberation Committee.

Among the independent states there was a question of borders and Mwalimu was instrumental in saying, "The liberation of the continent is more important to us than what the colonialists drew up as our borders". He was key in the resolution that we should respect each country's borders as they are laid out by the colonialists; this worthy agreement meant that the potential for border conflict was minimised then and until today.

It is difficult to convey the effect and power of Mwalimu over Tanzanians; people held him with such great respect. He was carefully listened to, his instructions carried out almost unquestioningly. He was head and shoulders above everyone, there is no doubt about that; though to be fair the opposition in Tanzania was weak in those early days. He was the perfect leader for that epoch.

What was most impressive is how he brought our young nation behind this struggle for the liberation of other countries. How he achieved this I will never fully understand, it was almost divine inspiration and it took a lot of courage on his part. The achievements in the liberation struggle for South Africa by Nelson Mandela and others is another example of courage and tenacity; but where would these liberation movements have been without Mwalimu? He even helped the movements to set up camp in our country to train; we used our own small army to help them, our nation's support was notable. It did help that we were very anti-colonial; yet Tanganyika was a small country on the world's stage and a desperately poor one, sacrifices were made by Tanganyikans to support the causes of other African countries. There was some criticism that Mwalimu should concentrate on his own country, that he spent too much energy and resources on the liberation struggle, but I think he was what the continent, especially southern Africa, sorely needed at that time.

Later, I think around 1972, some aircraft flew over Dar es Salaam and dropped leaflets warning us about supporting the Mozambican freedom fighters. The Portuguese rulers misguidedly thought we were a weak country; these leaflets carried a warning which stated how can you fight against the might of Portugal? Mwalimu was a very strong character and none of us were intimidated; the Portuguese had underestimated the depth of our commitment to the cause.

It wasn't till later when I was more knowledgeable that I could make a valid personal judgement of the leaders I observed, though at this early stage there were certainly many I respected and admired for their courage and dedication to their cause. For example, Dr Eduardo Mondlane of the Front for the Liberation of Mozambique (FRELIMO), which was established in Tanzania in 1962. My home village was only eighteen kilometres from the border with Portuguese Mozambique and FRELIMO's base was at Nachingwea, which is not far from Masasi. Naturally I had a personal interest, particularly as the struggle was organised to start from the north of Mozambique and move southwards. Dr Mondlane's assassination in Dar es Salaam by a parcel bomb in February 1969 showed me what great risks my country was facing by supporting the liberation movements. I was also concerned whether the FRELIMO movement would be able to find a suitable leader to take his place. Mondlane really was above any of the others; it was a great loss indeed. We all assumed that it was the Portuguese administration in Mozambique which had carried out the assassination. Kenneth Kaunda[18], KK as he was known, who was organising Northern Rhodesia's independence in 1964; was another impressive leader. He is a nice man, though his working style was very different to Mwalimu's.

What was it like in the early days of public service? It was characterised by a commitment to implement government policy. We government employees didn't really mix politics and administration; we concentrated on implementing government policy. We had minimal proactive participation in the evolution of policy, unless it was solicited for by our minister. There is no doubt that there was a very serious commitment to serving the government and there were strict and well-defined rules in terms of financial accountability and other matters of governance. There wasn't such corruption amongst government employees as there is these days.

During these early days of independence the civil service was strict in observing regulations. For example, you did not move confidential files by hand, rather a messenger would come to transport a locked box containing files and the person at the destination would have the key to open that box. You were not allowed to talk of confidential matters outside of the office or at meetings unless specifically authorised to do such. You were very carefully vetted at that time; such matters seem much more relaxed nowadays. Promotion in the civil service followed the stipulated grade levels and your promotion depended upon your immediate superior, but above all the permanent secretary. A minister's regard for your work and potential had minimal influence; the 'political voice' did not count within the civil service during those days, what did count were the civil service regulations.

The initiation for forming or changing a policy always came from leaders and politicians, who would seek the opinion of the top civil servants. We had a well-defined formal system of seeking or giving opinion. For instance, if you were a foreign service officer grade 3 you wrote to the head of the section who would modify or rewrite afresh. He would then send the revised version on to the principal assistant secretary for his modifications before he passed it on to the permanent secretary. The

---

18   Zambia's first president October 1964–November 1991.

real political fine tuning would be between the permanent secretary and the minister. You had to go through this hierarchy if you felt that there was a need to start a new line of thinking. Yet we didn't find this process inhibiting; we accepted it as just a matter of routine. As time went on, our first president was in the habit of inviting top civil servants who were experts in the field of reform to attend some ruling party meetings. The president would pose questions so that the ordinary members of the national executive committee or central committee could benefit from the experts' answers, though the decision-making was entirely by the politicians.

Our first Tanzanian chief justice was Augustine Saidi, appointed in 1971; he had a fine legal mind. Prior to him we had Justice Philip Telford Georges[19] from Trinidad and Tobago, who Nyerere had recruited. Telford Georges set standards for our judiciary; he was a first-class scholar and judge, brilliant. He also had a good political streak and would warn leaders if what they were proposing to do was unacceptable legally; this takes courage and high integrity.

The civil service's relationship with the civil service in United Kingdom at that time was very cordial; largely because many of the senior staff from both countries already knew each other, it was after the Arusha Declaration when this relationship waned.

As so often happens, I met my wife Anna Joseph Maro at work. She was secretary to the minister of home affairs, I was personal assistant to the minister of foreign affairs, and our offices were in the same building. From time to time we would meet in the corridor and I became interested in her. A good friend from school and university, Philip Magani, was interested in Anna's cousin, who was the daughter of Chief John Maruma from Rombo, who knew us two as the troublemakers who had agitated for an increased allowance at Makerere University College, so that made matters a little difficult at the beginning. Philip and I dated these two cousins and after two and a half years Anna and I decided to marry. Incidentally, Anna's grandfather, Mzee Joseph helped me to always think matters through, I enjoyed his logical approach to matters,

---

19   Chief Justice 1965–1971.

as well as his humour. Besides courting Anna during my leisure time and avidly reading of course, I read the news in English on Radio Tanzania. They had asked me to do this because of my fluency in English.

I was a tiny fellow within the government at the time of the Zanzibar revolution[20] in January 1964, so I have nothing to recount from my work then. I was worried about how much life would be lost and whether the ensuing violence would descend upon us in Tanganyika. I was overjoyed at the overthrow of the sultanate, which went absolutely against the spirit of African independence. Nonetheless I was concerned whether this would breed antagonism between the races, because although there were few Europeans here, there were Indians and Arabs, and indeed most of those who were killed in Zanzibar were Arabs. The Indian and Arab merchants and clove plantation owners were powerful and visible but it was the Arabs who constituted the ruling class. The potential impact on race relations was worrying, as what happened in Zanzibar could affect the ordinary person's attitude to Arabs and Indians.

I have pondered on the extent to which the revolution in Zanzibar affected the subsequent mutinies by the armies of Tanganyika, Kenya and Uganda. I think these armies were dissatisfied as there was still a large European contingent of former civil servants and administrators, with most of them being in the armed forces. More British than Tanganyikans held rank, with no Tanganyikan above captain. The living conditions of the Tanganyikan troops were poor. Within a week of the revolution we had the uprising of the army[21] in Dar es Salaam. Solomon Ole Saibul, a friend from Makerere University College days, who would later rise to be minister of natural resources, and I were renting a house on the main road to the airport, not far from the TAZARA railway station. That morning when Ole and I were driving to work, we met a detachment of soldiers who pointed their guns at us and ordered us to go back. Saibul resisted at first, almost arguing with them, he was a Maasai after all, but I exclaimed "Hey wait a minute, these fellows have guns, let's turn around"! On our way home we saw two trucks loaded with white army

---

20   The Zanzibar revolution commenced 12 January 1964, with estimated deaths ranging from 2,000 to 20,000.
21   The mutiny in Dar es Salaam commenced 19 January 1964.

officers heading for the airport. The next thing we heard were shots; we became very apprehensive, thinking that if they had shot those white officers then all hell would break loose. After a while we heard a Dakota DC3 flying out and fervently hoped that the white officers were alive and on that plane on their way to Nairobi, as turned out to be the case. I was apprehensive that there would be loss of life and, being a foreign service officer, that we should not hurt relations with our former colonial master. I had not sensed that something was building up to result in this uprising by some of the army, I had absolutely no idea; I was just too new to government at that time. The mutiny lasted around six days and was quelled with the help of the British army.

On 26 April 1964 Tanganyika made a union with Zanzibar, which led to the birth of our combined nation: The United Republic of Tanzania. There was a sense of great relief when it took place because we trusted Mwalimu's absolute ability to cool things down. Though he didn't gain immediate influence over the islands and there were incidents here and there with people disappearing, and there was apprehension that some of the unrest might pour over to the Mainland, thankfully this didn't happen. This union strengthened my commitment to African unity because it showed that it was possible for two countries to unite and safeguard an African independence which was tolerant of other races. I am sure that if it wasn't for this union we would have had a very troubled Eastern Africa. It would have attracted attention from the Americans because they were fearful of the influences of the Soviet Union and China upon Abdulrahman Mohamed Babu[22], who was seen as a key driver of the revolution. He became a minister in the union's cabinet.

Another event which sticks in my mind is the disagreement between Kwame Nkrumah[23], Ghana's first president and Mwalimu at the Organisation of African Unity's (OAU) summit in Cairo in July 1964. Nkrumah was pushing for the adoption of one continental African government, a

---

22 Secretary General of Zanzibar Nationalist Party 1957–1963; founder of Umma Party of Zanzibar in 1963; Foreign Minister of Zanzibar January–April 1964; Minister of Economic Planning of the Union government 1964–1972.

23 First Prime Minister of Ghana March 1957–July 1960, President of Ghana July 1960–February 1966.

'United States of Africa', while Mwalimu preferred taking this in stages, forming regional governments first. Nkrumah launched an 'attack' on Mwalimu's stance and Mwalimu was furious; he shut his hotel room door and wrote his own response. By the time he had finished delivering his response to the summit he had won. I think he won the hearts of the Francophones, who didn't like Nkrumah much, they thought he undermined them. Despite this public disagreement, Nkrumah and Mwalimu maintained cordial contact, and I recall that Mwalimu was furious when Nkrumah was overthrown by a military coup in 1966.

Then there was the Rhodesian Unilateral Declaration of Independence (UDI) in November 1965. Mwalimu was incensed at Britain's acquiescence. He told them: "We are going to break relations because this is inconsistent and unprincipled. You can't commit yourself to fight racism and change the regime in Rhodesia and do nothing". From this I learnt the strength of courage, a quality every leader must possess. If you have courage you will summon the will to see things through; which is what Mwalimu surely did. His stance did require explanation by him in the media, but at the end of the day the people were with him as we were united and firm in our anti-colonial struggle.

One evening after reading the news on Radio Tanzania I left the recording booth to be told: "*Mwalimu wants you at Msasani*[24]". I was deeply shocked and drove to his home in Msasani, which we all called 'The Clinic', wondering all the time what have I done wrong, and why hadn't he taken my misdemeanour up with my permanent secretary or my minister, which was the usual way? I was in awe of him, I couldn't believe that I was being called by the president to his residence. After nervously greeting him he told me to sit down and said he was unhappy with the way the English newspaper of the party, *'The Nationalist'*, was being managed. He said, "Ben, I think you can help us, I want you to be the editor of 'The Nationalist', I think you can do it, can you?"

I nervously replied, "Mr President I know I can write, but this is a newspaper, I know next to nothing".

"That's alright", he responded:

---

24   Suburb of Dar es Salaam where Mwalimu had his private residence.

What I shall do is to contact Barbara Castle[25], whose husband Ted (Edward) is on the management of the Mirror newspapers in the UK. I have a good working relationship with Mrs Castle and my personal assistant Joan Wicken knows her well. We will write to tell her that we want you to go there for a couple of months to learn about newspaper production and management. Then you will come back, and I will appoint you as editor.

I consented, "Ok sir, if you think I can help you, fine".

Mwalimu was astute in reading people, he must have seen some potential in me and had recognised my interest in politics when he asked me to become the managing editor. I suspect he must have known of my political interest during my time at Makerere and then followed my progress at the ministry of external affairs. This shows that Mwalimu was observant and followed people's progress carefully. He was a leader who could quickly recognise the qualities and potential of others, even when that person had not recognised this.

---

25 Later known as Baroness Castle of Blackburn.

CHAPTER 6

Writing to Serve Our Nation

TANU had established the English language newspaper *'The Nationalist'* in April 1964. The tone of *'The Nationalist'* was more outrageously nationalistic and pan-African than Mwalimu, who was a man who weighed his words carefully, who was not flamboyant in his promises or his demands of people of other nations, being down to earth about such matters. The editor of *'The Nationalist'* was a Ghanaian called Jimmy (James) Markham[26], the sub-editor was also a Ghanaian and there were two Irishmen working there as well. It was time for the party's English language newspaper to be run by Tanzanians; so after around five months in England learning about the newspaper industry from employees of The Mirror Group I was appointed as the managing editor of *'The Nationalist'* in May or June 1966. The other TANU newspaper at that time was '*Uhuru*', which was published in Kiswahili.

Some of the journalists who came to work on my team were Kabenga Nsa-Kaisi, Costa Kumalija, Damien Chokungokela who came from the Kiswahili Catholic Weekly '*Kiongozi*', (*The Leader*), and Gray Likungu Mataka, who was related to Oscar Kambona, the minister of foreign affairs. Those responsible for information at State House were Hashim

---

26 Formerly of the '*Accra Evening News*'.

Mbita, who was followed by Paul Sozigwa as press secretary to the president. Hashim Mbita joined the Tanzania People's Defence Force and rose to brigadier general and executive secretary of the Liberation Committee of the Organisation of African Unity, (OAU).

The staff at the newspaper had to accept me because they knew this was a political appointment; my editor in chief was Mwalimu, the president himself. I did feel immense pressure though; I was being watched by those at the top, by my peers and those who worked under me at the newspaper. It was also tough because our newspaper had little funds while our competition, *'The Standard'*, was an established commercial exercise. Staff working at *'The Standard'* were better paid than we were, even receiving a travel allowance while at *'The Nationalist'* we would come to the end of the month and sometimes if our sales had been low then we would have to wait for two weeks before we could pay salaries. But the staff were very patient, they were committed to working for the party and their nation. It was worrying for me though, at times I didn't know what my future would be.

This was the first time I was responsible for leading others and I strove to build a camaraderie amongst the journalists and editorial staff. We shared the drive to help our country and we worked long hours, seven days a week. It was tough, no doubt about that, it hardened me well for my future work. My personal car was the office car; with the journalists often joining me at home for dinner. Anna was very supportive indeed, offering hospitality to all who came to our home. By then she was working for UNICEF and liked her job.

Now I was thrown into politics, for Mwalimu expected me to advocate the policies the government was adopting. My role was to ensure that the newspaper supported the party's views and to educate readers on aspects of socialism and development. For we were heading to a massive change for the country which would be laid out in the Arusha Declaration. Those who were against the concept of African socialism would say, "Where are you taking this country, what is this thing you are writing about – ujamaa?" We didn't falter at all, we were steady for socialism, African socialism, as we put it; we had to defend the ideology and write well. From this experience I learnt the importance in leadership of being resolute in one's conviction and conveying the vision for your nation.

'*The Nationalist*' was also expected to underscore the party's support for the liberation movements, which required two of our reporters to have good connections with the major movements. The first was Kabenga Nsa-Kaisi, who would years later become my special assistant to the president for regional administration, as he had risen to be regional commissioner in three regions. The other reporter who worked with the movements was Ferdinand Ruhinda who worked at the radio station where I was still reading the news. I had noticed that when he was on duty there was a positive difference in the news writing and presentation, I had much less corrections to do than usual, so I sought him out and thanked him for doing a great job. Later he came to me and asked, "Do you think I could find a place on your newspaper?" I was happy to welcome him to my team. When I left '*The Nationalist*' and its Kiswahili counterpart '*Uhuru*' to take over the management of a government newspaper '*Daily News*', I had Ferdinand appointed as the managing editor of '*Uhuru*'. When I later left the '*Daily News*' to become press secretary to the president he was appointed as managing editor of '*Daily News*'. Years later he would manage my campaign to become president.

Mwalimu used '*The Nationalist*' and '*Uhuru*' to explain a lot of issues. From time to time he would write an editorial, other times he would discuss an issue with us and we would write the editorial or articles ourselves. Some of these editorials were to a certain extent a window to Mwalimu's mind; he would air his thoughts trying to stimulate people to start thinking about an issue. Occasionally he wrote articles under a nom de plume. Once the Americans were quite angry about our coverage of the war in Vietnam in '*The Nationalist*' and complained to Mwalimu that '*The Nationalist*' was expressing anti-American sentiments which were different from Mwalimu's and the government's stance. Mwalimu's disingenuous response was that this was the right of '*The Nationalist*' to do so because of the freedom of the press, it had nothing to do with him or the government.

I encountered a backlash from some of Tanzania's small middle class, with many flabbergasted by the position I took. I recall Dr Wilbert Chagula[27] who was the vice-principal and registrar of the then University College of Dar es Salaam; we knew each other from the TANU Club at Makerere University College. He admonished me, saying I had received a good education, yet now I was writing contentious material and associating with radicals. "Ben, I just don't understand", he complained. Some government ministers were openly hostile to me, or regarded me with suspicion, erroneously believing I was trying to influence Mwalimu against them. But I remained committed, my experience as a district officer cadet registering people in the villages to receive food relief was my call to arms so to speak, our citizens had to be helped to gain a better standard of living and I firmly believed that Mwalimu would achieve this.

Perhaps the minister who most enjoyed encounters with me and my reporters from '*The Nationalist*' was Amir Jamal[28], the Minister of Finance. The Minister of Economic Planning and known communist, Abdulrahman Mohamed Babu, had a regular column in '*The Nationalist*'. Yoweri Museveni[29] was another regular columnist, he helped form the University Students' African Revolutionary Front and was its chairman while he was studying at the University of Dar es Salaam. He was a frequent visitor to '*The Nationalist*' where we provided him with a lot of information; our newspaper was influential amongst the university students.

Prior to the momentous meeting of TANU in Arusha in January 1967 Mwalimu had a whirlwind tour around the regions and by the time he

---

27 Vice-principal and registrar of University College of Dar es Salaam 1963–65, also Dar es Salaam University's first indigenous principal 1960–1970. Minister for Water Development and Power; Minister Economic Affairs and Development Planning; Minister for Water, Minerals and Energy; Minister for Finance and Administration of the East African Community; Chairman of COSTECH, and Ambassador to the United Nations in Geneva.

28 Minister Finance 1965–72, 1975–77 and 1979–1983; Minister Commerce and Industries 1972–75; Communications and Transport for approximately two years 1977–78; Minister without Portfolio 1983–1984; Minister of State for Cabinet Affairs 1984–1985. Joined TANU as its first non-African member in 1962.

29 President of Uganda since 1986.

met the central committee and the national executive committee of TANU at Arusha he knew well the reality of life for the people, especially those in the rural areas, who were the majority of the population. At the meeting in Arusha he gave an overview of the living conditions he had seen during this tour, then stressed that the people were looking up to TANU and the government to at least define the meaning of *uhuru* and proceeded to explain his concept of African socialism. This time in Arusha was perhaps the most critical two weeks of his career, but he was an extremely articulate leader, advocating strongly for equal opportunities for all. Initially his concept of *ujamaa* did not receive the full support of his cabinet, but he persisted. There was little discussion amongst us civil servants, but it certainly was a hot issue of debate amongst politicians.

In addition to Mwalimu's deep concern for the living conditions of the populace I could see from our reporting of his speeches around the country that he was unsettled by the emerging trend of politicians using their positions to better themselves; I sensed that something was brewing. Mwalimu tabled this matter for discussion in Arusha as well, resulting in two days of intense debate. Some agreed that the temptation to use public office for self-promotion and self-aggrandisement existed, noting that some politicians were being enticed to be on boards of companies as a way of security for that company, while others said that we should not constrain the initiative and talent of politicians. This discussion led to the drafting and subsequent adoption of the Leadership Code.

The Arusha Declaration[30] was adopted in Arusha on 29 January 1967; nowadays it is discounted by many, perhaps because of its socialist connections. But it still bears worth examining today, and much is still relevant, such as the importance of self-reliance and the dangers of relying upon aid from third parties; as well as the vital roles sound policies and good leadership have in this nation's development. Nsa-Kaisi and I attended the meeting and helped draft a few paragraphs. It was Nsa-Kaisi who came up with the name 'Arusha Declaration'. We used this in '*The Nationalist*' and Mwalimu liked it and adopted the name. We two were

---

30 Part One of The Arusha Declaration is in Appendix One.

considered trouble makers by some politicians, some suspected me of being the brains behind the declaration, which is not true.

What was most unpopular was part five of the declaration, which ruled that no TANU leader or government leader such as an employee, councillor or member of parliament and their spouse could be directly associated with capitalism, whether by way of their own business, company directorship, holding shares or even renting houses. This measure was specifically introduced as there were people from the government and party who were abusing their positions to enrich themselves and Mwalimu foresaw that this would "…alienate the leadership from the people". After its adoption by the party we returned to our hotel and sat in the lobby. Two members of the national executive committee came upon us there; one of them was Michael Kamaliza, I think he was the minister of labour and secretary general of the National Union of Workers at that time; he was vehemently opposed to the declaration. He took off his sandals and presented them to us, declaring, "Take them you fellows, you decide that everything belongs to you, even my shoes, so take them!" There were some people who were truly upset, especially those who were aspiring to be new capitalists, own property or be big farmers. What's more with nationalisation many ministers lost their houses and businesses. The ideology was not embraced wholeheartedly by the party elite. I think it was worse in the civil service, they just didn't understand and were protective of their positions. The equality being espoused by Mwalimu was seen by many as a threat to their livelihoods.

In 1998 Mwalimu was asked by Dr Ikaweba Bunting if the Arusha Declaration, then over thirty years old, was still valid. Mwalimu's response was that it was, adding:

> The Arusha Declaration was what made Tanzania distinctly Tanzanian. We stated what we stood for, we laid down a code of conduct for our leaders and we made an effort to achieve our goals. This was obvious to all, even if we made mistakes – and when one tries anything new and uncharted there are bound to be mistakes. The Arusha Declaration and our democratic single-party system, together with our national language, Kiswahili, and a highly

politicized and disciplined national army, transformed more than 126 different tribes into a cohesive and stable nation.

He added later during that interview: "...I still think that in the end Tanzania will return to the values and basic principles of the Arusha Declaration".[31]

The Arusha Declaration is ignored today because of its strong association with African socialism. It is seldom heard or incorporated in political discourse, in articulation of state policy or in advocacy of national fundamental philosophy, perhaps because few leaders support it. It is wrong for the Arusha Declaration to be thought of simply in terms of the leadership code, that code was designed specifically as a restraining instrument for people who were using their government offices to enrich themselves. I regard the declaration deserving of attention from Tanzanians today. The challenge is for young people to understand the ethos of the declaration and determine how to adapt it for today's environment so that it can be used as a framework to achieve economic, social and cultural objectives. I accept that there cannot be a society without differing incomes, though this inequality should not be great. The ethos of the Arusha Declaration remains, you must involve the people and the land in development; you must plan, and encourage a society which values hard work, intelligence and self-reliance.

Mwalimu was making a significant change in our society, introducing concepts new to the majority of the population. Our role in the media was to 'translate' these concepts so they would be understood by the citizens, though of course it would be for the minority, those who could read. The biggest challenge was to open the minds of the well-educated; they were an elite minority who thought they would be the new ruling class and here was Mwalimu speaking of equality and shared resources. We of '*The Nationalist*' and '*Uhuru*' were well aware of our responsibility. To educate the peasantry, most of whom were illiterate, Mwalimu would

---

31 Extracted from the article '*The heart of Africa*' by Ikaweba Bunting contained in the January/February 1999 issue of the *New Internationalist*.
Downloadable from: https//:newint.org/features/1999/01/01/anticolonialism

travel throughout the country twice a year; one of our reporters always accompanied him.

Oscar Kambona, TANU Secretary General and Minister of External Affairs did not attend the meeting in Arusha, but once he realised that this ideology was eventually going to be adopted, he went to the Civil Service School in Dar es Salaam to publicly support the ideology; I regarded him as an opportunist. Kambona would resign later that year, flee from Tanzania and condemn the Arusha Declaration, saying that Mwalimu wanted to adopt the ethos of communism rather than socialism. I remember being surprised hearing his announcement that he had resigned, naturally this was very newsworthy for the newspaper, so we closely followed what happened next. Around two or three days after his announcement he called a public meeting in his constituency of Morogoro where he withdrew his resignation and said he would return to cabinet. I found this odd, so requested to see my editor in chief, the president. He saw me immediately and I told him of Kambona's withdrawal. Mwalimu said, "No way, I have withdrawn his appointment". We reported that while Kambona had initially resigned, it was now out of his hands as his appointment had been withdrawn. I regarded his actions as somewhat treacherous, they were not positive for the nation's development and unity. He ended up in England, where he tried to foster an underground movement against Mwalimu.

My work was helped by the fact that I was allowed to attend the meetings of the central committee of the party. Non-voting of course and I didn't speak unless I was asked to; but at least I heard the discussions and learnt the underlying rationale for the decisions made. It also provided me with a good insight to the thinking of Mwalimu and within the leadership of the party. Even though we were a one-party state there was space for debate amongst the politicians, they felt free to suggest initiatives. Pros and cons would be analysed, experts sometimes called in to contribute and the senior party members would work together to come up with an appropriate strategy or policy. There doesn't seem to be the same quality of debate nowadays, the emphasis seems to be more on political grandstanding or point scoring.

One of the consequences of my attending those meetings was that sometimes when there was a policy paper issued from the national executive committee I was part of the team drafting the policies because of my editorial experience. For example, a meeting of the national executive committee was called to discuss the potential of irrigation in boosting agricultural production, especially in those areas where there was ample water and the policy on farming with irrigation arose from this meeting: '*Kilimo cha Umwagiliaji*' *(1974)* (Irrigation Agriculture). Similarly, the policy '*Siasa ni Kilimo*'*(1972)* (Politics is Agriculture) arose from our realisation that we were thinking of development as industrialisation, forgetting that agriculture can be the basis of value addition. We saw the need to disabuse people of the notion that the deployment of agriculture was solely the preserve of the professionals such as agricultural officers and veterinarians. Furthermore, it was acknowledged that it was important for the politicians to know about agriculture because they were the leaders of people who were predominantly peasant farmers. Pretty soon the politicians would ask each other where there *shamba* (small farm) *was*. You had to show that you could live off the land, rather than just leading those who lived off the land. I learnt from this that as a political leader you must be actively involved in promoting policy to the citizens.

A great quality of our first president was his capacity to listen; he would patiently listen to all kinds of rubbish, especially when politicians were essentially showing off their ability to express themselves. Some of us would be impatient and send notes to each other asking why Mwalimu would not stop them from talking. But he would sit and listen very carefully to everyone; he was conscious of allowing them to have their say. This ability to listen was a notable aspect of his leadership style, no question about that.

It was Mwalimu and his assistant Joan Wicken who taught me about socialism. I read everything he wrote, reproducing some of his speeches in English so they could be published in '*The Nationalist*'. What appealed to me in socialism was the emphasis on the principle of equality and the importance of self-reliance. The principle of equality was important for our populace because our nation was comprised of over 120 tribes. If you emphasised our people's diversity, rather than equality, this could be problematic for national unity. It also appealed to me that there shouldn't be such a large gap in incomes. The concept of self-reliance, that we shouldn't depend too much on aid, that we must use our own energies and resources also had a strong attraction to me. My conviction in the importance of self-reliance lasts to this day.

'*The Nationalist*' and '*Uhuru*' were vehemently against the occupation of Vietnam and Mwalimu sent me there to demonstrate our solidarity with the Vietnamese people in their struggle against American occupation and for unification. I visited North Vietnam during 1968 as editor of the party newspaper; travelling to Hanoi from southern China. One afternoon in our hotel there was an air raid siren and I was so surprised to see one of the waitresses pick up her gun and guide us down to the bunker. I had seen her only as a waitress serving us. Then came her sudden transformation to a soldier, this was real equality for women, it heightened my respect for women workers. Much later I enjoyed visiting Saigon (Ho Chi Minh City) when president. Some of the government officials mentioned then that I had been editor of the party newspaper which had strongly supported them; they keep score, they sure do.

On the home front we felt there was a need to improve the education curricula, particularly in terms of history and geography as it was too English oriented, students would be taught about the county of Northumberland in the UK, which was ridiculous. In my editorial I asked why, several years after independence, our students were sitting examination papers that were orientated to England. The Minister of Education, the late Solomon Eliufoo[32] was furious at what we published because he thought we had destroyed his credibility; he complained to the president, who responded, "Oh come on, these are young people, forget it". But when I next met Mwalimu he said, "The minister complained about this, you know, so find a way of asking for change in less abrasive ways. Your case is quite right but the language and presentation were a bit harsh". This was a good lesson for me in constructive criticism.

I became interested in the TANU Youth League because they were a very important pillar of party governance; we called them the 'Green Guards', so I became involved and was eventually invited to be on their general council. This helped to deepen my understanding of the workings and intricacies of the party. The reporters and I also joined the

---

32 Minister of Health 1959–1960; Minister of Education 1962–1967.

TANU study group which Mwalimu established to encourage intellectual discussion on aspects of socialism. We read widely and discussed adapting policies used by other socialist countries for our own country's development.

'The Nationalist' and 'Uhuru' supported national service, which had been introduced in 1964 on a voluntary basis. During 1966, we called for it to be mandatory for graduates of higher learning institutions. I believed in the case very strongly, but word started getting back to me that people were saying, "Mkapa and his fellows, they are just doing this to please the president; they themselves have not done any national service". So I went to my president and requested to join the adult intake for the national service; which was known as the 'Arusha Declaration Intake', which would have a term of three to four months. He was unsure, querying, "You are editing my party newspapers, who will edit the papers?" I replied, "I have assistants there who can do this". He remained doubtful until I mentioned Ruhinda and Nsa-Kaisi to him, adding, "They are the pillars of my work there. If you agree to meet them fairly regularly, as you have been meeting me as your editor, I am sure that they will do fine". So off to do my national service I went.

This was my first time as an adult to live and work with people from all walks of life. As I entered the gate to the army compound they ordered, "Take your suitcase on your head", and of course I immediately thought of my school days. "Now go quick march to the dormitory. Until you get your force number you are a recruit and recruits don't walk, they trot from point A to point B. Otherwise you will be punished. Anyone who has come with a degree, remember you have left your degree at the gate". One of the officers who took us for drill was a woman; she was beautiful, but tough, no-one would dare say any nonsense to her. We worked hard, particularly during the first month and a half, it was a good physical regime for me.

National service underscored the unity of our people; we were adults from all kinds of professions. In my intake one was a hotel booking clerk, a few of us had degrees, while others were peasant farmers barely able to read and write. We all worked as a team, regardless of our education or status outside of the army. You learnt skills of how to do things, when to do things, when to seek help and when to reciprocate. One night we were woken up and given hoes without handles. The officer said, "When you get on parade tomorrow morning we will inspect your hoe with a handle". I said to my colleagues, "How can I go to the bush in the night to look for something which could be a hoe handle?" A peasant farmer I got on very well with came to my aid, offering to go with me to find something, which we did. He then fashioned a handle for me so when I went on parade I had my hoe. My turn to help him came when he was asked to produce a short play using us adults. I reassured, "Don't worry, leave it to me", and helped him with the production of the play. This fostering of mutual support and cooperation was a positive outcome of national service.

National service encouraged our ardent support for the liberation struggle. A political commissar called Ali Mchumo[33] gave us lectures on governance and colonialism. The themes of our singing while we worked were against Portuguese rule in Mozambique and Angola, racist rule in South Africa and the then Rhodesia, and President Hastings Banda[34] – who we regarded a neo-colonial agent for his pro-Western stance and maintaining full diplomatic relations with apartheid South Africa.

Mwalimu came for the passing out of my adult intake and of a general intake. He inspected us on parade but didn't recognise me. Then we went to the assembly hall where a representative of the cadets would read a statement prepared by us describing our experience of the national service; I had been nominated to read this statement to our commander-in-chief, the president. I stood up in front of him to read the statement and he recognised me and started laughing because I had lost so much weight; I reckon at least four inches off my waist.

National service was a tough undertaking and I am very glad I undertook it. As a result of that experience, I think I worked more efficiently

---

33   Junior Minster Prime Minster's Office 1975–1977; Deputy Minster Home Affairs 1977–1981; Minister of Trade 1981–1083; Ambassador/High Commissioner to Australia, Swaziland, Ireland, Japan, Lesotho, Mozambique, the Philippines, UK and the United Nations in Geneva and Vienna; Deputy Secretary-General for France and Administration East African Community; Managing Director of the Common Fund for Commodities.

34   Prime Minister of Malawi July 1964–July 1966; President of Malawi July 1966–May 1994.

as managing editor of the party newspapers thereafter. What's more, no-one could say that I was arguing for a case that I hadn't experienced myself. From then onwards I was a great advocate of the national service and as president would later insist to my cabinet, "Now I don't care what anyone says, we are restoring national service". When I reinstated national service there was an effort by fundamentalist Muslims to have women excluded, which I refused as I did not want to lose that important integrationist benefit from the national service and I also recalled my experience with the waitress/soldier in North Vietnam. My camp commander from that time was the late Rashid Makame; he ended up as a major general in the national service with me as his commander-in-chief as I was president. I subsequently appointed him as ambassador to Malawi when he retired from the army.

I enjoyed my work as managing editor, though there were frustrations, largely due to insufficient funds. Occasionally we received support from central government, but our predominant source of revenue was advertising and sales, which were not very high. Sales did improve during my time, though I don't think we ever reached 10,000 copies with the 'The Nationalist', though we did better with 'Uhuru'. At times we were so short of funds that wages were delayed; I would appeal to the patriotism of the workers, asking them to bear with us. Eventually, we were able to increase the wages little by little as sales increased.

There was another English language newspaper, 'The Standard', which had been nationalised in 1970. Mwalimu had placed Dr Frene Ginwala as the managing editor, while he was 'editor in chief', as with 'The Nationalist' and 'Uhuru. She was an intelligent woman who would later become the first speaker in the post-apartheid parliament of South Africa. However, she was too socialist in some ways, and did not fully embrace our nation's policies or appreciate the policy and foreign relations inclinations of our president, particularly towards African countries. Eventually Mwalimu removed her as managing editor and merged 'The Nationalist' with 'The Standard' to form the 'Daily News'. He appointed me as the first managing editor of the 'Daily News' and our first publication was in April 1972.

I liked working in the world of the media because you were always producing something new; no edition looks like a previous issue. I enjoyed the mental stimulation of the editorial conferences where you were trying to reconcile a news story to the newspaper's policy, government policy and party policy. Was our article extremist? Was the language appropriate? Then of course the actual news stories, we enjoyed analysing the issues and digging into the background. We always insisted on trying to get both sides of the question presented, we were very strict on that. Otherwise our newspaper would have been too obviously propagandist and would have lost credibility. In addition, I found managing the *'Daily News'* less demanding financially because the returns on the sales and advertising were much better. The newspaper was self-reliant, we didn't need any intervention from the government, which was a relief to me. In the *'Daily News'* there was also less controversial coverage regarding the implementation of policy; rather it was a question of mistakes made by people, how to highlight them and whether they will think you are attacking them personally rather than their failure.

Other personal lessons from my time working on these newspapers which helped me as I took on greater leadership roles was that I learnt to work with people who were technically and/or professionally more knowledgeable than I was, particularly at *'The Nationalist'* where the typesetters knew more than me when it came to producing a newspaper. I learnt to adjust to working with people of different talents, and that, coming in from the top, it was important to have humility and not be seen as an oppressor. Furthermore, my teams were multi-religious which helped me to be inclusive, which is also necessary for leaders. Naturally our common socialist leanings underscored these benefits. The comradery and unity we achieved was a great thing; I believe these foster open communication and constructive dialogue within a team.

During this time I felt comfortable with my role, I did not have any specific goal for my career, other than I would continue doing good and remain in the public service, enjoying the confidence of my president, but other than that, quite frankly, I held no ambition. Also, we were bringing up our children, our first son Stephan (Steve) was born during 1967, and our second, Nicholas, during 1969, they were great fun. I hadn't really started thinking where it would end in terms of work and service; I just felt that I would continue and continue well. However, after a couple of years of absence from the civil service they forgot about me as a civil servant, and after my six years working on these newspapers I felt almost like a politician in limbo. Pius Msekwa[35], the party secretary general, had devised the notion that there was such a thing as a political civil servant, there was a government civil service and a political civil service, and this description of a political civil servant fitted me; I hadn't thought of standing for parliament. Then Mwalimu brought me completely under his wing as his press secretary, this was the beginning of my political career.

---

35   Speaker of the National Assembly of Tanzania 1994–2005; Vice-Chairman CCM 2007–2012.

CHAPTER 7

First Steps on My Political Journey

In 1974 the announcement was made, which was totally unexpected by me, that I had been appointed as Mwalimu's press secretary, then Mwalimu departed immediately for his home in the small village of Butiama, which is in the Mara Region of northern Tanzania. After completing the handover of the managing editor job to Ferdinand Ruhinda I wondered what to do, as Mwalimu was still away. When would he come back, should I wait for him to return? Sitting and waiting was not my style, so I found out that someone was going to Butiama with government papers for him and got a seat on that plane. I found Mwalimu hoeing in the field. He greeted me: "Ah, Ben, you have come to report. Very well, welcome". Obviously I could not say, "I will wait for you to finish", so I asked for a hoe and joined him for the better part of three hours, which was hard going for this desk worker. Thus my first job as press secretary was hoeing in the field each morning, followed each afternoon by my sitting in on the visits to his home; he received a constant stream of callers.

I was a novice as a state house employee, so was very careful in my relations with those who had been there 'forever', including his private secretary, Joseph Butiku[36]. I knew his personal assistant Joan Wicken well because of my prior job, who I got on beautifully with. During my two years in this position I travelled with Mwalimu and sat in on his meetings with the liberation movements in the frontline states, such as Zaire briefly, Zambia and Botswana. I also attended his meetings with the cabinet. I learnt a lot from two Indian ministers in the cabinet: Minister Amir Habib Jamal[37] and Minister Al Noor Kassum[38]. They would ask a lot of questions, they were thinkers, very development-oriented. Prime Minister Cleopa Msuya[39] was impressive, a very hard-working person. It was interesting work, but not arduous, as there was a ministry and director of information services. The minister of information had been arguing the case for a news agency which was finally approved by the cabinet, so Mwalimu asked me to start up the National News Agency, *SHIHATA*[40], which I did in 1974 and became the agency's CEO for two years.

The next job Mwalimu determined for me was to go to Nigeria to restore bilateral relations, not that they were broken, but there hadn't been an ambassador in Nigeria since the end of the civil war[41]. Relations had cooled because we had supported Biafra during the war, particularly Mwalimu. "I need someone there who can speak English well, who knows his diplomacy, who is educated and can compete with those fellows and I have decided you should go", he declared. I arrived as high commissioner late October 1976 and presented my credentials to General Olusegun Obasanjo, who was then head of the federal mili-

---

36 Private Secretary to Mwalimu Nyerere and later to President Mwinyi; Regional Commissioner; Executive Director and Trustee of Mwalimu Nyerere Foundation.

37 Minister of Finance 1965–1972, 1975–1977 and 1979–1983; East African Community Minister of Finance and Administration; Ambassador to the UN in Geneva 1985–1983.

38 Minister of Water, Energy and Minerals 1978–1979; Minister of Water and Energy 1980–1985; Minister of Energy and Minerals 1986–1988.

39 Prime Minister 1980–1983 and 1994–1995; Minister of Finance 1974–1975 and 1986–1989.

40 *Shirika la Habari la Tanzania*

41 Biafran War, also known as Nigerian Civil War, July 1967–January 1970.

tary government. He noted during our first meeting that Mwalimu was coming on a state visit for six days during the coming month. Fortunately Mwalimu's visit went well; I recall that a lecture he gave at the University of Ibadan was very well received[42].

Since I had left Tanzania so quickly to prepare for this state visit, I hadn't been able to say farewell to anybody in the ministries and discuss with them what relations they could establish with Nigeria. What's more, the new political party *Chama Cha Mapinduzi*, CCM (Party of the Revolution), was going to be founded on 5 February 1977. I had asked for permission from my ministry to come back to Dar es Salaam for a visit, which was denied. I said to myself:

> Wait a minute, I was the editor of the TANU party newspapers for six years, now these political parties TANU and Afro-Shirazi Party[43] are merging to form a new party and you are telling me that I shouldn't be there to witness it for myself? That I shouldn't say hello to anyone?

I called in my second-in-command and said, "Listen, this telegram from the ministry came after I had left, ok?" and set off for Tanzania. My arrival in Tanzania surprised the ministry, but then Mwalimu surprised me.

After the founding ceremony I was talking to my Minister of Foreign Affairs, Ibrahim Kaduma[44], when someone knocked on his office door and said, "Mwalimu wants Ben at his residence". So off I went again to 'The Clinic', wondering what was in store for me this time. Mwalimu said: "Ben, I have decided to make you foreign minister, my difficulty is how do I tell this to Obasanjo and how will he take it?" I replied:

> Mr President, you don't have to worry about Obasanjo. They treated you so well during your visit, they know there is good cause why

---

42 'The Process of Liberation', Ibadan University 17 November 1976.

43 From Zanzibar, founded in 1957.

44 Minister Foreign Affairs 1975–1977; Vice-Chancellor University Dar es Salaam 1977–1980; Minister of Trade 1980–1981; Minister Communications and Transport 1982–1982.

you are recalling me. You are calling me for higher office, in any case. So if you write a nice letter I will deliver it myself and give the explanation at the same time.

I took his letter with me, said farewell to my colleagues in Nigeria and returned to Tanzania. I had served as high commissioner for only three months. This upheaval was handled very well by my wife Anna, who had only recently joined me in Nigeria and found schools there for our two sons, when I told her that I'd been recalled. Fortunately it hadn't been long after she had left her job at UNICEF, so she was able to take up her old job when she returned.

I went to my soon to be permanent secretary, Antony Nyaki[45], and said, "You know you are looking at your next minister of foreign affairs". He was surprised. We were good friends, he had been my best man at my wedding. I asked, "Now how do I tell the minister to step aside, this is my seat now?"

"Well that's your problem", he replied. I didn't tell my minister, I just couldn't; Mwalimu must have told him. I was appointed minister of foreign affairs in late February 1977; this was the real start of my political journey.

From my past work I knew that foreign affairs were very close to Mwalimu's heart, being central to his management of state affairs. Given his intellect and his concern about relations with foreign powers it had to be like that; in a sense he was his own foreign minister; I was more like his assistant minister. At least he believed that I could listen, take notes of his meetings, attend meetings, deliver messages and report back to him. This working relationship worked very well, fortunately.

During my first year or so as minister of foreign affairs the number one issue was our interaction with other states on the question of the liberation of Southern Africa. We had what was called the frontline states – Angola, Botswana, Lesotho, Mozambique, Zambia and Tanzania – to speed up that process of lending support to the liberation movements.

---

45   Ambassador to the Netherlands 1968–1970; to Germany 1970–1972; High Commissioner to Zimbabwe 1980–1981; to UK 1981–1989; Ambassador to UN 1989–1994; Special UN Representative to Liberia 1994–1997.

There's no doubt that the heaviest burden for supporting the liberation movements rested on Tanzania and these frontline states. Mobutu Sese Seko[46] joined our group for a little while but his heart was not in it and he absented himself. Then the military government in Nigeria, which had a great sense of what the destiny of their country was in Africa, realised that the future for Africa was total liberation, so we became the frontline states and Nigeria. I worked very well with the Foreign Ministers, the late Major General Joseph Garba[47]; and Ibrahim Gambari[48], with whom I still keep in touch. The Nigerians did a splendid job of support, chiefly through finance and training.

Ministerial counterparts from that time who also rose to become president were Joaquim Chissano of Mozambique[49] and Abdelaziz Bouteflika[50] of Algeria. While Algeria was not a geographical frontline state it was firmly in the forefront of lending support to the liberation movements. The three of us were quite close, I suppose we were one of a kind: ardent nationalists, anti-imperialists, very much on the non-aligned side, analytical, and bold in our formal discussions, particularly with the major supporters of apartheid South Africa, such as the United States of America and the United Kingdom. These two men were brilliant, no question about that; they also enjoyed the confidence of their presidents. Another foreign affairs colleague I recall with respect is Archibald (Archie) Mogwe[51] from Botswana, a fine gentleman, he was older than us.

One challenge was to get the different members of liberation movements to agree on a unified front. It was particularly difficult and intense

---

46 President of Democratic Republic of Congo 1965–1997.

47 Nigeria: Minister Foreign Affairs 1975–1978; Permanent Representative to the United Nations 1984–1989; President United Nations General Assembly 1989–1990.

48 Nigeria: Minister for External Affairs 1984–1985; Permanent Representative to the United Nations 1990–1999; Chairman United Nations Special Committee Peacekeeping Operations 1990–1999; Under-Secretary of the United Nations 2000–2007.

49 President of Mozambique 1986–2005.

50 President of Algeria since 1999.

51 Foreign Minister 1974–1985, Minister Mineral Resources and Water Affairs 1985–1994; Ambassador to USA.

between the two political movements in Southern Rhodesia, with the Zimbabwe African National Union (ZANU) led by Robert Mugabe and the Zimbabwe African Peoples' Union (ZAPU) led by Joshua Nkomo. They came from the same country and held the same ambitions and aspirations, but you could sense that they couldn't stand each other. Usually Mwalimu would meet them separately, he found them frustrating to work with.

The West's perception of Tanzania at that time was that of an extremely independently-minded country, non-aligned, but very objective in analysing its interests, promoting them and fostering alliances. We did not have any serious opponents other than apartheid South Africa which did try to sabotage our efforts due to our support of the liberation movement.

With regards to the United States we would meet with President Jimmy Carter's secretary of state, Cyrus Vance[52], who was a fine gentleman. We also met with Donald McHenry[53], the U.S. ambassador to the United Nations, an African-American, he was brilliant, a shrewd diplomat, I have great respect for him. He was astute in his negotiations about Namibia and apartheid South Africa. His predecessor, Andrew Young[54], was also good, he was also an African-American. Sometimes you could sense that the Americans were feeling a little embarrassed defending their stance regarding the apartheid regime in South Africa. With the United Kingdom the underlying issue was that it was much more a matter of supporting kith and kin as there were many British people living in Rhodesia and apartheid South Africa. From Britain it was David Owen[55] I dealt with, he was the same age as me.

The Union of Soviet Socialist Republics' USSR involvement in Africa was mainly to provide arms and officer training in support of the libera-

---

52 Secretary of the Army July 1952–January 1964; Deputy Secretary of Defense January 1964–June 1967; Secretary of State January 1977–April 1980.

53 Ambassador to the United Nations September 1979–January 1981.

54 Ambassador to the United Nations January 1977–September 1979.

55 Minister of State for Health and Social Security July 1974–September 1976; Minister for State for Foreign and Commonwealth Affairs September 1976–February 1977; Secretary of State for Foreign and Commonwealth Affairs February 1977–May 1979.

tion movement. In a sense they were competing with China, which was a major supporter. In that regard we were quite non-aligned, we took anything anyone would give us for the struggle. The Soviets produced a lot of propaganda of course, but they did not try to influence us very much. They knew how strong Mwalimu was; you couldn't influence him; he looked only at the logic aimed at achieving agreed objectives. Though the Soviets did occasionally caution us about the machinations of the imperialists, which was helpful. I think that they viewed us as a dependable ally in their confrontation with the West in the sense that they would be sure that we would look at issues objectively and would not hesitate to support the Soviets if they were right, or to criticise the West if they were wrong in any confrontation between the two sides. Of course we respected USSR very much for its support for Cuba. The Soviets were not as sophisticated as the British or Americans when it came to propaganda. They undertook very little public relations in foreign countries as opposed to the work done by the British Council or the United States Information Services.

The Nordic countries were very reliable allies and I travelled there regularly as minister of foreign affairs. We had little to do with the French, though I recall the visit by Louis de Guiringaud, the French Minister of Foreign Affairs[56]. He arrived in his own plane, and, as customary, I was there to meet him at the airport. I found there around 200 university students holding placards denouncing France and its collaboration with apartheid, particularly the sale of weaponry to South Africa. De Guiringaud was furious, he had a very imperial manner. He said, "What is this? Is this the reception I deserve?" He said he held me personally responsible and demanded that I must tell the students to lay down their placards and leave. The students were well mannered standing in line, they didn't pose a threat to him, other than to his ego, so I responded that I would not do so, adding, "This is a free country, these are university students, they demonstrate just as yours do". He said this was unac-

---

56   French Permanent Representative to the United Nations 1972–1976; Minister of Foreign Affairs 1976–78.

ceptable[57]. Anyway, we drove past the students with their placards and I took him to his hotel where he said, "Now I must have an apology", to which I refused. He said, "Well, then we will not talk, nor do any business here". I calmly responded, "Fine, you think about it", and went straight to report to Mwalimu, who approved of my reaction, adding that it was provocative of De Guiringaud to ask for an apology. We cancelled the official dinner organised for that evening. De Guiringaud then sent a note essentially saying please let's forget this thing now, just send a little note to say that you are sorry for this unfortunate incident that happened and then we can resume. No way was I going to do this and Mwalimu backed me up. In the morning, I collected De Guiringaud and returned him to the airport. Upon his return to France he made a statement to the press, saying he held me personally responsible for the incident, that the demonstration had been "…organised with the complicity of the authorities". That's the kind of arrogance that France had towards its colonies in West Africa. He did not realise that this was Tanzania and Mwalimu was different, furthermore that our students had a right to protest against apartheid and its supporters.

We were alienated with the Israelis, largely because of Palestine. If the Israelis are entitled to a homeland, then why can't the Palestinians be entitled to a homeland? Mwalimu had severed relations in 1974, but I reinstated relations with Israel in 1995 when I became president. The Israelis helped us establish the national service and develop our agriculture; and also shared security information. They have more business in Kenya than here, though there is no political or legal bar against them here.

As minister of foreign affairs I accompanied Mwalimu on a visit to Saddam Hussein in Iraq during December 1979. The visit went well until their ministry came to us with a draft communique of our visit; a draft which condemned the American government for its oppressive treatment of African-Americans. My response was:

---

57   Link to a film clip at the airport with the students in view and De Guiringaud showing his displeasure: www.aparchive.com/metadata/youtube/e50429fd0fd2b-7cd410f84f8c57238ea

Do you think we can't condemn these people from our territory if we want to? Why do we have to come to Iraq to condemn them? We know there is racial discrimination, and there are places where Iraq can add its voice of support, but why do this on a bilateral visit between our countries?

Their response was that this was the way it would be, otherwise there is no communique. Did the Iraqis really think we were unable to examine issues and issue statements of our own; we had to be supported by Saddam Hussein and Iraq, or be used by them as their pawn? I said, "Ok, well, be prepared for no communique".

They responded, "Come on, you are our guests". I refused and then took the communique to our president, who had already retired for the night but got up to speak with me. I said, "Mwalimu this is what they are telling me, and I told them we don't travel to Iraq in order to condemn".

"You are quite right, there will be no communique", he replied. The next morning my Iraqi counterpart asked me what we had decided; he was shocked that we had not changed our mind and would end our visit with no communique. Before we left for the airport Saddam Hussein asked Mwalimu: "I understand there is a problem about our communique?".

Mwalimu replied, "Yes, because you are asking us to say things we cannot subscribe to, so there'll be no communique", and we departed. That was Mwalimu, a principled man. He was my teacher in every sense; when I became president I wouldn't tolerate such nonsense from anybody.

Regrettably my recall is not strong regarding the talks on independence for Southern Rhodesia. I do know that Robert Mugabe was very reluctant to reach agreement unless two issues were settled: one was the proposed size of the White representation in the independence constitution, which he thought excessive. Second was the question of the allocation of the land, "our land" he used to say. There was heavy argument during the Lancaster Agreement[58] negotiations, sometimes on the verge

---

58   Lancaster House Agreement signed December 1979.

of breaking up, but Mwalimu was able to persuade Mugabe to sign. He advised, "Don't you have majority rule? Well, you will be independent, so after a while you can change the constitution. Seize the power first". Mugabe agreed to this practical approach by Mwalimu, the agreement was signed, and Mugabe subsequently overcame these two issues of contention. The independence of Southern Rhodesia (now Zimbabwe), was a real culmination of my services as foreign minister. It was a very hard struggle and I admire Mwalimu's efforts, who persisted unceasingly.

Robert Mugabe is an ultra-nationalist with strong self-discipline. During the ten years he spent in jail[59] he obtained a Bachelor in Law and Economics, as well as a Bachelor of Administration, studying by correspondence from the University of London. He also taught his fellow political prisoners. He is also conscious of history, that Zimbabwe had been an empire in the past. But now he has got on in age, and a factor that has reduced his public image is this public perception, inculcated by the Western media, that he loves power so much that he will not leave. This has coloured people's perception of him as being power hungry. To understand my feelings towards Robert Mugabe, there is a speech I wrote for a public lecture at the University of Zimbabwe in 1999. I couldn't deliver this as Mwalimu was gravely ill at that time; so I sent Frederick Sumaye, my Prime Minister, to read it for me. Mugabe liked my speech *'The Quest for a Second Liberation in Africa'*[60] very much.

The general election in Southern Rhodesia was held during February 1980 to determine who would govern post-independence[61]. The major anticolonial political parties on the ballot were: ZANU-PF[62] led by Robert Mugabe and the Patriotic Front under Joshua Nkomo, which later became known as PF-ZAPU[63]. The British government under Prime Minister Margaret Thatcher had argued strongly before the elections that the voting would be manipulated, Robert Mugabe would steal

---

59 1964–1974.

60 Volume 2, Cluster 7 of 'The Mkapa Years Collected Speeches.' Dar es Salaam: Mkuki na Nyota.

61 Independence 18 April 1980.

62 Zimbabwe Africa Nation Union – Patriotic Front.

63 Patriotic Front – Zimbabwe African Peoples Union.

the elections and ZANU-PF would win. ZANU-PF's response was that their party was spread throughout the country and their party had more membership than Nkomo's Patriotic Front. Several election observers attended, including a team from the Commonwealth; their decision was that the elections had been fairly free. I led the delegation to celebrate the independence of Zimbabwe[64] and Peter Carrington, the British secretary of state for foreign and commonwealth affairs was there. At the pre-independence day reception, I went to Carrington and said, "So we have had a good election, free and fair".

He replied, "So I gather".

I then said, with grim humour, "Thank you, you helped us to steal the election". He was astounded; he didn't recognise I was making a joke. In his memoirs, '*Reflect on Things Past: The memoirs of Lord Carrington*'[65] he writes that I said, "The President wanted me to ask you why you made Mugabe win by so much".

I had the honour to receive Nelson Mandela after he was released from prison and came to Tanzania very shortly thereafter during March 1990. I took him to Dodoma where he met with Mwalimu and the central committee of the party. Nelson Mandela was fantastic, I was over-awed by him. When I went to brief Mwalimu before the two of them met I said, "Mandela is such a great personality, but what overwhelmed me was to look at him and say this guy has spent twenty-seven years in prison. That is nearly half my life, Mwalimu. I can't imagine spending half my life in prison". Four years later we went to his inauguration[66] and I said to Mwalimu, "I never thought I would step into a democratic free South Africa".

"Neither did I", Mwalimu replied; it had been such a long hard struggle for us all, for Mandela most of all.

Leaving foreign affairs for now, I'd like to comment a little on the internal politics during this period. I welcomed the merger of the mainland based political party TANU and the Afro-Shirazi Party from Zanzibar

---

64   18 April 1980.

65   London: Collins 1988.

66   10 May 1994.

to form CCM in 1977; it made sense of the fact that we were a one-party state. I also hoped that this would moderate the extremists on both sides of the Union, as there were some real hardliners and it could have become a whirlpool of ideological contest. Uniting would also give ascendency to Mwalimu, everyone would have to think hard before they took him on. What's more, I thought this would give momentum to democratic change and therefore also stem the excesses of those on the Mainland who were against the Zanzibaris and those from Zanzibar who thought the revolution had not been hard enough on their former oppressors. Knowing Mwalimu's skill in moderating differing interests, I thought he would bring a positive and calming influence.

When it came to building bridges between differing interests, Mwalimu could really bring people together. There was a lot of contest between the various wings of the liberation movements in Southern Africa and sometimes this would really get out of hand. Mwalimu would try to discuss the issue and encourage reaching a compromise, but if people were recalcitrant and Mwalimu was getting fed up he wouldn't lose his temper, rather he would walk out, calm down, and then return to resume the meeting. This was his way of telling them to think again.

Accomplished communication skills are essential for any leader and Mwalimu was an exceptional communicator. He was adept at finding areas of common interest when chatting with foreign diplomats, whether issue related or mere social chat to put them at ease. Certainly, I learnt the importance of listening from him. Often I would feel impatient listening to someone drone on and on and wonder why we were taking so long; why Mwalimu didn't tell the fellow to cease? His capacity to listen, even to the dullest member of the gathering, was extraordinary. He listened because something of value might emerge from whatever the speaker was saying, that person's florid presentation style might be obscuring some useful knowledge, so he would patiently wait. I definitely owe an immense debt to Mwalimu for teaching me the importance of listening.

Mwalimu was brilliant at using the talents of others to enrich his arguments. You would go to him and say I have an idea. He was always open to hear your ideas and would listen thoughtfully to what you said. Once you had finished he would respond by putting it another way and by the time he was through talking you thought why didn't I think of doing it this way? He was exceptional in this regard. Another of Mwalimu's superb communication skills was his ability to give arguments a simple, understandable and retainable presentation, distilling down to the key elements. You can see this in his speeches.

In 1977 I was nominated as a member parliament. As I recall, there were five different wings (*jumuiya*) of CCM: women's, youth, parents', cooperatives, and labour unions. Each wing had the right to nominate around five potential candidates to go into a pool for election to the special seats of parliament. It was the cooperatives wing which sponsored my entry into the election. When I was later appointed as high commissioner to Canada I could no longer be a member of parliament so on my return to Tanzania the president nominated me as a member of parliament under his allowance of ten seats. In 1985 the party political leadership from my district of Masasi asked me to stand for Nanyumbu constituency in Masasi District, to which I was elected and then re-elected in 1990. I had resolved that come 1995 I wouldn't stand again; it was time to retire as I felt I had been in politics too long.

When I had to tell Anna we are off to Canada as I had been appointed high commissioner there she was annoyed and frustrated because by that time she had really made her mark at the UNICEF office in Dar es Salaam and didn't want to leave her job. Anna is someone who likes work; even now in retirement she works more than I do. I was the high commissioner in Canada for only ten months; no sooner had my family settled then we all had to move to Washington DC where I was appointed ambassador to the United States of America. We had been there only fourteen months when I received a phone call from Dar es Salaam saying please come back as the President wants to see you. I said to Anna, "I have an instinct that we are going back".

"Oh no" she said, "no please; not again. Please can't we be allowed to settle in one place?" Naturally I sympathised with how she was feeling but I felt a strong sense of duty towards Mwalimu:

> How do I say no to my president when he asks me to do that? I can only hesitate if he's calling me to give me a whole new portfolio without explaining why. But if, for instance, he was to call me and

say I want you back at the ministry of foreign affairs, how do I say no? The struggle continues in Southern Africa.

Sure enough, Mwalimu wanted me to take over the foreign affairs ministry again. I had to tell Anna, "I'm sorry, I had to accept, so you will have to pack and come back again". To her credit she was understanding that I was needed and accepted to return. This time it was more difficult for her to rejoin UNICEF, but she managed to do so, which pleased her.

Mwalimu was quite demanding of me and my family with all these changes in positions and locations. Between 1976 and 1985 when Mwalimu left office I worked in Nigeria (1976), Canada 1982), USA (1983–1984) and of course Tanzania. I was appointed as high commissioner/ambassador, was twice the minister of foreign affairs (1977–1980 and 1984–1990) and once minister of information and culture (1980–1982). Under the reign of his successor, President Ali Hassan Mwinyi[67], I continued as minister of foreign affairs, then became the minister responsible for information and broadcasting (1990–1992), then science, technology and higher education (1992–1995).

Wherever in the world in the political arena, the spouses and children of politicians always have to make sacrifices. I am very grateful to Anna, especially when I think of her patience and strength during my frequent absences travelling as well as the long hours I worked. I'm not an easy person to get along with and she has really borne a lot throughout my career, she had to cope with many separations and carry the greater responsibility of raising our children. I salute Anna, for she was the glue which held our family together.

There is no doubt that these many changes during our sons' childhood was difficult on them and Anna. There were some people who recognised this and went out of their way to support us and I have several people to thank for contributing to the stability of our marriage and for our children's welfare. First is Mwalimu. When he asked me to return from Washington DC, I said to him:

---

67 Second president of Tanzania 1985–1995.

> Sir, as you know, I am always ready to serve you, but I ask you please to also take into consideration my children. They have been through three differing education systems: Tanzania, Canada and the USA. Now I'm going to take them back to Tanzania. How will they fit back in to that education system? They are approaching their final years of high school; please provide for them to finish high school there; then, if they qualify for university, they can come back to university in Tanzania.

Mwalimu immediately approved the financing of this, he was very good on that front for which my family and I were grateful for. Then there was the problem of school holidays when our sons were still at high school as we couldn't afford to fly them home to Tanzania for each holiday. We knew Mrs Perucy Butiku, who held the position of counsellor at the Tanzania permanent mission to the United Nations in New York. We asked her if she could take the boys in for the occasional holiday which she willingly did, even after she left the mission.

I was fortunate to have a friend, Peter Palangyo, who was a brilliant and creative man. He is known for his novel '*Dying in the Sun*'[68] which he wrote while still at university. I got to know him personally because of our shared interest in literature when I was his minister of foreign affairs; he was a foreign service officer. One of the things I really loved to do during trips to Europe or USA as foreign minister was to have a little time to myself to go to the theatre or a good bookshop. Anyway, Peter had a friend from his home locality of Arusha, Eli (Eliawira) Ndosi, who had studied in the United States and was now teaching economics at Augsburg College in Minnesota, and Peter had introduced me to him on one of my official visits to USA Much later, when Anna and I had a dilemma about how to find a college for our elder son Stephan (Steve) to go to, Eli generously offered that Stephan live with him and his family and go to Augsburg College. Stephan received his college education in the USA thanks to the generous and welcoming hospitality of Eli, his wife Barbara and their children. Thankfully, by the time our younger

---

68   '*Dying in the Sun*'. London: Heinemann 1968.

son Nicholas (Nico) was due to go to college and then on to study law we were able to manage this ourselves. Anna and I are very grateful for this kindness extended by Eli and Barbara Ndosi and Mrs Perucy Butiku to my sons over the years; I sincerely thank them for making it possible for my children to smoothly transition the periods of high school and then university.

Before Peter Palangyo joined foreign affairs he worked as a teacher at Tambaza Secondary School in Dar es Salaam, where Mwalimu's children attended; Peter shared this anecdote with me from his time there. One of Mwalimu's sons was particularly naughty; he thought that because he was the son of the president he could be disrespectful and disobedient to the teacher. So the teacher, who was also the headmaster, gave him corporal punishment and the boy complained to his father, saying that the teacher at the school was very disrespectful of Mwalimu. The next morning Mwalimu gave his son a ride in his car to the school, on his way to work. His son gloated to arrive at his school in the official car. Mwalimu asked, "Where is the headmaster?" Naturally this caused consternation amongst the school staff. The headmaster came forward, "You are the one who caned my son?", the headmaster said yes. Mwalimu said, "This fellow told me what he did yesterday at school; if he does it a second time give him a really good hiding"! Mwalimu would not tolerate bad manners and a lack of discipline.

The years 1978 to 1980 were tumultuous, truly tumultuous on matters of foreign affairs. We had the war with Idi Amin of Uganda, which I will cover in the next chapter. The second major issue was to do with our compatriot, Salim Ahmed Salim, who at that time was the permanent representative to the United Nations in New York. We successfully campaigned for him to be elected the 34th president of the United Nations General Assembly for the 1979–1980 term. Then, with the second term of the incumbent secretary-general of the United Nations, Kurt Waldheim, coming to an end, we wanted Salim to be the first African secretary-general. I led global efforts to canvass support for our candidate, receiving strong support from many countries in Africa, Asia, Latin America and the Pacific. He had the endorsement of the Organisation of African Unity and the non-aligned movement, which gave him a majority in the UN general assembly. I would like to record our gratitude for China's support, who were on the security council and repeatedly vetoed Waldheim's candidacy against Salim. Despite this strong backing, Salim was not elected as he was vetoed by the Americans, sixteen times in fact. I believe they regarded him as a dangerous radical. I still regret that we did not succeed as Salim would have been very good in this role. After all, he had been a diplomat since the age of 22, was well regarded and had been our permanent representative at the United Nations since 1970. The result was that he came back to take over from me as minister of foreign affairs and I became minister of information and culture.

CHAPTER 8

War With Idi Amin

"People are being massacred. You have bombed my house. Please tell the army to stop"! I had spent a year at Columbia University with Ugandan Matias Lubega learning about the art of diplomacy and international issues affecting developing countries. We were friends, our countries were neighbours; now we were on opposite sides of the war and he phoned me to complain. He was the minister of state for foreign affairs at that time; poor man, with Idi Amin[69] as his president.

Frankly, I couldn't believe that Idi Amin had decided to invade the Kagera region of Tanzania; I had not expected this invasion at all. For all his craziness, such as calling himself the *'Lord of all Beasts of the Earth and Fishes of the Seas, Conqueror of the British Empire in Africa in General and Uganda in Particular'*, I did not think that he would be so foolhardy as to invade Tanzania. Mwalimu had long regarded Amin a useless leader and had hoped that things would work out so that he could be removed from office. I think Mwalimu was also surprised; he knew that this man was mad, but this invasion shocked him and that may have helped to propel his strong will to stop him. Idi Amin harboured resent-

---

69 President Uganda January 1971–April 1979.

ment against Tanzania; we had provided shelter to both Milton Obote[70] and Yoweri Museveni and had been the starting point for the attempted return to power by Milton Obote during 1972, though they didn't even reach Uganda. Idi Amin was furious at this unsuccessful attempt and these factors may have germinated his idea to attack us in retaliation.

I was in Arusha when I received a phone call advising that the president wanted me to attend a meeting with elders at the Diamond Jubilee hall in Dar es Salaam; I was able to arrive just in time to attend the meeting. This was where Mwalimu stated:

> This man has invaded our territory and claimed it as part of his country, this is in contravention of international law, we are a sovereign country. We are a people of pride and we have the means, capacity and will to reclaim our territory. We are declaring that we are going to recover our land.

Later that night Prime Minister Edward Sokoine[71] instructed me to call the ambassadors, especially the USA, UK and the Nordic, as well as Egypt.

> Tell them this is it, we have been aggressed and we are going to recover our territory; we have no ambition to take on any new territory, we just want to recover our territory. See if they can help to talk this man out of his madness and withdraw. If there are those who are prepared to help us drive him out, let them do that.

Early the next morning my prime minister called me to his office and asked what their responses were. I said, "Mr Prime Minister, did you really think that I would call them at ten o'clock at night to give them this news and get a response from them? You must allow some time". This tells you of the efficiency of Sokoine, he always wanted to get things done right away, he was a no-nonsense person.

---

70 Prime Minister April 1962–April 1966; President April 1966–January 1971 when overthrown by Idi Amin, and December 1980–July 1985.

71 Prime Minister February 1977–November 1980 and February 1983–April 1984.

My principal object was to tell the ambassadors that we were not an aggressive people, but we wanted our territory back. The Western ambassadors were a little lukewarm, the Nordics a little more understanding, while the ambassadors from the Eastern countries were more understanding. For some reason the Western countries had some sympathy for Idi Amin. I don't know why; though the British did not like the idea that Milton Obote was, as they saw it, towing our socialist line. Obote's removal by Amin was no great issue for them. What's more, the excesses perpetrated by Amin hadn't really reached the highpoint. In any case, we were the frontline of helping the liberation movements in Southern Africa, so anything that restrained us was somewhat favourably viewed by those Western countries who were supporting the existing regimes. Algeria was supportive, in spite of the Islamic connection with Amin, but Libya and Palestine supported Amin. Egypt wasn't responsive, they kept a low profile, while Sudan was not understanding at all. President Gaafar Nimeiry[72] came to Tanzania to try to persuade Mwalimu to sue for peace. After they had met I talked to my president, who said, "This man has the nerve to talk to me about democracy, how did he get into power and what elections has he allowed on democratic terms? I said to him stop this foolishness, that man (Amin) is making carnage in Uganda". In addition to the frontline states such as Mozambique and Angola, which supported us, Ethiopia was positive. That's why for all the ills of Mengistu Haile Mariam[73] I still have a soft spot for him, for he enabled us to build our capacity to fight.

As foreign minister I took the diplomatic front of explaining the situation to countries, especially those in the African Union, though Mwalimu undertook a lot himself, travelling to set out our stance with other key heads of state in person. I was also sent off on missions to try to reinforce our requests for equipment and arms. We had a tough time sourcing arms; especially as the British would not give us any arms to strengthen our capacity to respond. They didn't like us due to our supporting South-

---

72   Sudan: President May 1969–April 1985.

73   Ethiopia: Head of the State of Ethiopia February 1977–September 1987; President September 1987–May 1991.

ern Rhodesia and opposing apartheid in South Africa; so, while they would not arm Idi Amin, they would not give us arms either.

Another major concern for us was how Tanzania could manage to sustain both the southern and the north-western war fronts? We had the front in Southern Africa, while Mozambique was now free it was really under threat from apartheid South Africa and Southern Rhodesia, and South West Africa (Namibia) were not yet free. Was this invasion a coordinated diversionary tactic to get us away from giving strength to the liberation movements in the South? Mwalimu was an extraordinary man, he was a God-given gift to us, really; imagine having such courage and conviction to undertake all these major events at the same time.

The mobilisation for the war was fantastic, so many people volunteered, some young men even cried when they were not taken up to fight in the army. Before the war our armed forces comprised of the Eastern, Western and Southern brigades, with each brigade having three battalions; though these were not a full complement before the war, there were only about 30,000 soldiers beforehand. Within a relatively short time we had around 100,000 troops, a dramatic increase in the number due to around 70,000 volunteers who came from the police and other civil servants, as well as non-governmental employees from all walks of life. Even some diplomats volunteered, though they were told they were needed to remain at their posts to support Tanzania's international presence. So many volunteers, Mwalimu was the only one who could galvanise the people this way. Business people supported as well, for example by providing buses to carry the soldiers up to the north-west.

The war showed the underlying strength of the Tanzanian people. Their unwavering support for the liberation movements had long been in evidence, but this was the first time that Tanzania's sovereignty had been attacked. The war with Idi Amin entrenched nationalism in Tanzania, no doubt about that. This is pertinent today when some people in Zanzibar say they are not part of Tanzania, yet Zanzibaris laid down their lives for our nation during this war. For most Zanzibari soldiers it was their first time on the Mainland, yet they still believed in one sovereign country and wanted to fight for it. It is said that in those early days of the invasion by Idi Amin's Uganda some in Kagera Region felt they were closer to Uganda because of their ethnicity, Baganda Kakwa. But there was no particular rejoicing after Idi Amin had taken that area and there was much celebration when we recovered the territory. Kagera Region is as far as you can possibly get from Dar es Salaam in this country, it's over 1,300 kilometres by road; but these people felt Tanzanian like any other.

The sacrifice by many during this war strengthened a sense of nationhood in me, beyond religion, colour and ethnicity. In my case, I married a woman from the slopes of Mt Kilimanjaro in the north of the country, while my home is only sixteen kilometres from the border of Mozambique in the south. Then I look at our children, who don't speak their mother's language or my language, but speak Kiswahili and English well. What are my grandchildren, except Tanzanians? The intermarrying of our peoples has helped unity a great deal.

There were 96 Tanzanian military casualties, and an estimated 1,500 Tanzanian civilians. We don't honour our war dead properly these days; we have the Heroes Day[74] in remembrance, but it is not a public holiday on the Mainland. When I became president I visited the war cemetery at Muleba District, Kagera Region, where soldiers from all around Tanzania, Christian and Muslim, had come together to defend their young nation. Reading their names at the cemetery you can see this represents the nation of Tanzania. I found my visit inspiring, so before I left office I insisted that I visit there again to pay my respects and pray. I also made sure that our soldiers who had died fighting for Mozambique and Zimbabwe were returned and laid to rest in the South, because Mtwara and Lindi were the areas which had sacrificed the most for the liberation movements by hosting them and suffering military attacks by the Portuguese. I felt a strong obligation to honour those dead; so we gathered their remains and reburied them in their home country.

After reclaiming our territory the army continued right up to Kampala. This advance was in large part due to Idi Amin's threats against his own people who had welcomed the Tanzanian army; Amin threatened that when he won the war he would deal with his own people. The possibility of genocide was a major concern of Mwalimu, who was worried that Idi

---

74 25 July.

Amin would massacre his own people if we only took back our territory and did not advance into Uganda. Mwalimu said it was very difficult for him to decide; but determined, "If we can finish this then let's finish it". Therefore, our troops advanced to Kampala.

I'd like to record some of the military leaders who should be remembered, (I have included some noms de guerre): Brigadier General John Butler Walden (Black Mamba); Brigadier General Silas Mayunga (*Mti Mkavu* (Dry Tree)); Major General David Msuguri (*Jenerali Mtukula*); Major General Ben Msuya; Colonel Tumbi (*Kamanda Radi* (lightning)); Major General Tumainiel Kiwelu; and Major General Mwita Marwa (*Jenerali Kambale* (Catfish)). Tanzanian troops had pulverised Idi Amin's army, and our Major General Msuguri was the commander of Uganda. The extraordinary thing is that after these men liberated Uganda and were effectively the military leaders of Uganda and could have pushed to remain in control there, when Mwalimu stated that the army had accomplished what it had set out to do and they were not there to occupy the territory, the army was well disciplined and returned to Tanzania. There was substantial fear in the West that we would not withdraw; but they did not know Mwalimu. He was not a military adventurist; Julius was a very peaceful person. What he did in aiding Uganda's transition after Idi Amin was quite remarkable, not just for Africa, but across the world. The fact that he did not want a military occupation of Uganda is the greatest tribute to him.

Neighbouring countries were very worried that this war might spread. After the flight of Idi Amin these countries became very jittery, suspecting that we Tanzanians wanted territory. I was sent on a mission to Malawi to meet President Hastings Banda[75]. His foreign minister took me to Nguru-ya-Nawambe palace at Mt Kasungu; Banda came in, we stood up and he sat down. The foreign minister said, "Your Excellency, our brother from Tanzania has sent his minister of foreign affairs with a message for you. I received him at the airport, took him to his accommodation, he was well received there they took good care of him. This morning I have the great pleasure to present him to Your Excellency".

---

75   President of Malawi July 1966–May 1994; Prime Minister July 1964–July 1966.

Banda responded imperiously, "Fine, thank you, now get out", and the minister left the room by walking backwards. I was shocked at the humiliating way Banda treated his minister of foreign affairs; President Banda regarded himself emperor, no doubt about it. Despite this startling commencement to our meeting I was well received by him; he was pleased to hear me say: "My mission is very simple, to tell you that we were repulsing aggression; we have no territorial ambitions; we have no quarrels with any of our other neighbours; please don't think we are irredentists; we are not going to try to take over territory". I also travelled to Burundi and Rwanda whose leaders were grateful for our assurance; they had felt vulnerable due to the small size of their nations. Kenyans held this notion that having finished with Uganda we would just move across the border to Kenya, the reason being our ideological differences between socialism and capitalism. President Daniel arap Moi was receptive to my coming to see him; I think the Kenyan leaders had been nervous of what would happen. I was a good errand boy for my president and this was an experience which I found very interesting.

Only one meeting of foreign ministers took place during the war, in late February 1979 in Nairobi; where my friend Matias Lubega implored me to stop, saying that the Tanzanian army was on the verge of taking over the country. I had a difficult time explaining to my friend that I was only a politician and not privy to military information, though this was the truth. It was all over within a few weeks anyway. The war lasted from 30 October 1978 to 11 April 1979.

Then came the challenge to get several liberation movements, including Museveni's Uganda Patriotic Movement, to agree on a common coalition to take charge of the country. We arranged for the putative liberation movements to come together in Moshi[76] and I attended as foreign minister. Essentially I said, "Listen, your country is about to fall, we don't want to occupy Uganda, we don't want to rule it, you have been fighting Amin for all this time, now you must come together and work out a leadership arrangement to take over from Amin". Yoweri Museveni initially opposed our request, wanting to continue his war of resistance

---

76   24–26 March 1979.

until victory. We demurred, saying it was all over, Tanzania was in charge and it was time to move forward. Museveni wasn't easy to deal with, but eventually he had to agree. We established the Uganda National Liberation Front (UNLF) and I encouraged them to pick an interim leader and interim constitution for the period leading up to when they could have an election. Professor Yusuf Lule was chosen as their leader. I know it is said that we picked him, but that's not true; it was the various liberation movements who all agreed on him, noting that he was somewhat untainted, was elderly and agreeable to the Western countries. Museveni was unhappy, but he accepted to be Minister of Defence.

But the new regime ruled badly, mainly due to Lule and his cohorts deciding that now was the time for Baganda people to assert themselves and be dominant. Mwalimu was insistent that we must leave them to sort out their own problems. Lule lasted only around two months[77] before they removed him and Godfrey Binaisa[78] took over. General Tito Okello,[79] who likewise did not last long. He flew to Kenya but they didn't want him; so he came to Tanzania and stayed with me at my home in Seaview, Dar es Salaam, for a couple of days before we agreed with the Ugandan Defence Force that he should go to a nominated residence. This was a sensitive time because we didn't know how Museveni, who was then the Minister of State for Defence, would react to our hosting Okello. Thankfully Museveni was very good about it, so it worked out well in the end.

Some accused Mwalimu of using the post-Amin interval to arrange for Milton Obote to return to Uganda. This belief was wrong, I assure you, as Mwalimu was sceptical about Obote's capacity to mobilise internal support. Perhaps he felt a sense of guilt because Obote had been removed from power by Idi Amin while he was at a Commonwealth Heads of Government meeting in Singapore in January 1971, a meeting which Mwalimu had encouraged Obote to attend. But Mwalimu was not a sentimental person and he was sceptical of Obote's capacity, particu-

---

77   13 April–20 June 1979.

78   President of Uganda June 1979–May 1980.

79   President of Uganda 29 July 1985–26 January 1986.

larly after his aborted attempt to invade Uganda during 1972. The armed forces in Tanzania were also sceptical about Museveni; however, Mwalimu instructed that he should be helped. There was a time when Museveni was held in the maximum security Ukonga prison in Dar es Salaam for two weeks until he managed to get word to Mwalimu, who instructed that Museveni be quickly released. Did we influence the outcome of the political settlement in Uganda? Many people believe we did, but I don't agree. Some expected that we would try to impose Milton Obote, but we did not. I think the impact of Museveni's guerrilla war and military takeover from Tito Okello is somewhat exaggerated. I think Ugandans were war-weary; they were hoping that this would be their salvation. There's no doubt Museveni did well then; he took care to form an inclusive government of leaders from all backgrounds, including Idi Amin's people.

I think we Tanzanians acquitted ourselves very well in terms of the war and subsequent handover to civilian government. Tanzania is a poor country, I know that Idi Amin did not have a very strong army, but it took a lot of sacrifice on our part and we Tanzanians were modest about it. We suffered a major economic disruption because of the war, which took us years to recover from. During my time as president I resumed talks on compensation and USD 9.6 million was repaid; however we then decided to let the issue go, it was better to move forward and concentrate on being good neighbours. I hope something like this never happens with any other country in the region. This is why I am frustrated now about the slow move to integrate East Africa politically and economically – why are we hesitating? Can't we learn from history?

The war with Uganda destroyed my naive concept that because we were all former colonies of the British and were friends then we would have no inter-country strife. The most valuable lesson I learnt was that a sense of national unity across ethnic, racial and religious groups was the crucial pillar of our survival. This is why I am so intolerant of any sectarianism. We are all God's people, I may not like your colour, but the Lord likes you, he created you and he created me. The readiness of many to sacrifice their lives for the unity of this country brought home to me the realisation of equality in our country, which is what Mwalimu was striving for.

Chapter 9

We Must Change Ourselves or We Will Be Changed

The first time Mwalimu discussed his retirement privately with me was in 1980, during a state visit to the United Arab Emirates. He said that he wouldn't stand for president in the general election set for October that year. I said to Mwalimu:

> Ok, you may have a good argument that there is no time when it is proper for one to leave, but definitely this is not the right time. We have just concluded the war with Idi Amin, there are major problems of reconstruction and people will say that you want to run away; you got us into all these costs, but you are not prepared to stand the task of reconstruction.

I could see he didn't like what I said. When we returned to Tanzania he went to the national executive committee (NEC) of CCM and tried to sell his idea that he should step down to let someone else take over, but the NEC vigorously protested and pressed him to stay, saying that he was needed during this difficult time of recovery after the war; so he remained in office.

Towards the end of that five-year term in 1985 he repeated that he wanted to retire. He explained:

> I am a human being and one day I may be run over by a bus. Secondly, if I don't step down as president and I die as president, no-one who follows me will accept to step down from the presidency. They will say the first president stayed until he died, why shouldn't I die as president? Third, I need to start the succession plan. If I don't do it there will be no succession at all. If we can do this succession peacefully four times, then we will have built a culture of peaceful succession.

The party leaders and regional chairmen tried very hard at a meeting of the national executive committee to persuade him to stand again for president. I didn't attend that meeting but was reliably told that he said, "No, please this time no. I have heard you, now I want to ask you. In 1955 I decided to leave my post as teacher to devote myself to politics 100% of my time. Which one of you advised me to leave my teaching to go into politics 100%?" Of course there was no one. "So just as at that time no one advised me, and I decided for myself, now I have decided that I'm leaving. Now let us talk about the real issue, which is how you can have a proper succession that maintains the stability of the country".

That was the end of the debate. Subsequently Samora Machel came from Mozambique to appeal to him not to leave; but Mwalimu remained firm. He knew he had an obligation to the nation to ensure there was a timely succession, rather than leave it too late.

There was great economic difficulty after the war because the country had made a substantial financial sacrifice, the impact of which was widespread and long-lasting. Times were very hard indeed; the foreign exchange situation was in crisis. Discontent started to emerge, especially with the shortage of imported goods. I firmly believed that we needed a change in both policy and implementation. I think Mwalimu recognised this too and that is why in 1985 he said to the national executive committee of the party, (CCM), that they needed a new president and it was time for others to try to put these things right. He told them that it was important to get someone who was agreeable to work with, acceptable to other leaders and sellable to the population, as well as someone who could embark on a reform programme.

I did not attend that central committee meeting of the party which preceded the CCM national congress where Mwalimu would announce his retirement and proposed successor; I was told that Mwalimu was absolutely shocked by the negative response of the members of the central committee to his preferred successor, Salim Ahmed Salim. He had to hastily change the last two paragraphs of the speech he wanted to deliver at the national congress to reflect the different successor chosen by the committee. Mwalimu was surprised by their preference for Ali Hassan Mwinyi. However, the fact that Mwinyi did become his successor shows the strength of the party, as well as the greatness of Mwalimu; he could have imposed his choice but did not. After that he was careful not to mention his preference for Salim.

Succession remains a sensitive subject till today; regrettably some African countries do not have a good track record, and this often attracts media interest in the West, rather than news of an ordered handover of power. Tanzania's limit for presidency is two five-year terms and I remember conversing about this with Joaquim Chissano, who concluded that perhaps it shouldn't be just two terms, rather three terms. During the first five years you gain a deep understanding of the systems and structures and you work on promoting the programme you have determined for the country. The next five years are taken up with implementation; while the extra third five-year term would be devoted to completing your programme and passing it on properly. I think that Chissano had a point, except that in Africa people are so restless for power, I don't know if they would allow you to remain for so long a time. Personally, I have no problem with a ten-year period of rule. When my two terms of five years were completed I was relieved; leading a poor country is not easy. In the 1970s and 1980s there was a prevalent idea in Africa and South America that the military taking over was the solution; due to the army's strength in focus and discipline. But military regimes proved just as bad, in some cases worse than the civilian ones.

Of course, successful succession depends on who you are passing the presidency on to. If you are passing it on to someone who has a personal ambition to establish a new base of his own and do away with what was achieved or is well on the way to successful completion, then you may have problems. Here Britain has strength in continuity, with stability and history not yet established in our kind of countries; this arises from Britain's long-established strong and professional civil service.

President Mwinyi tried to resolve the economic and financial crisis. One major change was that he led the opening up of the economy which he did well. Unfortunately, there was insufficient management of implementation and follow-through, you just can't open up then let everyone do their own thing; this resulted in problems. To be fair, this mismanagement can be attributed to our lack of experience, especially in business.

Another major reform which Mwalimu had fostered, which was instituted by President Mwinyi, was the change from single party to multi-partyism. I remember many of us in the party were unhappy about that, but he persuaded us. We had seen the agitation for change in the satellite Soviet states, and we recognised that on a smaller scale there was agitation for change in our country for moving from a single party to a multi-party political system. During the discussion within the party about this issue Mwalimu said it would be wrong not to respond to this desired change, adding: "We must change ourselves or we will be changed. If we don't change the world will change us and we will not have any control over those changes. We will be swept along as if by waves". Mwalimu was a visionary leader who took care to observe events beyond Tanzania's borders and consider their implications for Tanzania. His foresight remains pertinent even today looking at events around the world. Thus multipartyism was introduced in May 1992, under the eighth constitutional amendment, with the first multi-party elections held being by-elections during 1994 and the first multi-party general election held in 1995, when I stood for president.

Nevertheless, Mwalimu would resist change when he thought that the potential for causing damage was too great. After he retired the central committee of the party wanted to pass a resolution to have three governments. I was a member of the central committee at that time and could see that the overwhelming decision was emerging that we should go ahead. I queried, "You know, are you quite sure, have you talked to Mwalimu about this?" Everyone looked around and agreed I had a point.

"Well", I said, "if you decide to go ahead with this then I think it will be best to talk to him first".

They said, "No, you go and tell him", whereupon I left the meeting in Dodoma and travelled to Dar es Salaam to see Mwalimu. He was very unhappy and opposed the pending resolution, ending our discussion with, "Tell them I have heard them and explain my views on this. But what's more important tell them that I will not keep those views to myself; I will hold a public rally to explain my views". I rang President Mwinyi and advised that Mwalimu's response was unfavourable and he might call a mass meeting to state his views; whereupon President Mwinyi decided to bring him to Dodoma to speak to the central committee. Mwalimu and I flew there and when I got out of the plane I could see people looking at me and saying there's Mkapa the troublemaker. Mwalimu spoke with the central committee and it was eventually decided to call a special joint meeting of the national assembly, the Zanzibar house of representatives, and the party national executive committee. Mwalimu talked them out of introducing three governments at this meeting.

My parents passed away during the period I was minister of foreign affairs and then minister of science, technology and higher education[80]. My work and lifestyle as a minister and member of parliament was of course something completely foreign to them, and while I was conscious of my father's disappointment that I had not become a priest, doctor or teacher, my parents were truly amazed that I had attained the level of minister. They were fascinated at how Mwalimu judged me to be worthy of this senior position, particularly given the calibre of others from my region who were involved in politics. I had a feeling that they had more admiration for Mwalimu's judgement than for my own ability, but nevertheless, it gave them a great deal of satisfaction to see what I had achieved in my career. Though they did not approve of my constant absences from my family and that Anna bore the brunt of raising our sons. They missed us and their grandchildren during my postings abroad and were very happy to see us return to live in Tanzania. I built a home for them in the village of Lupaso which they were very happy with; it was amongst

---

80   May 1992–1995.

the first, if not the first, locally owned tin-roofed house in the village, which was notable in those days. It gave me much pleasure to be able to provide for them, as they had worked so tirelessly to raise us four children. When my mother's diabetes worsened, I rented a home for them close to St Benedict's hospital in Ndanda, as she required regular medical attention. My parents found it uncomfortable adjusting to living in the town, being such a different environment from their village of Lupaso; though my father was much more outgoing, so they were able to make acquaintances with neighbours. Eventually, her condition stabilised and they were grateful to return to their home in Lupaso.

Sadly, my mother's condition later worsened after some time and she was taken back to the hospital; and her doctor, Dr Mwambe, contacted us to come quickly as he could see that she was fading. The businessman and philanthropist Hatim Karimjee had a light aircraft to get to the family's sisal estate in Mikindani and he kindly gave Bernard and me a lift to their estate, from where we rushed to the hospital. I am grateful that my mother was still conscious, she was relieved to see us, and we spent a little time with her. My elder brother remained with her for the night while I went to my home in Masasi to sleep; she passed on shortly after I had arrived at my house. Regrettably I did not have such an opportunity to say farewell to my father, I just received the news that he had passed away.

Incidentally, whilst I was staying with my parents at the rented house near the hospital, I was sent a message by the district party leadership to come to see them. I went to see these leaders who said that I should stand for election as a member of parliament for their constituency. I was a little doubtful, saying I had never stood for elected office and was not well known in the constituency, but the leaders reassured me that that was not a problem and to leave matters to them. I returned to my parents at their house; who were naturally curious what this 'summons' was about. They were quite sceptical that the party leadership could deliver and fearful that if I were to stand and lose it might destroy my career and as I was already an appointed member of parliament, they thought it better to maintain the status quo. I told them that I couldn't turn down the request of the executive party of the leadership. My parents accepted my decision.

My father was not very interested in politics; he was respectful of authority generally, due, I think, to the fact that he had worked for the German missionaries all his life. Of my family, it was only Blasius, my eldest brother, who was keenly interested in politics. Bernard, my immediate elder brother, would follow politics because he was a good civil servant, but he was not politically minded; he certainly was a nationalist and admired Mwalimu very much, but, as with my sister Marcella, he was not interested in getting into the affray of politics. I was disappointed that my parents passed away before I rose to the highest office in the land. I don't think they ever expected that that would happen; they would have been proud of me. Blasius believed that I would go high in politics, but my parents had no notion of this at all.

Towards the end of 1994 I discussed with Anna whether it was worth continuing with my political career. We decided that we had had enough of the demands of politics, I had worked very hard from 1962 to 1995 and Anna had given a lot as well. I had made my contribution to public service as I had set out do, it was time for me to retire and for us to try something new together. Frankly, I was feeling a little disillusioned, as well as feeling worn out. But there was an undercurrent of unease about the way politics was unfolding in the country and how the party and government were operating. Public servant salaries were always paid late, revenue collections were poor, there was discontent in the trade union movement particularly the teachers, and our development partners were unhappy about the way things were. Several of my friends thought I should try my hand at the office of the president and kept on nagging me about it. I talked this over with Anna, saying that there seemed to be people who thought that I could help to put matters right in our country and I felt I had an obligation to try my hand at seeking nomination. Her initial reaction was, "Come on, really, is this fair to me?" But she consented; Anna has been so supportive to me throughout my career, for which I continue to be grateful.

My next step was to tell Mwalimu, I wrote a note to him as he was at his village Butiama, saying:

> Mr President, I hope you are well, I have decided to seek nomination and am sending this note to tell you this because I don't want you

to hear from a third party in case they misrepresent my reasons for doing so. I hope that the next time we meet will not be in the far distant future, so I will be able to explain to you why I am seeking nomination.

I gave the note to Joseph Warioba who comes from Bunda which is near to Butiama; though I didn't tell Mr Warioba what was in my letter and Mwalimu didn't discuss its contents with him either. I met with Mwalimu when he attended a meeting of the national executive committee of the party in Dodoma where I explained to him:

> I have decided to seek nomination for office for several reasons. First, relations between the party and its government on the one hand and the co-operative movement on the other are sour, because, I think, we have abandoned the essence of the co-operative movement. The leaders have become the owners of the movement themselves resulting in co-operative unions being owned by elected leaders. While they may be elected, they usurp power and I don't think that is fair; the result is that there is a lot of theft in the unions. You know that in the independence struggle one of the pillars of your struggle were the co-operatives – the peasants – and that is why our party is called the Party of the Peasants and the Workers (Chama Cha Mapinduzi – Party of the Revolution).

I pointed out that from the co-operative movement we had Jeremiah Kasambala[81] from the Rungwe African Co-operative Union, one of the largest farmers' unions in the country; from Bukoba, George Kahama (later to become Sir) of the Bukoba Native Co-operative Union for coffee; in Mwanza, Paul Bomani with the cotton growers' co-operative, Nyanza

---

81 Minister of Co-operatives and Community Development 1962; Minister of Industry, Energy and Minerals 1965.

Co-operative Union[82]; in Moshi-Arusha you had Nsilo Swai[83] with the Kilimanjaro Native Co-operative Union. I continued:

> We mobilised the peasants to support your struggle for independence. Now we have turned the principle upside down, the leaders in the co-operatives have turned themselves into the owners and are mismanaging the co-operatives for their benefit. The voice of the people is not heard enough. That's one reason, you can't have a party of peasants and workers where the peasants have been thrown out of the decision-making process.

> The second pillar was the trade unions where we had Rashid Kawawa, General Secretary of the Tanganyika Federation of Labour and Michael Kamaliza of the Tanganyika Government Workers Union; they were at the forefront of the trade union movement during the struggle. But now there is tremendous disaffection between the government and the trade union movement.

Earlier that year, 1995, there had been a threat of a general strike. I said:

> You ruled this country, you were the head of the government for over twenty years, during all that time there never was a threat of a general strike. It's a measure of the disaffection that exists between the party and this government and the trade union movement that we experienced a threat this year. That's another pillar of the relationship which I think requires attention.

> Thirdly, you built a very good developmental relationship with the Nordic countries and other bilaterals. We have now reached the point where our donors are no longer interested in lending support

---

82 Earlier known as the Victoria Federation of Cooperative Unions.

83 Minister of Commerce and Industry 1960–1961; Minister of Health and Labour 1962; Permanent Representative to United Nations 1962; Minister of Development and Planning 1962–1963; Minister of State 1964–1965; Minister Industries; Mineral Reserves and Power 1965–1967; Minister Economic Affairs and Development Planning 1967; Minister for East African Affairs 1967.

to our development efforts because they say we are misusing their funds, that there is a lot of theft and corruption. They have said they will not discuss any new development projects, though they will conclude the ones that are currently ongoing. You invested so much in building this relationship with donors. Although we have a policy of self-reliance, we still need the help of others for our nation's development. We can't let this soured relationship with donors continue as it is now.

Then there is the fourth issue, our relations with international financial institutions. I know you don't like the IMF and World Bank, but the fact of the matter is that they have invested in our country and we need them in today's world. As with our donor countries, they too have said no new projects to be discussed with this government. This is another area of disaffection or disconnect which is not conducive to our nation's development.

Finally, I have looked at the people presenting themselves as potential nominees; I know their record, I have worked with them. I feel that if I don't enter the ring then I might finish my career and later say why didn't I enter into the ring? But if I do enter the ring and am not selected at least I will have salved my conscience, I will have tried to serve yet been told that they don't want me. Whatever happens afterwards would be their problem to solve. I couldn't forgive myself if I didn't enter the ring, so I have decided to do so.

I then thanked him for listening to me; he was a great listener, he never interrupted. Mwalimu looked straight at me and responded:

Thank you very much for being so very frank with me; I shall be equally frank with you. It never occurred to me that you would seek the presidency, the thought had never entered my mind. Not only hadn't it occurred to me that you would seek office, but I had thought of someone else who would make good. But my efforts to get him interested have not succeeded, he's hesitating, he thinks he can have his nomination served to him on a platter, that's not politics, you've got to make the struggle. I have sent an emissary to him, but he still will not take up the challenge. Ben, all I can say to you is I will not stand in your way, I'm not going to oppose you. If you have made up your mind, go ahead as your conscience demands.

I replied, "That's all I wanted, thank you very much", and that was it.

In the weeks before this conversation with Mwalimu I had been repeatedly urged to run for the presidency by friends and colleagues. Foremost, among many others, were former editorial colleagues Ferdinand Ruhinda and Kabenga Nsa Kaisi; former member of parliament the late Patrick Qorro, then members of parliament Jared Gachocha and Edgar Maokola-Majogo; former ambassadors Saleh Tambwe, Adam Marwa, and the late Suleiman Hemed; party cadres Harrison Mwakyembe and Walter Bgoya, and businessman Yusuph Mushi. Ambassador Suleiman Hemed deserves special attention because he accompanied me through most of the campaign providing advice and evaluating the response of audiences at rallies. I remember Patrick Qorro and Jared Gachocha with nostalgia and loving respect; for they spearheaded the movement to recruit me and put together this campaign team. The team had formed during months of discussion about the future of our country and they mapped out the nomination strategy. Their commitment was such that they worked voluntarily, even paying some of the early costs from their own pockets. These good people helped me to firm my decision to meet Mwalimu to tell him I would go for nomination and I thank these friends and colleagues.

I suspect that Mwalimu came to the conclusion that I would be a better choice than his preferred man, who I understand was Salim Ahmed Salim. I have been told that Mwalimu asked a couple of former and current leaders of the party to look favourably at me when they started the selection process; but I can't confirm this. I also have been told that he commended me to others for my ability to make decisions. I was told he said, "Why Ben? Because he can make decisions. He will rely on advice, but the final decision is going to be his. Once he makes that decision it holds, he will never waver, never. Leadership is about making decisions, tough decisions sometimes". Mwalimu gave a speech at the national party congress[84] where nominations were taking place which some people think that he really was recommending my nomination. I don't know if this was so, but he definitely influenced some people, for which I was grateful.

Before the party's selection of the presidential candidate I travelled around the country taking the nominations papers to each region to seek their nomination. You must be sponsored from at least ten regions, two of which must be in Zanzibar; I think I travelled to sixteen regions talking to potential sponsors about what I intended to do. These visits in person, rather than sending an emissary as other contenders had done; as well as the fact that I travelled to so many regions helped me during the eventual vote at the party congress. By the time I got to Mwanza I had learned that Mark Bomani had also entered the fray. I met briefly with the sponsors there, saying "Please when you come to the conference I know your first choice will be your son, Mark Bomani. But should it come to a second vote I hope that you will vote for me". My modest request was well received by them.

Despite this extensive preparatory work behind the scenes I was not confident at all before the party run-off; and as it turned out the run-off between the three presidential candidates was close. No-one had an absolute majority in the first vote, Minister of Finance Jakaya Kikwete[85] was ahead of me, while former Prime Minister Cleopa Msuya was third; whereupon Msuya had to step down and then it was between Jakaya and myself. We voted again and then all broke for lunch, not knowing the result. I was so uncertain if I would win that during lunch I asked my friends if we should make a few notes of acceptance, just in case I got elected. We decided to prepare a couple of paragraphs, just in case, though I was fairly certain that Jakaya would win. When we returned to the hall it was announced that I had won, so I ended up using those hastily prepared notes for my acceptance speech. I won by twenty-seven votes

---

84   Mwalimu's speech at this CCM meeting can be viewed at: https://youtube.be/GAEpisZ3Cuk

85   Minister of Finance 1994–1995; Minister of Foreign Affairs November 1995–December 2005; President December 2005–November 2015.

on the second round. Unfortunately, the youth wing of the party had backed Jakaya strongly and suspected that the results had been doctored, but Jakaya nobly calmed them down. They had wanted a younger person like themselves to win, but the party was very disciplined then, so thankfully the youth got into the spirit of the campaign and supported me during the campaign for the general election.

Once chosen as the presidential candidate that person must then consult with the leadership of the party, particularly the central committee, on who their running mate should be. In my case it had to be someone from Zanzibar who would run as my vice-presidential candidate, as traditionally there must always be this balance between the Mainland and Zanzibar. The central committee chose who was then the Chief Minister of Zanzibar, Dr Omar Ali Juma[86]. He was a wonderful person, it was a pleasure travelling together and addressing rallies one after another. He became my vice president and we worked very well indeed, though sadly he passed away during our second term[87]. After consultation with the President of Zanzibar, Amani Karume[88], Dr Ali Mohamed Shein[89] became the new Vice President.

I have been told that Mwalimu was relieved when I won the party's vote to be the presidential candidate. Mwalimu supported me as I campaigned for the general election, his first time to be so actively involved in campaigning since he left office. My campaigning was issue based, focusing on the election manifesto; something that is not done so much nowadays, rather campaigning seems more personality based. Unfortunately, once I took office and learnt the true state of affairs the country was in, I realised that the party's manifesto was too ambitious. I felt obligated to travel around the country during my first year and explain to the people that we could not raise sufficient funds to implement some of the manifesto promises; they were too ambitions and the

---

86   Chief Minister of Zanzibar 25 January 1988–1 November 1995; Vice President of Tanzania 23 November 1995–4 July 2001.

87   Dr Omar Ali Juma died on 4 July 2001.

88   President of Zanzibar November 2000–November 2010.

89   Vice President July 2001–November 2010; President of Zanzibar from November 2010.

revenue base was too narrow. This openness to the citizenry resulted in the opposition jumping on me, saying that we had lied to people during the campaign. I was vilified for being so frank and open with the people; with some colleagues from my party expressing the opinion that I was not a politician, because I was not speaking as they believed a politician should. *Ukweli na uwazi* – truth and transparency – is what I believed in then and still do now.

This was the first post-independence multi-party general election for Tanzania so there was concern about the outcome, resulting in us undertaking vigorous campaigning[90]. Despite the campaign being principally issue based, from time to time we would make a little jab at my principle opponent, Augustino Mrema of the National Convention for Construction and Reform (NCCR – *Mageuzi*) Party. He was a defector from our party, a decisive man who made decisions rapidly, but not sufficiently competent. His most senior positions had been Minister of Home Affairs and Deputy Prime Minister[91], so he knew well the workings of government. He appealed to the public because of his decisiveness; when he was minister of home affairs he was strict with the Indian community, saying things like: "Pay your taxes. I summon you to come to see me at my home in Kilimanjaro". He used to order, "Arrest that man", even though he had no powers to do so. So the public felt that this was a strong man who could drive the nation forward. Because of the widespread discontent with the performance of the CCM government, the party was fearful that the voters might elect Mrema by default. What's more some people were saying, "We don't know this Mkapa, we know he's been foreign affairs minister and so on, but he's not a politician".

Campaigning wasn't altogether new to me, I had campaigned in my constituency, of course. I also saw Mwalimu at mass rallies when I was his press secretary. However, this time I confess it took a while for me to get used to meeting so many people on such a massive scale as I am shy. The children who came to the rallies encouraged me and helped me

---

90   Associated Press video of campaigning: www.aparchive.com/metadata/view/739 b48fa33379b71ef57466e60fb5040?subClipIN=00:00:00&subClipOut=00:03:35

91   Minister of Home Affairs 1990–1994; Deputy Prime Minister 1993–1994; Minister of Labour, Development and Sports 1994–1995.

to overcome my shyness; they had only seen pictures of me and were excited to see me in person and I recalled how excited I was as a child when the bishop or someone else important came by car to our village. Some adults believed that they would have good luck if they touched you, which was odd to me. I disliked photo opportunities but you have to do them. I was accustomed to this when I was press secretary; only now it was me who had to be at the centre of it all. It took quite a while to adjust to that kind of adulation; it made me feel uncomfortable. People, especially women's, enthusiasm at campaign rallies, coupled with CCM's skilled organisation of the events makes an exciting time for all. Political contests are cultural extravaganzas as well; with poets, musicians, artists and dancers expressing their preference for a political party and its candidate(s). The songs, dances, and colourful attire result in an event similar to festive carnivals in other countries; with participants striving to put on the best show for their region. The origin of the colourful nature of these events dates back to the days of the anti-colonial political mobilisation, when music and dance were used to bring people together in a peaceful demonstration of opposition.

Should a CCM candidate fail to visit a district, or not stop to greet the multitude who throng the roads and the meeting grounds then this is received badly. I was reminded, this when I had to cancel at the last minute a scheduled appearance at Ifakara town in the Morogoro Region. The CCM leadership told me that I had disappointed our supporters there. Furthermore, not going at all would be seen that I did not consider those people important; especially as in their view I had visited places they considered less important than Ifakara. Naturally I could not offend CCM's supporters in Ifakara, so I squeezed in a visit into my tight schedule by flying there to save time.

As it turned out, I well and truly proved my commitment to the people of Ifakara by my tense arrival in a Cessna plane. It had rained heavily and the pilot was unsure if we could land safely on the soggy track on a grassy field which served as the landing strip. The flight was quite bumpy and as the pilot first attempted a landing in the rain, he decided to abort the landing only a metre or so above ground. We then circled above the landing strip several times while we discussed whether we should try to land or give up altogether and return to Dar es Salaam. Below us we could see hundreds of umbrellas shielding those people stoically waiting for us in the rain. How could we disappoint them by turning back? I decided we should chance it and instructed the pilot to land.

The plane lurched from the left to the right as we descended, despite the pilot's brave efforts with the plane's rudder. The closer we came to the ground the more the plane seemed determined not to cooperate. It was frightening enough when we were still airborne; but there was no relief when the plane finally touched the ground. The ground was slippery, and worse still, uneven, which meant that the landing gear was unable to keep straight. After what seemed like an eternity the plane finally shuddered to a stop at right angle from our line of landing.

The crowd gave us a roaring welcome; they were very happy that we had taken the risk to be with them and thankful, as were we, that we had landed safely. Later, before we took off, the pilot told us to brace ourselves as our take-off would be worse than our landing. When we were finally airborne our skilled pilot told us that there had been a ditch in the ground in front of the plane and he had to lift off seconds earlier to avoid crashing into the ditch and overturning the plane. Luck was on our side that day.

Campaigning began each day around 8 a.m. with breakfast with elders from the locality, then one rally after another until evening when it fell dark, when we concluded with a dinner with elders. District after district, travelling on rough unsealed roads; it was mentally and physically tiring. Anna wasn't required to campaign but decided to do so in support, campaigning in the Lake region with her friends.

Mwalimu followed our campaign closely; but when he learnt that the campaign management were thinking of hiring a helicopter so we could cover more territory he was furious. He rang to speak to my campaign manager, Ferdinand Ruhinda, who was out. So Mwalimu told the second in charge:

> I hear that you people are thinking of using a helicopter to do campaigning. Well tell Mr Ruhinda that I have told you that even if God had ordered you to get a helicopter for this campaign, sent an

angel to tell you to get one, you would have to decline. You want to get close to the people and a helicopter will prevent this.

So that idea was swiftly dropped.

When Mwalimu came to join the campaign from Mwanza to Tabora he went by road, that's a tough long way for someone well in his seventies and the road was in poor condition then. He would be surprised about the use of helicopters nowadays, everybody uses them. Though helicopters can be misleading because in some of the rural areas people come just to look at it, fascinated by the helicopter rather than interested in the political message or the person campaigning, and the candidate might be fooled into thinking they had drawn a large crowd. My principal opponent, Augustino Mrema of the National Convention for Construction and Reform, (NCCR – *Mageuzi)* party, liked to be carried shoulder high so everybody could see him, so people would carry him to the stage at rallies. Our people were getting annoyed about this, but Mwalimu was unperturbed, saying, "Don't be bothered by that; if people decide that they would like to carry their candidate in a coffin then by all means let them".

A highlight of the presidential campaign was the first ever held presidential candidates' debate. Four candidates took part, my opponents were: Augustino Mrema, Professor Ibrahim Lipumba[92] of the Civic United Front (CUF); and John Cheyo of the United Democratic Party (UDP).

This three and a half hour debate, broadcast live on national radio and television was a game changer. It exposed Mrema as a charlatan who had no inkling of what a president and his government should and can do. While Professor Lipumba could do no more than lecture as if the national audience was an economics class, his replies were often unrelated to the issue being debated. Mr Cheyo was at least humorous with his promise to fill the pockets of Tanzanians with money – *mapesa*. I was

---

92 Chairman of Civic United Front 1995–2015.

amazed at the shallowness of these three, whose campaigning seemed to be based on their personality, rather than their party's manifesto.

I stuck to CCM's policies and manifesto and how I would go about implementing these. I believe my rational explanations and thorough knowledge of my party's manifesto meant I won Tanzania's first broadcast presidential candidate debate. I was told that Mwalimu was impressed by my sound grasp of the issues. This was a pivotal moment; as beforehand I was not well-known by the public. Afterwards many recognised me as a strong contender and began talking about my merit.

The result of the 1995 general election was that I received 61% of the vote, while my principal opponent, Mrema, received 27%. CCM gained 186 seats in parliament, while four opposition parties shared 46 seats. Voter turnout was 76% of those registered to vote.

After the election I held a party to thank my campaign team and other key supporters. During my speech of gratitude for their hard work, I made it clear that their work was done and they should not expect to be involved in the new administration. I needed a new team now, drawn mainly from those who worked for the institutions of state. There were around five to ten key supporters who expected to be awarded high office, or called upon as counsellors, but I would not indulge in cronyism. I knew that I now needed people with different skills and did not want to begin my term creating resentment within the civil service and the uniformed service, as I respected those institutions of the state.

It was a relief that the stress of the campaign was over but when I read the government briefing notes from President Mwinyi I was overwhelmed at what lay before me; but I had sought the presidency and I was resolved to do my duty.

CHAPTER 10

Mzee Ukapa and the *Askari wa Miavuli* (Paratroopers)

As the Kiswahili saying goes, *mwanzo mgumu* – all beginnings are difficult, but I had no inkling how difficult mine would be. I was sworn in on the 23rd of November 1995 and on the next day my Chief Secretary, Matern Lumbanga[93], held a frank meeting with me which really shocked me – the economy was a shambles. You don't appreciate the gravity of the problems facing a country until you are the one who has the power to make the ultimate decisions. Soon after I asked some staff at State House if the salaries had been paid to the public servants. They looked at me aghast, "Do you mean if the salaries have been paid? Sometimes we don't pay them until the first week of the following month; that is how late we can get with the wages".

I responded firmly, "No, we will make a start now. Ring up all the major tax collection points all over the country and let them bring the money in, I want us to start paying salaries in time". Public servants

---

[93] Chief Secretary to the president, Secretary to the cabinet and Head of public service February 1995–January 2006; Ambassador to UN in Geneva and Vienna 2006–2012; Governor of The Commodity Fund for Commodities 2006–2012; Chairman of the Public Procurement Authority 2013 to date; Chancellor of National Defence College (Tanzania) 2014 to date.

needed their salaries to live on, how can you get government to function if the workers are not being paid? To make it worse for these government employees inflation was extremely high at 27.4%. I could sense that there was something wrong in the economy that made revenue collection difficult, I thought it was either corruption or the people in charge of collections were lazy. Then I began to suspect that maybe this lack of collection was not wilfully done, perhaps the money was not there. Prior to being elected president I had been the minister for science, technology and higher education and was not in the inner cabinet of my predecessor, President Mwinyi, hence did not know much about the government's dire financial state. It was a nasty shock to discover how grave our government's financial state was. Had I known this beforehand I am not sure I would have sought nomination. Thus I began my term facing a far-reaching problem that turned out to be essentially a combination of incompetence and the economy not growing.

Prior to selecting my cabinet, I went to see Mwalimu, who congratulated me on becoming president. After thanking him I asked, "Now Mwalimu, have you any ideas about who should be and who should not be in the cabinet?" He declared:

> Ben, this is your cabinet, not mine. Your government, not mine. So go and form it. The only advice I can give you is that, first, you must remind yourself that we are multi-ethnic, so you cannot ignore this altogether, you must try to produce a balance. Second, we are also multi-religious, we have two major religions, you can't ignore that fact. Other than that, it is your government, your cabinet; go and form it.

This illustrates that Mwalimu was not an interventionist, despite what some people say. My predecessor and I had felt we worked under Mwalimu's shadow, which is understandable as he had ruled the country for over twenty years and truly was *Baba wa Taifa* (Father of the Nation), as he was known. Yet while Mwalimu kept a keen interest in developments and we spoke often, he did not interfere. The nearest thing to intervention I experienced was when I was about to appoint the governor of the central bank. I was taking a while to decide and when Mwalimu was told

I was thinking of someone he did not think should be a governor he rang me: "I understand you are appointing a new man to the central bank. Can you give me his name?"

I replied, "Daudi Ballali is the one that I want".

"Oh", he responded, "this is a relief because I had been told that you were appointing another person". And that was the end of our conversation and the closest Mwalimu came to intervene during my time as president.

My choice of the cabinet, including the exclusion of two former prime ministers was a controversial decision; unpopular with some people and it certainly surprised very many, causing them to realise that they didn't know me. I have heard that when Mwalimu realised that two former prime ministers were not included, he said, "I didn't know this fellow could be so bold". There was an underlying reason for my decision of who would form my cabinet, I wanted to clearly show the prospect of change with this new government by introducing a new face to the government. I had to be decisive and act boldly and it would have been very difficult to argue the case for speedy and major changes if cabinet had included the former Prime Ministers, Cleopa Msuya and John Malecela, who were strong characters. These two omissions really signalled change. My appointment of Frederick Sumaye[94] as Prime Minister was also totally unexpected.

An advantage I possessed, which meant that I could be so bold, was that I had not been anyone's candidate, hence was not expected to reward anybody with a position. Those who might have claimed a benefit were put off by my campaign manager Ferdinand Ruhinda saying, "Keep your distance, let the man govern. We got together in order to help him get elected so he could do a job, not so that we will join him." What's more in those days elections didn't cost that much. Voluntary contributions were made, though these were not substantial, and I was not expected to reward someone because they had made a large contribution to the party to assist with campaigning for the election. Consequently I had a free hand, which was very helpful.

---

94 Prime Minister November 1995– December 2005.

Sadly this is not the case nowadays, I have been told that even to get a councillorship in Dar es Salaam you must have several millions of Tanzanian shillings. I don't like this one bit; though I suppose it is inevitable the more you monetise the economy. Elections cost money, whether being held in a developed or developing country and we have seen government ministers having to resign in many countries because of the misuse of election funds.

There were no favourites in my cabinet, I called them the *'Askari wa Miavuli'* (the paratroopers). "You hit the ground running", I instructed them. I felt comfortable discussing particularly difficult issues with my first Vice President, the late Omar Ali Juma[95]. He was a very dependable person and we built good trust in each other. It was a great loss when he died. Fortunately his successor, Dr Ali Mohamed Shein, proved to be dependable as Vice President as well. It was a good team; they were paratroopers all right.

I had some good deputy ministers on my team as well, it is they who had to deal with the donkey work. Some of these deputies have since advanced well, especially John Magufuli, who became Tanzania's fifth president. He began as deputy minister of works during my first term and rose to minister of that portfolio during my second term. Tanzania's fourth president and my successor, Jakaya Kikwete, was minister of foreign affairs throughout my two terms.

I suppose it was my upbringing at school which implanted my drive for efficiency and timeliness. Early each morning I would go through all the newspapers to read the pulse of the people. If I read something I did not like or understand I would contact the relevant minister to ask for their explanation. My ministers quickly learnt to be prepared for my phone call early each day. They also learnt that I would not accept a paper tabled at cabinet unless that paper had been properly prepared. I expected each minister to have sat down with their permanent secretary and senior staff to discuss the preparation of the paper and have a thorough understanding of the issue, with attention to detail and proper

---

95   Vice President November 1995 until his death on 4 July 2001.

analysis. I also liked to walk about State House popping into offices, this created an alert atmosphere.

If I chose not to express my displeasure directly to a person then this task fell to my prime minister, as it was part of his role as the day-to-day leader of government business, particularly when the problem concerned a minister or regional commissioner. If the problem was more than a misdemeanour, such as an over inflation of their powers or a disregard for the limits of their powers, which was affecting the development of their ministry, then I would call them in and we would have a straight talk. I also called upon the attorney general to do this a few times because he could explain the law. Ministers must know the limits of their powers and when they may or should exercise them. Looking back now, I can see I made mistakes with some people I appointed during my two terms in office.

I was open to my ministers as I could possibly be, more I suspect than my predecessor had been. I had learned from Mwalimu to be patient, to listen, to find common ground as much as possible and strive for a collective working atmosphere. Those of us who had worked with Mwalimu for some time could see when our president had made up his mind on a matter but would still make an effort to discuss it, for he wanted us to understand. I tried to continue his culture of consultation with my cabinet; it may have even worked better for me because there wasn't much age difference amongst us, which meant that discussions were more open. However, it was a challenge at times to solicit views from some of my ministers, as there was a tendency to be acquiescent. I was pretty thorough in consultation when it came to policies; I made a conscious effort to consult widely and it was rare for me to make an abrupt decision.

In the end, the cabinet members defer to your judgement, as we have a very strong tradition that the cabinet advises the president and the president decides. The president can ignore any advice given and in return the minister has the option to resign from cabinet if they disagree strongly with an issue. Thankfully no minister felt compelled to resign for this reason during my time. I knew that the ultimate responsibility was always mine, as former USA president Harry Truman so rightly had on a sign on his desk: '*The buck stops here*'.

I asked four ministers to resign, three of them during my first term, though I later asked the Minister of Natural Resources and Tourism, Juma Ngasongwa, to rejoin cabinet after an investigation cleared him of wrongdoing. I asked my Minister of Finance, Simon Mbilinyi and his Deputy, Minister Kilonsi Mporogomi to leave as they were often in conflict with each other, something I could not allow during those crucial early days of trying to get on top of the state's finances. The Minister of Industry and Commerce, Iddi Simba, resigned during my second term; it seems that he had trouble distinguishing the promotion of government business with his personal interests. The Minister of State, Hassy Kitine, left when it emerged that his wife had made false claims for medical expenses incurred in North America.

Being a leader who is regarded as approachable is important, though it is tricky to get the balance right, especially in developing countries, where if you are too close with someone then there is the potential that people take you for granted – ignoring your status or exploiting closeness for their personal aggrandisement. You might listen to someone giving you advice, yet when he leaves he tells others, "You know, I've told the president…". Or casually dropping into a conversation, "As I was saying to the president last week…". Thus I learnt to be careful who I fraternised with, as well as from whom I sought counsel. I also learnt to be wary of flattery, because people wanted to please me and would answer what they thought I wanted to hear, which is not useful for a leader.

When I needed to mull over issues with someone I would call upon my personal assistant for political affairs to discuss affairs of the party and politics generally. The late Brigadier General Moses Nnauye[96] worked with me during my first term as my political advisor; he was a real professional, very discrete. During my second term I relied upon Kingunge Ngombale-Mwiru[97], a revered party activist, who, after Mwalimu, was

---

96 Deputy Secretary General of CCM 1990–1996; Presidential Advisor Political Affairs 1997–1999.

97 Secretary to the NEC of CCM 1982–1996; Deputy Minister of State Prime Minister's Office 1984; Minister of Local Government and Cooperative Development 1986–1987; Minister (no specific ministry) 1993–1995; Minister of State – Prime Minister's Office – Information 1997–2000; Minister of State President's Office Social and Political Affairs January 2006–February 2008.

the party ideologue. I appreciated working with my chief of intelligence, Cornel Apson Mwang'onda[98]; I think he may have dissuaded me from taking action on two occasions. I also called upon Nsa-Kaisi, who I had known since my days as managing editor. I was guided by the late governor of the Bank of Tanzania, Daudi Ballali, on matters of the economy, particularly regarding relations with the World Bank and IMF. During those tough economic times I relied heavily on him, as well as the head of the Tanzania Revenue Authority, Melkizedeck Sanare[99]. I had only studied economics at high school so much depended upon the Minister of Finance, Professor Simon Mbilinyi, as well as Permanent Secretary to the treasury, Gray Mgonja.

When I reread the party's manifesto after I had learnt about the true state of government's coffers, I wondered how our manifesto could be implemented. At a regional thank you for electing me rally I decided it was the time to frankly tell the people that we would not be able to achieve the goals in the party's manifesto because we simply did not have the financial base to do this. Certainly the government would endeavour to do so, but the finances were not good at all. That kind of bluntness was unheard of; everyone queried what was wrong with me, asking if I was determined to have a one term presidency. Some even admonished me that that this was not the way to conduct politics. I was not criticised by my party; though of course the opposition said this was an example of me being duplicitous during the campaign. I replied that I was trying to modify the people's expectations; after all, *ukweli na uwazi* (truth and transparency) had been my slogan during the campaign. Should the people decide they did not want me for a second term, well, I was ready for that and would be fine with such an outcome. I declared, '*Ni bora mnichukie kwa kuwaambia ukweli kuliko mnipende kwa kuwaficha ukweli*', essentially this means: I would rather that you hate me for telling you the truth than you like me for not telling you the truth.

There is no doubt that those first two years were the toughest time of my ten-year tenure. As I came to grips with my new job, I encountered

---

98   Director General of Tanzania Intelligence and Security Service 1996–2006.

99   The Tanzania Revenue Authority commenced on 1 July 1996.

much I did not like: inefficiency, sloth, irresponsibility and corruption. Despite this, I never had doubts that I had taken on too much; I had made a commitment which I was determined to see through. I knew I had to show strength and work hard; *ora et labora*. My leadership style during this period was described by someone who had known me for a long time as fearless; that I didn't do anything in fear, nor do anything out of fear. A leader must be courageous when necessary.

My biggest burden was turning around the economy, including the management of government revenue and expenditure. I remember a visit in 1996 by Baroness Lynda Chalker,[100] the United Kingdom's Minister for Overseas Development and Africa; she was quite blunt, she really gave me a piece of her mind. Britain was a major development partner and they didn't like the way we were managing our development funds; I assured her this was going to change. She said somewhat disbelievingly, "How do I know it is going to change?"

I responded with conviction, "What proof can I give you except my word? We have no option, either you believe me or don't believe me; but you will see in due course". Thankfully she believed in me and released funding from the UK government.

Understandably, the World Bank and IMF would not work with us unless we showed financial discipline. I said we would show discipline; naturally they wanted proof I could achieve this. Hence in the early months we worked as a government on a monthly cash budget system, with everything closely supervised and followed up. The measures I took to monitor public expenditure made me unpopular with many Tanzanians. Things got so difficult that I was being blamed for what was called '*ukapa*' – when you play a game of cards and your opponent gets all the cards while you wind up with nothing we describe this in Kiswahili as '*anakula kapa*' – you have nothing. My nickname became *Mzee Ukapa*. I hope those who criticised me during those times now have some sympathy for me. Thankfully after a while the World Bank and IMF relaxed their demands so by the beginning of my second term we could move to a three-monthly budget cycle.

---

100   Minister for Overseas Development and Africa 1989–1997.

One example of financial irresponsibility I learnt was that some government employees would wait until the month of June, which was the end of the financial year, and write post-dated cheques to pay for government services that they had received, in the full knowledge that those cheques would not be honoured until the new financial year. This skewed the government's finances and records. It also affected businesses because their income was delayed. This bad practice had a negative impact on the whole economy, which incensed the World Bank and IMF people, and rightly so. To show I was serious about stopping this unacceptable practice I had to threaten that anyone who wrote a post-dated cheque in June would lose their job.

It was not easy arguing the case for a close working relationship with the World Bank and IMF because these organisations were the bête noires to many Tanzanians, indeed many Africans. Nevertheless, these relationships were vital if I was going to get our country on a stronger footing. Tanzania was heavily indebted and I could not keep international debtors at arm's length, hence I moved quickly to improve relations. I am grateful for the helpful personal intervention of James Wolfensohn, the president of the World Bank[101]. He phoned me and said:

> Mr President, we haven't met. Well you know our people don't seem to agree about the way forward. I suggest that you call your people in, talk to them, nail them down about the real difficulties between the World Bank and the Tanzanian government. I will call them in on my side and will also pin them down about what their difficulties are. Then if you can manage to be in Washington we can sit down together and sort this out.

That is exactly what we did and from then onward we worked together well. This is a fine example of James Wolfensohn's proactive leadership, positive communication, and willingness to find common ground; I have a soft spot for him. I maintain contact with his then country director, Jim

---

101   President June 1995– June 2005.

Adams[102]; as we had worked well together. I also reached a good understanding with Horst Köhler[103], the IMF managing director. Though I am sure there were some Tanzanians who looked askance at me, saying 'this man is collaborating with the enemies', the World Bank and IMF. When it came to country support, I found China and the United Kingdom very helpful, as well as the Netherlands, Norway, Sweden, Denmark and Finland; the Germans helped a little as well.

A major achievement I was proud to gain for my country was debt relief under the Highly Indebted Poor Countries Initiative run by the World Bank and IMF. Our country's external debt was around USD 7 billion in mid-2001; this behemoth had grown over the years, being fed by such factors as drought affecting Tanzania's agricultural production, the war with Uganda, the global rise in oil prices during the 1970s, and our mismanagement of fiscal affairs. It took four years of hard work to earn debt relief, we had to prove our commitment to sound economic policy, followed by producing a Poverty Reduction Strategy Paper and undertaking associated institutional reforms. This concerted effort meant that in late 2001 we were granted USD 3 billion in debt relief. The relief reduced our total external debt by some 54% and reduced interest payments from around USD 193 million for the 1999–2000 fiscal year to an average of USD 116 million during the 2001–2002 to 2010–2011 fiscal years[104]. I regard this as a milestone in my unwavering drive to improve our economy and embrace financial discipline, transparency and sound management.

There is also a personal aspect to my securing debt relief for Tanzania, as I know that it brought comfort to Mwalimu when he was nearing the end of his life. The Paris Club members had positively viewed our economic reforms and efforts to put the state's finances in order and thought that we had fulfilled the conditions to qualify for consideration of debt relief, but I was frustrated as the Americans were resisting; perhaps they were recalling my days at '*The Nationalist*' newspaper and

---

102 World Bank country director for Tanzania 1995–2002.

103 Managing director of IMF 2000–2004; President of Germany 2004–2010.

104 Financial data obtained from the IMF: www.imf.org/en/News/Articles/2015/09/14/01/49/pr0148

were suspicious of me. When I attended the United Nations General Assembly in September 1999 I asked to meet with President Clinton, who was also attending. Bill Clinton queried the state of relations between our two countries, to which I replied, "That's precisely why I asked to see you; I want you to tell me why your country is putting its foot down against Tanzania getting debt relief?" Initially he denied this, so I explained that we had met the stipulations laid out by the World Bank and IMF, but when we attended the meeting of the Paris Club it was the USA that blocked us from obtaining debt relief; why was this? He turned around to his people who eventually conceded that this was true. Bill Clinton assured me that at the next meeting of the Paris Club the USA would endorse Tanzania receiving debt relief. I enjoyed working with Bill Clinton, at times I felt there was a genuine meeting of two minds.

During the next recess from the United Nations General Assembly I went back to my hotel and said to my assistant, "You must get me Mwalimu on the phone". Mwalimu was at the flat in London receiving treatment for leukemia, he hadn't yet been admitted into St Thomas hospital. I said, "Mwalimu, I want to tell you that now I have a commitment from President Clinton that we will get debt relief, the Americans will no longer block us".

"What?" he exclaimed, "are you sure?"

"Yes" I was pleased to reply.

"And you think Clinton is serious?" I said I was quite certain.

He replied, "Well, thank you, congratulations, thank you very much." Our conversation was just three days before he was admitted to hospital, yet even at this serious stage of his leukaemia he was still thinking of Tanzania. He died three weeks later. I like to think that this conversation provided some comfort, however small, to him during his final days.

The British Prime Minister, Tony Blair, kindly offered to provide transport to bring Mwalimu's body back to Tanzania, but we had a dependable Air Tanzania aircraft, so we dispatched that as we felt that Mwalimu's remains should return home on a national plane. It is a credit to our uniformed services that the organisation and the funeral ceremony itself went so well, this reflected the high regard they held for their first commander in chief. I was moved by the high-level attendance at his memorial service, over four hundred leaders from sixty-one countries and eight international organisations attended, a reflection of his recognised greatness. Leaders included Robert Mugabe of Zimbabwe, Sam Nujoma of Namibia, Joaquim Chissano of Mozambique, Thabo Mbeki of South Africa, Yoweri Museveni of Uganda, Olusegun Obasanjo of Nigeria, Isaias Afwerki of Eritrea, Meles Zenawi of Ethiopia, Daniel arap Moi of Kenya, Vice-President Krishna Kant of India, and U.S. Secretary of State, Madeleine Albright. The Finnish president, Martti Ahtisaari, attended as the head of the European Union, with Princess Anne representing the United Kingdom. This august presence gave me strength to carry on. I determined to uphold Mwalimu's conviction of what our country could evolve into. By leading Tanzania well I would sustain the honour and respect that had been shown to Mwalimu by all these mourners. I received hundreds of messages from all around the world, a few of which I read during my address[105] at the state funeral[106]. I closed my address with, "Our world is composed of givers and takers. The takers may eat better, but the givers sleep better. In death, as in life, Mwalimu sleeps better. For his entire life was a life of giving, not taking".

The death of *Baba wa Taifa,* Father of the Nation, as he was also known, was a significant event in the history of our country, his funeral a sorrowful yet unifying occasion. It was a very sad time for us all, with people from all religions, tribes and age groups genuinely saddened. I was determined not to cry at the funeral, my sense of duty prevailed for I felt I must show the country that life had to go on. However, I am told that Mwalimu was so devastated when he was told about the fatal car accident of his Prime Minister, Edward Sokoine, that he cried.

Besides my personal grief, his passing caused me to reflect on my leadership. For I felt subdued in terms of authority, because, despite it being twelve years since he had left the presidency, Mwalimu's presence would always deter others. I knew that his departure would embolden some.

---

[105] '*State Funeral for Mwalimu Julius Kambarage Nyerere, 1999.*' Speech (pages 493–499) included in Volume 3, Part Two, Cluster 1 of '*The Mkapa Years Collected Speeches*.' Dar es Salaam: Mkuki na Nyota.

[106] A portfolio of press coverage of Nyerere's death, including statements by leaders from all around the world is available at: https://www.juliusnyerere.org/uploads/nyerere_press_covarage_1999.pdf

But I would not give up, I had to go on. I knew I must have stronger arms to hold the torch which he had passed on to us.

Later I was honoured by being adopted into Mwalimu's clan, the Burito clan of the Zanaki people, which is a rare occurrence. Chief Japhet Edward Wanzagi knew how I had worked very closely with Mwalimu, serving him faithfully, and also appreciated how I had honoured Mwalimu when he died, with the state funeral and accompanying his body for the burial at his village. When I was press secretary, Mwalimu would visit Chief Edward Wanzagi Nyerere to pay his respects and converse with him. When this chief died, Mwalimu continued to show respect to his son, Chief Wanzagi. Drawing the distinction between the head of state and the tribal chief is important. When I became president I followed Mwalimu's example and paid the chiefs due respect. He had divested them of their governance, but this was done in order to push forward national unity, for entrenched tribal leadership could have hampered his drive for this. He certainly valued Tanzania's chiefs as cultural leaders.

Returning to economic matters, I was criticised for my commitment to paying off the nation's debts – many said I should have spent the money on building resources for Tanzania instead; decrying that I had embarked on repaying the debts to the detriment of other services. Yet we received more in debt relief than we repaid in debt and saved more resources by way of debt relief. Otherwise the debt burden would have been impossible. Equally important, this was our way of demonstrating to lenders and development partners that we were earnest in our commitment to honouring agreements. Beforehand there had been a lack of interaction, for example when the World Bank advised that money was due; we had kept quiet and not made the required payment. My actions led to us restoring the confidence of private national and international institutions. In turn this cleared the way for us to plan the expansion of the economy.

My first term was dominated by change. Reforms touched everywhere, I believe I reviewed over fifty policies and 205 bills were passed in parliament during my two terms. By the time the first five years were coming to an end even my detractors realised that change was inevitable and that there was a prospect of things really looking up. The fact that we got an increase in the presidential vote in the second term from 61% to

71% of the vote shows that the people had recognised the need for change and wanted me to continue.

Of course the politics started whether I would have a second term or not, especially since Mwalimu had passed on. There was much speculation of who else would seek nomination as the party's candidate. Some thought that it might be easier now for them to get nomination. However, I think that they looked at my record from the first term and decided they didn't stand a chance against me. Overall my memories from my second term are much more positive. Prime Minister Frederick Sumaye knew my work style and we had a good team, in a sense a better team, as those who remained with me had proven their worth during the first term. Although it is not a criticism of the prime minister, I brought the ministry of regional administration and local government under the president's office and appointed the late Brigadier General (Rtd.) Hassan Ngwilizi as minister of state for this portfolio, which he ran well indeed.

These ten years of my term represented a change of course for Tanzania, particularly with regards to the fostering of the private sector. No president before me had really embraced the concept that the private sector could drive economic change in our country; while I saw it as the only way forward. To be fair President Mwinyi had initiated some steps in this direction, but he had not been articulate enough in explaining the rationale and necessity and his approach had not been sufficiently bold. I saw that I must be strong and push change through, that was my mission and I believed in it.

While president I was committed to making tough decisions and taking the actions necessary to advance my country. You must be consistent with and persistent in your leadership; you must make decisions and then act on them. Decisions that lead to actions mean you are going somewhere, even if only one step, at least you are going forward instead of standing still. I had learnt from Mwalimu; some of his decisions were not easily palatable, but people knew his unwavering commitment once a decision was made.

In my view the interpretation of the policy of self-reliance and self-development was to enable people to help themselves, so my perspective of the economy was focused on empowering the people. I would promote equality through creating or increasing opportunities for them.

The underlying rationale for all the reforms I instigated was that I would help the people to help themselves. I acknowledge that some of the changes were tough for people to understand and embrace, especially for those who didn't understand the context. Some criticism was to be expected because we all still had a socialist outlook. Those who knew me from the days when I was managing editor of the party's newspapers couldn't understand how I could be now driving these changes.

I could well remember when I was high commissioner to Canada and would come to Tanzania for meetings, I would receive many requests to bring basic goods such as bath soap and toothpaste because products such as these were unobtainable in Tanzania at that time. I did not want Tanzania falling further behind and I would not allow a return to those days of hardship during Mwalimu's time. We were in a tunnel; I sensed that something had to change, we couldn't continue along this tunnel.

I firmly believed that we needed a re-examination, a rethinking and re-strategising of how our country was being run. This required a significant change of mindset and attitude for the people of Tanzania, so it was inevitable that I would take a lot of flak; especially as often my leadership style had to be a 'telling and directing' form of situational leadership. We had to adapt and adopt new ways which many did not have sufficient knowledge of, or experience with. As the leader of this momentous change I had to be confident; I am conscious that some saw my confidence as bordering on arrogance; but I had to show absolute conviction in the path we were taking. Could I have achieved so many reforms if I had not appeared so determined?

CHAPTER II

Reforms and Yet More Reforms

Bringing the government finances into a healthy state required an attack from two fronts: I needed to increase government revenues and stimulate economic growth, as well as reduce unnecessary operational costs, including remove support from non-self-sustaining capital assets.

My continual message, my mantra if you like, to ministers and public servants was that we must use what resources we had and prioritise the many problems we faced. Our focus on sound financial management showed results in many ways, for example: government revenues for the 1994/95 financial year were only 331,238 million Tanzanian shillings, which was equivalent at that time to USD 612,587; (I took office in December 1995). This was not enough to pay our country's operating costs, let alone finance capital costs necessary for the country's development. Ten years later, the government's revenue was for the 2005/06 financial year was 2,124, 843 million Tanzanian shillings, equivalent to USD 1,796,862, (I left office in December 2005). There were only sufficient foreign exchange reserves to cover imports of goods and services for under a month and a half. This grew to foreign exchange reserves to cover 5.3 months in 2005. We lowered the interest lending rate from 36% in 1995 to 15.2% in 2005.

Addressing the bottom-heavy taxation system, which also suffered from widespread tax evasion, was an obvious area to start with. My predecessor had begun efforts, with his presidential commission[107] resulting in the Tanzania Revenue Authority, TRA, being established in the last piece of legislation passed by parliament before the general election of 1995. The TRA commenced full operations July 1996 and we introduced a Value Added Tax in July 1998. Then we passed the Public Finance Act in 2001 to ensure there was transparency on tax collection and tax expenditures.

Good governance and sound financial management are matters which I care deeply about, they are the foundation stones for any sound government. Furthermore, it is important to ensure that laws and regulations are strictly adhered to, for the betterment of good governance. It is important to understand the reason for each law, which must be drafted with a clear purpose.

Some measures I fostered to encourage these critical mainstays of government were introducing the Public Service And Public Ethics Act[108], as well as the Public Procurement Act of 2001 and associated Public Procurement Regulatory Authority[109], which set out the rules for purchases by government. I wanted to promote transparency, to show that public funds should be publicly accounted for.

People were pleased with these and similar legislation and regulations I introduced as they had become accustomed to politicians speaking about corruption but doing little, now they saw punitive legislation with clear rules being put in place. I also took care to amend some legislation introduced during my time when shortcomings emerged as new acts were implemented.

Another element of good governance is human rights, so the Commission for Human Rights and Good Governance commenced operations in July 2001. How effectively it is operating now I don't know, but at least

---

107 Presidential Commission of Enquiry into Public Revenues, Taxation and Expenditure, 1991.

108 Ethics Division established 1998 along with Code of Ethics and Conduct for the Civil Service, as well as Public Service Act No. 8 2002.

109 Public Procurement Regulatory Authority PPRA 2004.

its establishment was my expression of intent at that time. I started the Prevention of Corruption Bureau of Tanzania[110] as part of my many reforms; 'Mr Clean' became my name.

It is inhumane when someone asks for a bribe from a poor person who has absolutely nothing, so they can receive basic health delivery or education. Sometimes a poor person even had pay something to receive a government form. That really annoyed me; still does. One example I see nowadays is the sudden increase of traffic police officers on the roadside a few days before a public holiday. My friends tell me these policemen are seeking bribes so they can celebrate during the coming public holiday. At least that bribe is being taken from someone who has money, otherwise they wouldn't own a car or motorcycle, though this is still unacceptable. But seeking a bribe to provide a basic service such as access to water, or treatment at a hospital, that kind of corruption really upsets me. This was particularly bad in my time because public service salaries were so inadequate; even then it was not justified, but you had to accept that it was happening.

Fighting corruption is hard because you are fighting people's livelihoods. There were times when I wondered why I had entered this fray as I upset so many people. Then I would remind myself that my actions were to help the vulnerable poor who could not afford to pay bribes. I have been told that since I left office corruption has gone up the ladder into politics. If the use of money during campaigning is corruption, then this is widespread now. This also disturbs me because during my two times of campaigning to be elected as president I didn't spread money around to win favours. I did spend money travelling whilst campaigning, for I wanted to show my personal commitment by travelling to districts to ask for their nomination. At most, at the end of the day, I would spend money on having a meal with elders and local representatives. But I didn't hand out money; actually, we didn't even have the money to do so. It seems that money is driving politics now, we have learnt fast from American electioneering, I suppose. I had known corruption in the West has been there all along, but I did not know it was on such a large scale

---

110   Later renamed as The Prevention and Combating of Corruption Bureau PCCB.

in Western countries to the extent that it has been revealed lately, it is incredible.

Considering corruption in politics, Mwalimu tried to keep very wealthy people from obtaining leadership positions within the party. He made it difficult for rich businessmen to seek to become members of parliament, though I recall there were two wealthy Tanzanian Indians in cabinet, Amir Jamal – who was Minister of Finance for twelve years and Al Noor Kassum, who held several posts. I tried to follow Mwalimu's tradition. I recall blocking some wealthy Tanzanians, such as Yussuf Manji, when I saw his name on the list for consideration to be nominated as the CCM candidate for Kigamboni, yet I had not met him at any party function and he hadn't been actively involved in the party. There was also Abulaziz Mohamed Abood from Morogoro.

I saw this as the beginning of the encroachment on the party elite, the decision-makers in the party, which was based on money, which is not tenable. There is nothing wrong with being wealthy, and I am not saying the sensible thing is to have a poor man's party, but to have a leadership elite characterised by their wealth? This creates the possibility that these people may use the instruments of state and the structures of government to enrich themselves and their friends. Nowadays there are some who want to get into politics because they believe that this is where they will make money; though there are some wealthy members of parliament who use their wealth for their constituency; being people and service orientated.

Under other efforts to promote transparency and protection for consumers as the markets were opening up, we set up several regulatory agencies, such as: the Tanzania Airports Authority[111], Business Registrations and Licensing Agency[112], Energy and Water Utilities Regulatory Authority[113], Tanzania Communications Regulatory Authority[114], and the Surface and Marine Transport Regulatory Authority. We ensured

---

111   Tanzania Airports Authority TAA 1999.

112   Business Registrations and Licensing Agency BRELA 1999.

113   Energy and Water Utilities Regulatory Authority EWURA 2001.

114   Tanzania Communications Regulatory Authority TCRA 2003.

that these authorities did not depend on government to fund their operations and there was the added benefit that they streamlined or trimmed the role of government by taking on the regulatory responsibilities. My intention was that by having specially dedicated independent agencies we would reduce bureaucracy and reduce the civil service, though I now fear that maybe we just created a different outlet for bureaucracy to operate from.

I tried to foster business, including the introduction of Export Processing Zones in 2002. However, understandably many in the private sector viewed this large-scale introduction of new legislation and regulations with concern; particularly as the influence of *ujamaa* (socialism) still held strong. Also, few within the public service had experience of doing business themselves, or interacting proactively with businesses, resulting in many misunderstandings about how businesses function and how they should be regulated. Thus I established the Tanzania National Business Council[115] to enable those from government to be in direct contact with the private sector, to encourage dialogue between government and business, learn their problems and gain their ideas on how to improve the taxation system. I found the input from the Tanzania National Business Council very useful indeed, and a bonus was that this helped many business people to realise that despite my close relationship with Mwalimu and past editorship of socialist newspapers I was not as antagonistic to business and the concept of capitalism as they had thought. Many business owners were prejudiced that I was a diehard communist, or socialist, that my inclination would be to dispossess people, rather than to enable them to own something. Some thought that I would assert dominance, which is the communist way, rather than promote equality and justice.

There was this notion that only communism could create a fair and equal society, but the pursuit of fairness and equality cannot be ascribed to the communist system alone. Even in the capitalist system you have that. Then there were those who thought I had experienced a dramatic conversion, like Paul on the road to Damascus, yet this is not what

---

115   Tanzania National Business Council launched April 2001.

happened. I held the same commitment to fairness and equality throughout, it was just that now I saw stimulating the economy as a means to aiding the people to achieve a fair and equal society.

TANROADS[116] was born out of my frustration at how long it was taking to solicit funding from the World Bank to improve the network of our major roads. A good road infrastructure was a necessary element of our strategy to bring about economic growth and the World Bank was the lead institution in providing funding for roading, yet nothing was forthcoming from them. Each time I raised the important matter of sealing the major roads I was told our economy was not right, or the evaluation studies had not been done. Yet how could we progress when most of our roads were unsealed? So, as our tax revenues increased, I determined to show the development community how serious we were about improving the roads by using our own money to build roads. Therefore, we set aside an amount each month which we then used to build roads, for example from Mwanza to Shinyanga, Shinyanga to Kahama, and Busega to Igunga.

When the World Bank representative Judy O'Connor's term was coming to an end, she found some money so that she could leave evidence of the World Bank's contribution; hence the section of the Singida–Nzega road, from Sekenke to Igunga. I confess I had found it difficult at times to deal with Judy O'Connor, but I was pleased to see the World Bank realise that we were serious about improving the main road infrastructure. John Magufuli[117] was terrific as Minister of Works during my second term, he got things done. His strong performance in this area was recognised when he sought presidential candidate nomination in 2015. These improved roads not only helped the economy, they also helped the people access services more quickly; travelling long distances on an unsealed road makes any journey arduous.

You may recall my discussion with Mwalimu about my proposal to

---

116   Tanzania National Roads Agency TANROADS came into operation July 2000 as a semi-autonomous agency under the Ministry of Works.

117   John Magufuli became President of Tanzania in 2015. He served as Minister of Works 2000–2006 and 2010–2015; also Minister of Lands and Human Settlement 2006–2008 and Minister of Livestock and Fisheries 2008–2010.

stand for nomination, where I spoke of the problems of the co-operatives and trade unions. I thought the party had distanced itself from the co-operatives, which had been a pillar in the independence struggle. I don't think they were given enough ideological cognisance after Mwalimu stepped down, their presence had diminished under my predecessor. The result was that magnates of co-operatives emerged. The peasant farmers kept sending their produce to the co-operatives but there was a lack of accountability, enabling some people to undertake large scale thievery. This upset me and now I was able to address these problems; as it was important to transform these co-operatives into a pillar for development. The co-operatives represented the voice of the rural population – the peasant; therefore I determined that they must receive greater attention. I wanted to address accountability and restore the co-operatives to be a real political voice, contributing actively to policy and political matters in our party. I am an ideologue, the workers and the peasants – this is what my party, CCM, is about.

I established a commission to investigate the status and practices of the co-operative movement, this was led by Sir George Kahama[118] and Anne Makinda[119], who is an expert on co-operative accounts. Many thought it odd that I had appointed Sir George, as he was old, but I knew he was a staunch co-operative person who knew so much about this subject. They produced a good report[120], rather critical, but also helpful with suggestions on how we could improve the co-operative movement. We followed their recommendations, establishing a co-operative audit department and a ministry of co-operatives and marketing, of which Sir George Kahama became minister; he did well there. We cleaned up the co-operatives, paid off their debts, some of which were substantial, and allowed them to start afresh.

I was determined to tackle the strong co-operative movements. One

---

118 General Manager of the Bukoba Co-operative Union; Minister of Home Affairs; Minister Commerce and Industry; CEO of the National Development Corporation; Director General Capital Development Authority; Minister of Co-operatives and Marketing; Ambassador; MP.

119 First female Speaker of Parliament 2010–2015.

120 Report of Special Presidential Committee on Reviving, Strengthening and Developing Co-operatives in Tanzania, February 2001.

recalcitrant co-operative I recall was the Nyanza Co-operative Union in the Lake Region, which was headed by Paul Ng'wani. He was a prominent and successful businessman; how come he was the chairman of that co-operative union for small farmers? He was a force to be reckoned with, politically and financially, and had a strong ethnic solidarity which he could call upon. It was difficult to decide if we should challenge him, so I consulted widely about this, yet finally determined that we must break the back of irresponsible leadership of co-operatives.

Having a close relationship with co-operatives is useful for gauging the feelings of peasant farmers in the rural areas, as well as being able to organise their access to markets and improve the quality and quantity of their produce. A co-operative gives the peasant farmer a sense of belonging to the growth of the nation, which is important when many in the rural areas feel marginalised.

Frankly, I was disappointed when the succeeding administration removed this ministry and placed co-operatives as an appendage to the ministry of agriculture.[121] Many of the civil servants there were mainstream, having little knowledge of co-operatives, which once again became a side-lined presence. At least I know I kept my promise to Mwalimu that I would tackle the problems of the co-operatives.

I attended every May Day celebration of the trade unions and met with them at the trade union congress. Trade union leaders would also come to talk with me at State House and I enjoyed these interactions. I always started off on the premise that they were all true nationalists and if they were against exploitation then they would be against exploiting the peasant. I found the teachers' union the most difficult to deal with, hence was frank communicating with them:

> Here are the government finances, now you tell me where I should cut in order to increase your allowances. It will take time for us to build the economy to where we have enough money to increase your salaries and retirement benefits. Let's get the economy going first.

---

121 Ministry of Agriculture, Food Security and Co-operatives.

I felt strongly about local government reform as the district administration level is really where you can get things moving, especially in the fight against poverty. On entering office, I held strong views that the position of district commissioner had become too politicised; with district commissioners being appointed who had insufficient qualifications or experience; it was no longer a professional role. Sadly this became even more so during my successor's time. In the old days there was a strict system of progression, building up from the lowest grade district officer, studying and sitting exams as you moved up, even studying law, because sometimes you were a third-class magistrate. This long preparation meant that when you became a district commissioner you knew a lot about how a district is properly managed and governed.

I vowed to try to reinforce the system of progression and the need for professionally trained and experienced district commissioners. But I had to restrain myself, and I much regret that I failed to achieve all my desired reforms in this area. If we had been still operating under the one-party system it would have been easier to reform, but, I couldn't achieve as much as I wanted now that we were under the multi-party system. Nowadays you have a week's seminar upon appointment as a district commissioner and you are supposedly ready for this important job. Those appointed come from all spheres – from newspaper men to foreign service officers. I think this is carrying politics too far, many of these political nominees have little experience and knowledge of administration and governance, yet this role is so important to the community and you have much interaction with the citizenry.

I became extremely unpopular in Dar es Salaam when I suspended the elected city council due to bad governance. The councillors had been elected the same time as I had been, but their corruption and mismanagement could not be allowed to continue. I did compromise by letting them keep their titles and the like during this period of suspension, though they could not hold council meetings. The executive team I appointed, which was led by Charles Keenja, did a good job and eventually the city council was restored after three and a half years[122].

---

122   Suspended 28 June 1996, restored 1 January 2000.

The most controversial of the reforms were the privatisation of nationally owned businesses, the reform of the public service and the sale of government housing. Some privatisation had been started by my predecessor President Mwinyi[123]; the most prominent government owned entities being the Tanzania Breweries and the Cooperative and Rural Development Bank. Yet his actions had been tentative; while I undertook privatisation almost wholesale and was heavily criticised for doing so. But this had to be done, I was convinced that this was the right path for the nation. I have always strongly believed in self-reliance and self-development, but we had strayed to total dependence on development partners and international financial institutions, without a sound revenue base of our own. Our economy was not functioning properly; furthermore, it was described as socialist but was not delivering socialist benefits. Moreover, some had carried the idea of social enterprise too far, for example during Mwalimu's time the Dar es Salaam city council was running butcheries. This was stopped by Mwalimu; there was no reason why there should be public ownership of butcheries. There were many potentially viable nationally owned business enterprises, though they were mismanaged and had run into heavy debt; drastic action had to be taken.

I was saddened by the incompetence shown in running these state-owned enterprises. I think this incompetence resulted from our not knowing enough about managing business, we didn't have good advisors I suppose, and I am sorry to admit that there was a general attitude of *laissez-faire*. We had entrusted the management of these enterprises to people with a government service mentality; in those days a civil servant just passed paper from one person to another, he was not innovative, nor a driver of business and we needed people like that to run these enterprises.

Socialist education was very much at the heart of this nation, from the classrooms to the national service. Public enterprise meant public ownership, this was very much inculcated in our minds. The generalised attitude seemed to be that it was evil to make money; which is wrong,

---

123 Presidential Parastatal Sector Reform Commission established 1992.

an economic enterprise should be an enterprise making money; but to those who had embraced *ujamaa* this was heresy. Even now you can see socialist indoctrination in newspaper articles, for example a tutor at a university criticising 'rampant capitalism', accusing Tanzanians of being agents of 'Western capitalist growth'. I had been a teacher of socialism dating back to my time as editor of the party's newspapers; the theory was one thing, but to have enterprises costing the government money to keep running, was simply unsustainable and unjustifiable.

Reflecting on this just before leaving office, I said in a speech[124]:

> Our experience is that the virtues of socialist inclusiveness were sometimes exaggerated, and their benefits were often eroded by the inefficiencies of socialist production. We also learnt that the exclusiveness of capitalism could actually be ameliorated through a people-centred development vision: targeted fiscal measures, better regulation and an improved business environment.

I had to face reality and correct this major problem affecting the economy; I would move ahead with widespread privatisation; notwithstanding that I was facing a battle with societal attitude. Being a leader requires an openness to new ideas and courage to push things through. My socialist influenced conscience was at ease as I was convinced that I was going to help make those institutions work better and the results would show to the people that there was nothing wrong with the reforms that we were making; this was the right path to self-reliance and self-development.

It was difficult to point to any parastatal that was making money, even the National Insurance Company was failing to do so. The National Bank of Commerce was called a bank of commerce but was in debt. The National Agricultural Food Corporation (NAFCO) was making a loss; the Canadians had tried to help us with the large scale Manyara wheat farms, yet this project had failed. There was the National Ranch-

---

124 *International conference on Reforming the Business Environment, 29 November 2005.* Volume 3, Part One, Cluster II of *'The Mkapa Years Collected Speeches'*. Dar es Salaam, Mkuki na Nyota. Also available online at: www.businessenvironment.org/dyn/be/docs/5/OpeningSessionMakapa/pdf

ing Company (NARCO) with big ranches, though none were making money. There was much incompetence with debt management at the national power enterprise, the Tanzania Electrical Supply Company Ltd (TANESCO), with parastatal companies, state institutions and the government not paying their electricity bills, yet still receiving electricity.

There was no option but privatisation really. Enterprises should have been making money and helping with government revenue, yet they were dependent on government handouts. People were fed up with those parastatals which were taking money out of the treasury, instead of generating money for the treasury. Some socialist ideologues were uneasy, but no-one could offer an alternative. What else was there to do other than to try to find businesses to partner with, or to sell these enterprises outright?

There is a misperception that Mwalimu was not happy with my push for privatisation. Certainly he did not like this policy and programme of privatisation of public enterprises, which is not surprising since many of them had been established under his presidency. He had been heavily critical of President Mwinyi's efforts on privatisation, though I suspect that may have been based on the process used, rather than the decision. If his criticism was based on the actual decision to privatise then I think that was unfair. I honestly do not know why Mwalimu did not upbraid me or my government. Perhaps, when it came to my time, he restrained himself because he realised that his earlier criticism of my predecessor had not helped solve the growing problem of the poor performance of the parastatals.

Above all, Mwalimu was a pragmatist, as leaders must be, especially in developing countries. While Mwalimu may have been disappointed that these enterprises could not continue being run by the government or governmental agencies following his socialist principles, he could see the scale and pervasiveness of the problem. We had reached a point where many of the parastatal enterprises were looking to the government for subsidies to keep operating, yet these were supposed to be business enterprises! Furthermore, the decision to privatise any public enterprise was the culmination of a process of extensive introspection and comprehensive re-appraisal; it was now time to take firm action.

Of my contemporaries, President Yoweri Museveni has also displayed pragmatism, for he was a committed ideologist when he lived in Dar es Salaam; but changed his stance to encourage private enterprise to aid the development of Uganda.

The catalytic moment when things really turned around on privatisation arose from Mwalimu's meeting with Jim Wolfensohn, the president of the World Bank. I had asked Mwalimu to discuss the matter of World Bank interference in the privatisation process, as the World Bank officials were trying to dictate everything. Ambassador Charles Sanga, who was Mwalimu's personal assistant then, was present at this meeting and narrated the following to me:

> Actually the conversation during this meeting didn't start with matters of the privatisation, but with the Washington Consensus[125] and the structural adjustment programs (SAPs). They discussed how the ten years of the structural adjustment programs had proved to be a loss decade for the development of Africa. Mwalimu called it a disaster and Wolfensohn acknowledged this, saying how even in Washington they were embarrassed by the failure of the Washington Consensus and the structural adjustment programs to work out the way they had expected.

Mwalimu had been vigorously opposed to the World Bank/IMF structural adjustment programmes. He will be remembered in this regard for his rhetorical question, "Should I pay debt and let my people die?". He was later proved right, with the World Bank and distinguished economists such as Joseph Stiglitz admitting that SAPs did not work!

> Then Mwalimu said to Wolfensohn, 'I hear that you are now trying to privatise everything in Tanzania', that's the way he put it. Wolfensohn denied this. Mwalimu became quite angry saying 'you guys sit here in your fancy offices and plan things for Tanzania without any idea of how people might react to whatever you are planning.

---

125 Ten economic policies prescribed by the IMF, World Bank and United States Treasury to constitute a reform package for developing countries.

> You really don't know the reality on the ground; if you tell me, Jim Wolfensohn, you know Tanzania better than me, I'll be surprised. You say this is the best thing for us to swallow, you just push things down our throats without even allowing us to chew. This is not right, please don't do that. We have determined the implementation of the privatisation process, leave us be, instead of breathing down our necks and trying to dictate everything'. Wolfensohn replied: 'you know Mwalimu there are a lot of complaints that we are the ones who are doing everything. But Mwalimu, let me tell you, some things that are done in your country are not our initiative, it is the initiative from your own people. Sometimes we are surprised and wonder why do they do that? Is there a hidden agenda?'

I suspect that there may have been some Tanzanian government officials with a hidden agenda, perhaps in order to better themselves financially. Mwalimu said that's where people go wrong, privatisation should be for the benefit of the nation, not just for private profit. There was another issue as well which I believed compounded this breakdown between ourselves and the World Bank, a problem of poor coordination. Sanga says that:

> Wolfensohn admitted that there was a problem with coordination, not just between Tanzania and the World Bank, but including other institutions such as the IMF, UNICEF, WHO and major international NGOs. It was an issue Wolfensohn had to deal with in more countries than just Tanzania.

Poor coordination within government and between government and other institutions remains an ongoing problem in Tanzania, as well as for many other countries.

This meeting proved to be a watershed between Mwalimu and Wolfensohn; it helped Tanzania's future development. Ambassador Sanga narrated:

Mwalimu said now let's forget about the past, now you have my president {me}, work with him. He's going to lead Tanzania to somewhere where we want to be. Please work closely with the president for the good of the country. My president is a very decisive guy who analyses issues well and is not going to come up with a decision without any analysis; he will be good for the nation.

From that point on we had a positive working relationship with the World Bank.

Returning to the privatisation of public enterprises, individuals and entities would submit their tenders; a board would evaluate the offers and make a recommendation. The larger tenders would come to cabinet for discussion and then I would approve or reject the offer. I think there was enough transparency in the process, but I am not sure if we had sufficient skilled experts to make a competent analysis of the offers. Perhaps we should have sought more stringent appraisal or due diligence. I had never run a business and was a bit naïve about business, the local Indian private sector was more experienced and fast-moving than many of us when it came to business.

Our follow-up was weak as well, especially with those entities which were privatised to local investors. For example, we expected the fruit processing factory in Korogwe to be developed into a major fruit canning enterprise; but disappointingly the new owners cannibalised the equipment and installed it in their existing factory in Dar es Salaam. They would not have won their bid for this factory in Korogwe if we had known their intention to do this. I acknowledge that once you have handed an enterprise over without conditions you must accept that you have no say, but I regret that I concentrated more on regulatory agencies than on the performance of the entities. I should have given equal attention to monitoring the reawakening of these privatised entities. We simply believed in the good faith of everyone, that they had the money, that they certainly would do what they had undertaken to do, and that they would be fair. We just disposed of the entity and then left it at that. We should have had a mechanism for monitoring what was going on in these privatised industries.

Furthermore, as I pointed out in my 2003 May Day speech regarding privatisation in the world of globalisation[126]:

> We did not always succeed with every privatisation of a public enterprise. There have been successes, and there have been challenges. But that cannot justify going back, even if that was possible, because the decision is basically right. On balance, the direction we have taken is more beneficial than retaining these loss-making public enterprises. The waters of globalisation are all around us, whether we like it or not. Unless we learn how to swim, we will sink; and learning to swim requires trial and error, and conquering the fear of water, while taking all necessary precautions.

A major criticism which persists until today was that I privatised more state-owned enterprises to foreigners rather than to Tanzanians. This is simply not true; this unfair criticism of me still rankles. We privatised 319 individual enterprises; of those 121 were privatised and owned 100% by Tanzanians – that's nearly 38%, while just under 54% – that's 171 enterprises were bought by partnerships of foreigners and Tanzanians. Only 27 enterprises, 8%, were privatised wholly to foreigners during my time. You will find that the capital required for these 27 enterprises was very substantial, well beyond the means of Tanzanians. Thirty-seven enterprises had not yet been privatised when I left office.

There was the question about whether there were enough Tanzanian buyers, and whether we could postpone a sale until there were, but some loss-making enterprises had to be dealt with quickly, as they were a drain on our perilous government finances. Nowadays when the citizenry see how much money some of the privatised entities are making they say the government should have continued with the public enterprises. At that time we simply didn't have the business capability and financial capacity to turn these enterprises around, particularly the largest enterprises, for example those in the mining and banking sectors.

---

126   A transcript of this broadcast, which is in Kiswahili, can be found in a published collection of my national broadcasts 'Uwazi na ukweli: Rais wa Watu Azungumza na Wananchi'. Vol III, 2005. Dar es Salaam, Mkuki na Nyota.

I was criticised for giving away our gold and tanzanite because I opened up the mining sector to foreign direct investment, but the upfront capital investment required for commercial mining is huge and no purely Tanzanian entity had the resources for this. A few years later I was criticised that the royalties were too low at 3% for minerals and 5% for diamonds, though these rates were not too low at the time we passed the legislation in mid 1998. How could we have known that the gold price would rise so dramatically in the future? That is what market forces are about. One can set in place that a certain percentage of those earnings must remain in that district to help with local development projects, though this has the potential for creating problems in the future, with natural resource endowed districts becoming better-off than those districts without minerals and other natural resources, such as the poorer districts in the centre of the country. Mwalimu's ethos of sharing wealth nationally is still relevant here, as the attitude that assets are national rather than local is a big factor for stability and governance in developing countries. We must take care not to give preference to local demands, rather we should rationalise the issue within the context of national development.

Aside from the mining sector, perhaps the most controversial privatisations were the National Bank of Commerce (NBC) and the Tanzania Electric Supply Company Ltd (TANESCO). Mwalimu did have some concerns about privatising NBC. The reason given to him was that NBC had branches across the country, which would make it difficult for any new banks which wanted to establish in Tanzania; we needed to have a level playing field so that there would be free and fair competition, which in theory would benefit the people. Mwalimu was not amused by this justification; why should another bank fear competing with NBC? He didn't oppose privatisation; it was the reasoning behind it. However, we needed to create a more diverse banking environment; so, we decided to split NBC into two banks. One would focus on commercial banking and high and middle-income customers; while a second bank would serve the low-income earner.

Once Mwalimu learnt that NBC would be split with one bank specifically established to serve the peasantry and small businesses people, he was pleased. We wanted to give this lower income class of society the opportunity to place their savings in a bank in an effort to encourage their saving and Mwalimu endorsed saving as part of his ethos of self-reliance. The National Microfinance Bank (NMB) was created out of the NBC in 1997. It performed so well that the government could divest 49% of the shareholding to a consortium of strategic investors led by the Dutch Rabobank Group in 2005. I am pleased to say that since then the bank has registered steady growth and continues to focus on serving the common man.

One thing that disappoints me when someone criticises our privatising NBC is that they do not acknowledge how indebted it was. It was in financial trouble; reaching a point where it was going to have to obtain a subsidy from the treasury to keep operating; that is not what government revenues are for.

The arrangement with TANESCO was one of the first public-private partnerships, we brought in management from South Africa – the NETGroup Solutions. This created an uproar; especially from the workers, but I had a good man, bold too, Professor Juma Kapuya, Minister of Labour, Youth Development and Sport, who helped me a great deal. I remember the day the NETGroup Solutions people were to move in to the offices, workers and other protestors had threatened that blood would be shed, but I stood firm and had the police there to escort the employees of NETGroup Solutions on to the premises if necessary. Fortunately, they entered without encountering any violence.

The critics were against this public-private partnership of the electrical supply company for two reasons. The first criticism was why did we have to contract with a third party to chase up debts and to force the government to pay its own outstanding electricity bills? We would be better to train our Tanzanian staff and discipline the debtors. But I knew the lackadaisical attitude of many government workers, it was time to show that I meant business and would deal with this serious issue of non-payment of the electricity bills. This general criticism that I underestimated or looked down upon the talents and the ability of those Tanzanians working for public enterprises was a condemnation I had to bear until we could shape a plan to reform the public service and create a working environment where talent and commitment to work would be recognised.

The second issue was a cultural one, Tanzanians had not forgotten our commitment to fighting the apartheid regime of South Africa and although South Africa was now free, there were still *Kaburus* (Boers) in that country. I understood this sensitivity but knew that it was more important to get the government finances in order and these South Africans seemed the right ones for this task. NETGroup Solutions proved to be successful in raising revenues and recovering debt from government departments, public enterprises and parastatals, even from State House!

As the country opened up to foreign investment there was fear that the economy would be dominated by South Africans. This fear was real, Mwalimu spoke at the University of Dar es Salaam to dispel the notion that we couldn't allow these people into Tanzania because they were *Kaburus*. "The days of the Kaburus are over, it is a free country now", Mwalimu told students and academics. He added that there were no longer *Kaburus* governing South Africa, it was now a government of the people. He also addressed parliamentarians in South Africa emphasising that they must consider themselves as Africans. Despite there being individual countries, we were recognised abroad more as coming from the continent of Africa rather than from a specific country. Still, it did take a while to adjust to this new coexistence, to welcoming the South African investors and traders.

There was also some sensitivity regarding whether we should privatise the projects which had been funded by the Chinese, I know Mwalimu was concerned as the Chinese had given freely to Tanzania. I didn't discuss privatisation with the Chinese, rather I told them that I recognised the era of aid was all but over and invited the Chinese government to look at possibilities of investment between their private sector and the Tanzanian private sector. There had been a strong relationship of dependence by African countries on the Chinese and it was time for Tanzania to move towards a productive business relationship on an equal footing.

Turning to my work on reforming the public service, I think there was a tendency those days to move people around ministries and parastatals rather than punish them for being incompetent or negligent in their work; we did not demand accountability from our government employees. I was battling a lack of skills, experience and accountability, as well as culturally influenced attitudinal issues within the public service. Those public servants who cared about their work were disheartened, many public servants did not value their job as they had not been trained to appreciate that their role was important. Some even moonlighted in other jobs; there was little respect for government employees generally. One cultural aspect was that there could be reluctance to openly discuss a problem because people did not want to humiliate someone. Secondly, some were too proud to ask for help to learn something as they thought once they had completed their education and secured a job their learning was finished. Thirdly, it was not appropriate to interrogate or challenge an older person. What's more the civil service was bloated; we had to reduce employee numbers so as to improve the conditions of service for those who would remain. It was not easy to explain these factors and retain my credibility and the trust of the public servants; yet a leader must be prepared to weather unpopularity.

Looking at the character of the civil service, I believe that it must have its own professional identity, you should not politicise it. I hope that with the evolution of democracy we will see a move away from efforts to politicise it, or to build it in the image of the ruling party, and instead to make it an integral organisation of itself. Unfortunately over the past decade or so I have become concerned that some senior appointments have been politically influenced. This creates the danger that when a new president comes there is a total overhaul of senior staff, even though the civil service is supposed to be characterised by continuity. This continuity means that well-established standards and procedures continue to be adhered to, regardless of who is president, and perhaps more importantly, knowledge from experience is not lost. When I was president I couldn't just wake up one morning and declare that I will appoint a particular person as a judge, established and time-tested procedures for appointment must be protected and respected, and not tampered with. Relations between the civil service and the political leadership are always delicate because there is a tendency for political leaders to behave as if they are the civil service, yet the civil service has limitations on power, as well as regulations and procedures to follow, which must be respected. Unfortunately nowadays you can see a government minister declaring to their permanent secretary: *'I am the boss here, go and do this'*, which is not appropriate.

Another aspect of the independence of the civil service is that they must be prepared to offer their technical expertise to the political leaders and make recommendations, even when these may not be what the minister wants to hear. I recall being taught this when I was a junior foreign service officer by the then Permanent Secretary, Bernard Mulokozi[127], who was very good. He said that our job was to advise and seek a decision. Even if we believed that the final decision made by the minister was not correct, we were still obligated to implement it. The civil service does what the minister says, but they play a vital role in guiding the minister. You cannot have obsequious civil servants who blindly follow what a minister says, the civil service should be a cadre of professionals. What's more the public service has the experience and benefit of knowledge gained from continuity. On the other side, some civil servants are too confident, arrogant even, regarding themselves as the expert compared to their minister, despite the minister's education and background. My message to the ministers and civil servants was clear: elected and appointed officials must always respect each other and recognise that they depend on each other, and that no one of them is indispensable.

My first step in reforming the public service was to involve the development partners as the proposed reform would be a substantial undertaking. The visit of the four development ministers from, Norway – Hilde Frafjord Johnson; Germany – Heidemarie Wieczorek-Zeul; the United Kingdom – Clare Short, and the Netherlands – Eveline Herfkens, was another key funding moment during my first term. They had been disillusioned by the state of the economy at the end of my predecessor's time and had taken the initiative to visit me to give me a piece of their collective mind. Our conversation was polite, though I could sense their strong scepticism. I laid out my plans, which they closely probed, but eventually agreed to resume our development assistance relationship. This was a welcome encouragement for me to continue with my plans. We agreed

---

127 Permanent Secretary: Ministry: External Affairs; Defence; Natural Resources and Tourism; Lands, Housing and Urban Development; Public Service, and Chairman Civil Service Commission.

to address areas such as reducing the number of public service employees, improving salaries and introducing a sound human resource system for training and career advancement.

One of the first steps we took was to offer early retirement with a reasonable payout for those who chose to leave, especially the older employees. I am grateful that this assistance from the development partners meant that we could offer a reasonable sum. There was no money in the government coffers to do this otherwise, and I was conscious that we were removing the source of livelihood for some employees. We emphasised that efficiency would now be the hallmark of public service, which likely encouraged some to opt for early retirement.

This retrenchment cleared the deck for a more competitive filling of positions. Decent salaries were being paid on time to government employees and I was bringing inflation down. These improvements eased somewhat the pain of my changes to the public service. By the time I left we had a better functioning civil service, no question about that. The chief secretary, thus head of the public service, was Matern Lumbanga,[128] a no-nonsense person who adhered strictly to the rules, he brought discipline to the public service. I regret that some of my public service reform initiatives were subsequently changed during my successor's time, especially those relating to the size of parliament and civil service, both of which grew to become too large again. It is better to have a small government because this improves efficiency in delivery and reduces operating costs.

Providing properly maintained and sufficient housing for senior government employees was an issue dating right back to Mwalimu's time; he had called in a Ghanaian senior civil servant during the 1960s to review the housing situation for public servants, as well as other aspects of public service remuneration. This consultant noted then the substantial disparity between the right to housing and actual availability of housing. A later investigation by the Presidential Salaries Review Commission[129] also found that the housing situation was untenable. Only 3%

---

128   Chief Secretary February 1995–January 2006.

129   1988, also known as the Nsekela Commission.

of the civil servants and government employees who were entitled or eligible to government housing were actually housed; there were around 6,000 properties, most of which had been built pre-independence and had subsequently not been well maintained, many were in a deplorable state. There was also a problem with some occupants not respecting government property, some were not kept clean, I have even been told of people keeping their cows and chickens inside their government house! So we identified certain government officers whose dignity and authority required that they were in a secure location and/or their house could be used as accommodation by the president when touring the regions. This set our baseline for entitlement to government housing, other civil servants would have to provide their own accommodation.

Mwalimu had established a National Housing Corporation (not the current one) which built houses that were sold to public servants, so I was not the first Tanzanian leader to decide to sell public housing to public servants. There was also the precedent of Mozambique, Lesotho and Zambia selling government housing. I recognised that we had a gap in the housing market, so the Tanzania Buildings Agency was established in 2002 to build, rent and sell accommodation to civil servants. The agency's accommodation could be sold on credit to the public servants, though they could not transfer ownership to anyone else for at least 25 years.

My decision to dispose of these excess properties was controversial and had an impact across the country, it even affected senior people who worked for me and no longer would be provided with housing, I showed no favouritism. I wanted to give existing residents the opportunity to buy the property they were living in, as I feared developers would have an advantage over the lower income earning public servants who would not have been able to buy their properties at a commercial rate. Thus we devised a formula for costing each house which enabled public servants who lived in those homes to purchase them on credit. The ownership of a home is a cultural issue, a matter of pride, it was important that we gave this opportunity to public servants. I received a letter, I think it was from a regional education officer from Morogoro, who was about to retire: "Sir thank you very much, at least now I have something to show for my service – a house of my own". The outcry over the disposal of these properties was understandable, but I believed strongly then and now that I had made the right decision. It would cost an exorbitant amount of money to restore all the properties and then maintain them, too much money for a poor country like ours.

Another issue which caused public debate within and outside of Tanzania was the decision to buy a replacement presidential plane. Our government plane was a Fokker jet, but it was somewhat slow and expensive to maintain. The jet was twenty-four years old, with the manufacture of this plane having ceased in 1987. What's more, because of its large size there was a tendency to travel with large delegations, which was against my drive for austerity. I decided that if we had a smaller, faster and long-range plane it would enable the president to travel quickly to the countries in the Southern African Development Community (SADC), which is worthwhile for neighbourly diplomacy and important in times of a potential crisis. You can move more easily, stopping here or there to talk with key figures. Furthermore, a smaller aircraft would reduce the size of your delegation, thus saving costs, you could easily travel with only twelve passengers. This would also minimise the complaints of those who were not included in a delegation, for the lure of allowances and free travel could be too attractive to some.

There was quite a discussion amongst my cabinet, parliament and donors, with many against the purchase, especially as we had recently received debt relief. The World Bank, IMF and some other development partners demanded an explanation as to why the president needed a new plane, despite knowing the unsatisfactory condition of the Fokker jet. My Minister of Finance, Basil Mramba, was strongly for the purchase; I am told that he said, "Even if we have to eat grass we will buy this aircraft." He retaliated to media criticism saying, "The fact that we have been forgiven our debts does not mean that our president has to use the donkey as a means of travel".

I don't believe we would have seen such criticism of this proposed purchase in a developed country. There was some resentment by donors that we were spending government money to buy this; although our economy was not too bad during my second term, certainly the finances were in a much better shape than when I started. Much of the criticism within Tanzania stemmed from our socialist heritage and our cultural desire for modesty. Despite the criticism I pushed ahead, confident that as I was soon to complete my second term at least the media could not say I was purchasing a jet to satisfy my ego. I also knew that the incoming president might feel embarrassed at ordering one, so I said to him, "I am leaving office, so they can throw the mud at me, but it will be you who will be able to use it."

Despite my many unpopular reforms, including those I have mentioned above, we had reached the point where nearly everyone acknowledged it was inevitable that we should reform in order to work towards our goal of an efficient and growing economy. The fact that I received a 10% increase in the vote for my second five-year term was an endorsement of what I was doing, a way of saying *'go ahead, continue'*.

CHAPTER 12

Struggling with The Dependency Syndrome

All leaders face the challenge of being consumed by the everyday demands of leadership and thus fail to look well beyond their expected term as a leader. It was important to me that I gave to my nation a framework which included my and others' vision for Tanzania's future. The key attributes I desired for Tanzania provided the framework: a high-quality livelihood; peace, stability and unity; good governance; a well-educated and learning society, and a competitive economy capable of producing sustainable growth and shared benefits. During my second term we produced three major documents which set out strategy, policies and goals towards realising these attributes: Vision 2025[130], MKUKUTA[131] (National Strategy for Growth and Reduction of Poverty) and MKURABITA (Property and Business Formalisation Programme)[132].

We began work on Vision 2025 the year I took office, 1995. It was the

---

130   Approved and launched 1999.
131   *Mkakati wa Kukuza Uchumi na Kuondoa Umaskini* Tanzania, approved by Cabinet February 2005
132   *Mpango wa Kurasimisha Rasilimali na Biashara za Wanyonge* Tanzania, launched October 2004.

first twenty-year national strategy document for this country, the Arusha Declaration of 1967 had had no timeframe. The creation of Vision 2025 was a more inclusive process than the Arusha Declaration and I believe it better addressed the complexities of policies and incentive structures. I hoped the process of creating this document would help to show I was aware of the concerns of those diehards who felt I was abandoning the socialist values which were inculcated in our development philosophy. As a leader of change it was important that I made it clear that my drive for reviving the economy would not be at the cost of the social welfare needs of our people, for I was heavily criticised in the media that I was forgetting the poor. People from across all levels of our society contributed to this important masterplan; discussions began at the district level, then progressed to involve the cooperatives, trade unions, members of parliament, religious leaders, non-governmental organisations, civil society organisations and major political parties. Vision 2025 was passed by a multi-party parliament in 1999. The subsequent United Nations Millennium Development Goals, which were adopted in 2000, tied in well with our vision document.

I introduced the Tanzania Mini Tiger Plan 2020 to parliament in 2004, with the period set for 2005–2020. This economic plan focusses on industrialisation and seeks to increase exports, using concepts used by developing Asian countries. However, I now think that it was too much to introduce it at that time. The government machinery was not geared to start on a new project such as this. It takes a certain degree of discipline, confidence and hope and the general reaction of the civil service was that starting this new thing was too much, they preferred to concentrate on the pillars of the economy. Furthermore, they were getting tired, for I had brought in so many reforms.

I knew that the consequences that would come from the kind of reforms that we were undertaking would be positive for our citizens and not just from an economic perspective. For example, increasing the representation of women in government; after all they represent around 51% of our population and this should be reflected in a democracy. The special seats for women in parliament were 15% in 1995, we raised this to a minimum of 30% by 2005. To make sure we kept women's issues in the forefront of our minds I expected every cabinet paper to include at least one paragraph that explained any potential impact on the advancement of women, as well as any obstacles to be overcome.

To my regret MKURABITA was received with great cynicism. The inclusion of new plans such as this as part of the development path was very tentative indeed, simply because it was all new thought. There was always a bottleneck, a barrier that had to be broken down to allow new ideas and projects to come in. With MKURABITA I think part of the problem was that it was not clearly defined. We had articulated this as a philosophy but had not translated this well into practical terms.

I had learnt about the positive benefit to the poor from property and business formalisation during my time as co-chair of the ILO World Commission on the Social Dimension of Globalisation[133] with Tarja Halonen[134]. One of the members of this commission was Hernando de Soto[135], who is well known for his work in formalising business and property ownership in developing countries with the aim of including the poor into the mainstream of the market economy. Providing the poor with legal access to business registration and property rights means they can obtain legal proof of their ownership of an asset. This gives them a sense of ownership and responsibility for development, as well as reducing marginalisation and offering some protection against unlawful seizure. Putting it simply, this is a way of acknowledging and enabling the contribution by the poor to the economy, which is a positive factor for self-reliance. After sharing Hernando de Soto's book, '*The Mystery of Capital: Why Capitalism Triumphs in the West and Fails Everywhere Else.*'[136] with my cabinet members, I brought de Soto to Tanzania to speak with my cabinet and the legislature in 2003 and again in 2005. The parliamentarians were particularly cynical, the concept was so totally novel for them, and they thought it strange that I was advancing this concept of private ownership when by law our land is public land, you only have

---

133   ILO World Commission on the Social Dimension of Globalisation, established 2002, final report 2004.

134   President of Finland March 2000–March 2012; Minister of Foreign Affairs April 1995–February 2000; Minister of Justice February 1990–April 1991.

135   Economist, president of the think tank Institute for Liberty and Democracy, Peru.

136   London: Bantam Press 2000

the rights to use it. Then there was the fear that with the formalisation of businesses the poor would have to pay taxes; my response to that was that they would only start paying at a certain threshold. This had worked in Peru and Egypt, why not here? A leader must be open to innovation and new concepts; especially nowadays with the impact of globalisation.

Mwalimu preached self-reliance, self-development and the mobilisation of local resources at the village, ward and district level. Self-reliance was the pillar of dignity for him, an ethos I firmly believe in as well; though I acknowledge a criticism of Mwalimu that the Nordic governments admired him so much that we came close to becoming too dependent on their help. When I read the newspapers nowadays it seems there is a preoccupation with which government ministry, development partner or corporate body is giving how much to a school, etc. Where is our development paradigm? Why is our nation's development centred on what government, development partners or businesses can do for us? I think that the development model has become skewed to one of automatically expecting help from others, rather than seeking first to help oneself, whether on an individual or national basis. Government should be a facilitator to development instead of being the one which brings development. Furthermore, grants from donors should be a tool for development, not the cause for development. With hindsight, I wish I had done more political and civic education in this area during my term so as to buttress the policies of self-reliance and self-identity for the nation.

Yet as a major driver of development, self-reliance and self-development have not sufficiently taken root in our development endeavours and philosophy; I feel this strongly. I do not regard this as a failing on Mwalimu's part, he tried some form of devolution of power and responsibility, though he also retained the authority to ensure that development would be egalitarian. The degree of the devolution and its outcomes remains an ongoing discussion.

Development dignity requires self-worth, that you take on responsibility for your own development as much as possible. Yet during my second term in office, it seemed people were becoming more demanding and less willing to help themselves. I became tired of this attitude, and sadly this seems to have become entrenched and widely accepted nowadays. Unfortunately, this attitude is fed during political campaigning when politicians say I will do this or give this to you if you elect me. No one says do this yourselves and we will help you to do it. I am concerned to see a trend of abdication of self-responsibility for development towards placing the responsibility on government, development partners or corporates to help you. You should ask yourself, why don't I have an iron roof on my house, instead of this thatch which lets the rain seep in? What can I do to get a better roof? Instead, the person asks when is the government/development partner/ business coming to give me money for a new roof? This marked reduction in, if not abandonment, of self-responsibility distresses me.

There is a potential danger too, why shouldn't a substantial donor think that as it provides much help then it should have the right to some influence on the management of your affairs? The media portray a bonanza – the British are giving us this, the Chinese are giving us this, but there is no such thing as a free lunch.

Another peeve is when people say in parliament that the government should increase the budgetary allocation to this institution or sector, without suggesting how this money could be generated, or which institution could bear money being taken away so it could be diverted to this new allocation. It seems like government is viewed as the munificent benefactor, which is immature of parliamentarians who should know better; indeed I regard this a weakness of my fellow citizens and their leaders. It seems that this unfortunate trend grew during the time of my successor; though to be fair during my time the opposition parties were not as strong, so criticism tended to stem more from within my own party. On the other side, government has an obligation to explain to parliament, and of course the citizens, why a promise made cannot be implemented.

Alongside this is the increasing tendency since I left office to raise expectations of achievement. For example, the phenomenon of the annual budget – its content, manner of presentation, manner of examination and review are not transparent and sufficiently concrete in facts. I see the tendency to giving oral propositions rather than practical reviews. We must temper the expectations of our people, especially since our country does not have a very large private sector and the economy does not grow fast enough. A government should be open and honest about financial matters, I tried to be so.

The concept of development for us is in the same term as used in developed countries, as if we are starting from the same base as those developed countries. When they talk of growth for the developed countries this comes from a well-established foundation, in the sense that they have an assured national health service, education service, water supplies, etc. Whereas for us the real development is to come to the point where we can say we provide education for all, that safe water is available in all our villages, that access to health services is assured for all. We haven't attained this, despite some people saying to me that Tanzania now has real development and growth, you can see this from the number of high-rise buildings in Dar es Salaam. This is not real development, because rural life hasn't changed that much. There seems to be an even greater disparity between urban and rural life now. I acknowledge that you do see more iron-roof houses in villages nowadays, which implies permanency and some development. But the access to education, healthcare and water continues to be a problem despite the number of years of development efforts that have passed.

Reflecting on development in African states, one of the trends that fill me with some discomfiture is the speed with which we are quick to start committees, commissions or regional enterprises that have not been thought through properly. Often they lack from careful preparation, and there is also little follow up of what they commit to undertake, with substantial outcomes rare to find. We tend to get a problem, we get together to discuss it, set up a committee and then think that the problem has been solved; a sort of development and governance by form, not by action. There is a whole cluster of organisations which hold costly meetings with delegates well-compensated to attend, free travel and accommodation, plus allowances. This is not only wasteful, but it can make people disillusioned and unhappy at the poor governance. This practice is one of the things that is holding up development. Why can't we have fewer meetings with smaller groups of delegates who demonstrate a real commitment to following up on decisions and their implementation?

Anyway, back to my time in office, when although we were gradually seeing success with reforms, the flow-on effects were not percolating far down enough to the people, especially those in the rural areas, who are the majority of the population. This led to the introduction of the catalytic Tanzania Social Action Fund (TASAF). I had learnt about this concept during a visit to Malawi, when Bakili Muluzi[137] showed me how his government was helping villagers to self-develop. The principle was that the villagers themselves decided their priorities for a development project, they contributed to it with manpower and some funds while the Malawian government supplemented their effort. The project was owned by the villagers themselves, who managed it and kept the accounts. This seemed a wonderful idea that could also work in Tanzania where we had long-established governance from the village level dating from Mwalimu's time; consequently I arranged for my assistant Mrs Eileen Swai to spend time in Malawi to investigate their Malawi Social Action Fund, which had commenced in 1996. After reading her report I was convinced that this framework would work in Tanzania and sought to introduce it.

I encountered a lot of scepticism within my cabinet, the party and the public service. We were used to the culture of receiving rather than giving; however, I was determined to get a social action fund introduced. I tried to sell this concept to the World Bank, who were very sceptical, they did not think that this was a paradigm for development at all. I responded that I knew what Tanzanians can achieve together. The vice president of the World Bank for Africa at that time was Professor Callisto Madavo, a Zimbabwean, so I broached this with him and thankfully he was able to persuade his colleagues to give it a try. That is how we obtained the first credit of USD 61.69 million for the pilot TASAF project.

When the project began, Mrs Swai would go to the village and gather the women as they were the ones who did much of the work such as fetching water and firewood; they still do. She would tell them that they carried the burden of development and the Tanzania Social Action Fund offered an opportunity to them. After this initial meeting she would encourage the women to get the men from the village to attend the next meeting, when they would determine what particular problem they wanted to solve, for example: a road to link the village to a highway,

---

137   President of Malawi 1994–2004.

or a water bore hole with piped water because they were walking long distances to fetch water, or an additional classroom because the number of school children had increased. The villagers would decide how they would contribute, whether by offering their labour, money or a combination of both. At that point a staff member from TASAF would come to help them write up the project for submission to the government.

In the beginning I put TASAF directly under my office, to counter scepticism and help push the fund along. I chose a politically savvy man to lead the fund, Emmanuel Kamba, who did a great job. I was pleased to see that the fund was managed carefully, resulting in good audit reports. I regard TASAF a high point of my ten years as president. It brings together a new approach to development, the strategy to achieve it and self-reliance. When you have such a very poor country with a large population, it is difficult to infuse a lot of financial capital, you must depend on the resources that are there – the human resource. This framework upheld the concept of self-reliance, self-management and self-development; underlining that the philosophy of self-reliance was indeed inherent in us, as instilled by Mwalimu, now we were translating it into action and visible results. What's more you can define successful leadership by outcomes, especially in the livelihood of the people, and TASAF was one way I could improve livelihoods with the government's limited funds.

Furthermore, development must belong to the people, they must participate and take responsibility. It was the villagers who identified their needs, prioritised them, determined how much they could contribute financially and/or physically and then the government came in and helped with the rest. Usually the villagers contributed about 25% of the cost of the development project, sometimes only 15%. Not only did the villagers end up with an improvement to their living environment, it also taught them skills of organising and financial management as they had to provide regular reports of progress. Furthermore, as the villagers actively participated right from the outset in bringing their development project to fruition, this fostered their sense of ownership. One time there was a village in Tanga with a TASAF project where the village chairman was gifted a bicycle by a relative from elsewhere and in those days owning a bicycle was something notable in the poverty-stricken areas.

When he returned to his village with this bicycle the inhabitants accused him of using the money from their TASAF project to get himself a bicycle. He was forced to prove that those funds were untouched. A TASAF project also brought a little cash to the villagers if there was a public works project; as those who physically participated would get 20% of the fund's grant for the project in recognition of the physical work they did on the project. Cash was usually in short supply in these poor areas, it was always welcome.

At the completion of phase one of TASAF we had development projects in forty districts on the Mainland and in Zanzibar; it worked so well that members of parliament would ask, when are you going to bring TASAF to my constituency? I am pleased to say that TASAF is now in phase three and has grown to extend beyond considering the poorest villages as candidates to looking at how to help the poorest individuals in that area. Unfortunately, TASAF projects rarely make the news because there is no development partner or company seeking publicity of their generosity; yet TASAF continues to make tangible difference to the lives of poor people. Furthermore, TASAF strengthens the operation of democracy – we choose our own way, our strategies and speed for development, day by day. This is democracy which brings about social development. I regard TASAF as one of the greatest achievements I initiated.

During my term the peasantry looked up to government as if it had a paternal role; which I struggled with. First, because I simply didn't have the money required to implement the myriad of desired improvements. Secondly, I wanted to destroy this attitude of dependence. In my ethnic group, the Makua of Bantu extraction, your manhood was judged upon by your capacity to maintain your family. It would have to be a dire situation before you would ask for help; otherwise it was considered almost shameful to ask for help; my parents certainly didn't expect help from others. Though if you were expanding your cultivated area then you would ask people to help you clear the site, but you always rewarded your helpers with a meal and some traditional beer.

Perhaps this attitude of dependence on the government began during the independence struggle when we declared to our fellow citizens: get us into government and we will build hospitals, schools and roads; perhaps this message was driven too far into the psyche of our people beginning from then. This attitude had not begun under the colonialists; for although their government had complete power over us, they did not encourage dependency. Indeed, it was the contrary, for any ruler wants to share failure, and our colonial government shared failure with us through the Native Authority. This government agency was a way of managing us. It was chiefly concerned with gathering cash crops to supply the colonials, as well as imposing a tax on our produce. The Native Authority offered a useful fall-back position for the colonial government, for if something went wrong, it provided the government with a way to assign failure. Granted that if you had a strong Native Authority then the colonial government would devolve power to it, which would have a minor and incidental developmental aspect. However, I believe the missionaries fostered dependency with their schools and hospitals, especially in the early days. It was only when they started having indigenous clergy that we woke up to the fact that we couldn't depend on everything coming from Europe; before then everyone and everything did. Mwalimu placed a lot of emphasis on local government and the policy of decentralisation, not only to devolve power, but to increase responsibility. You could see then that in those areas which produced good cash crops the local government delivered development results; while, in the poor areas the local government was forced to concentrate on ensuring food security. But against all this, because of Mwalimu's successful articulation of socialism with an African face, he attracted assistance in the implementation of this philosophy. We had no pride, we had a dependency syndrome, depending on the state, with the state in turn depending on foreign aid in those early days.

It disappoints me a great deal that this dependency attitude seems even stronger now. It is ridiculous to hear members of parliament asking for funding for improvements in their constituency during parliamentary debates and question time. Most of these projects could be implemented through TASAF, yet members of parliament ask central government to take responsibility. I believe this psyche of dependency has held back Tanzania's development. How else can you explain that, close to sixty years after independence, you still have schools that don't even have pit latrines? For example, a member of parliament does not say we will build this latrine together, rather they say I will talk to the Japanese ambassador so a Japanese aid programme will build a pit latrine for us. I know this is oversimplification, but this dependency attitude pains me a great deal.

On the other side, I fondly recall an encounter whilst on a tour of the Coast Region. When touring I would often ask my driver to stop so I could have a close look at the environment and chat with the people. I saw a sign painted on the side of a peasant farmer's humble home by the roadside: '*Mtaji wa masikini ni nguvu zake mwenyewe*' – 'A peasant's capital is their labour'. This saying had originated from Mwalimu and how true it is, even today. I cited this as an example of using what you have for self-development during a later address. Self-reliance and self-development, I cannot repeat this enough.

Another way to help the poor in a direct way was the National Health Insurance Fund[138] which offered health insurance to families. I learnt about this scheme from Rostam Aziz[139], member of parliament and successful businessman. In 1996 he started a health insurance scheme for the residents of his Igunga constituency. For a small sum, around TZS 10,000, a family with four children could be insured for a whole year. We introduced this countrywide. The scheme wasn't understood well to start with because people said, "I will never get sick. Why should I give money away to this fund?"; eventually this scheme caught on.

Around this time the government became sensitive to the scourge of HIV and AIDS. First diagnosed in Tanzania in 1983, by 1986 cases were reported across the Mainland. My predecessor had established the National Aids Control Programme[140], but we needed a body to advise on policy, as well as advocate, monitor, and share information. Hence I established the Tanzania Commission for AIDS[141], known commonly as TACAIDS. My concern about the severe impact of this unrelenting disease led to my establishing The Benjamin William Mkapa Foundation after I left office, which I will mention later.

---

138   The National Health Insurance Fund commenced operations during 2001.
139   MP for Igunga constituency 1994–2011.
140   The National Aids Control Programme was established 1988.
141   The Tanzania Commission for AIDS (TACAIDS) was established in 2001.

We started the process of qualitative change in education – particularly in text books, infrastructure and enrolment. This was so worthwhile; I look back on our progress in providing education during my term with great pride. Especially in primary education, where the net national enrolment rate increased from 55.4% in 1995 to 94.8% in 2005, with an increase in primary school students from 4.8 million in 2001 to 7.5 million in 2005. Some classrooms were as old as me, dating from the colonial times, yet our population had increased and there was greater enrolment; we needed new classrooms. Due to the positive response to TASAF we got the idea to build classrooms using the same methodology of the villagers taking ownership, though this time we allocated funds from central government rather than from TASAF funds. It was pleasing to see new signs outside new schools or new classrooms stating that the school/classroom belonged to the village, a clear indication of the local community taking up the concept of self-development. We increased the number of classrooms in both primary and secondary schools by more than a third, these new classrooms were dubbed by many as 'Mkapa's classrooms'. We also reduced the number of children sharing a textbook from twenty pupils per textbook recorded in 2001 to three children per textbook in 2005. My Minister of Education, Joseph Mungai[142], was great. I regard him as one of the most dynamic persons on my cabinet during my second term. The Primary Education Development Programme (PEDP) which we introduced in 2001 is probably the development programme I am most known for; I was pleased to see this programme continue into phase two which ran up to 2009. Towards the end of my time as president we embarked on the Secondary School Development Programme (SEDP) and I am also thankful this was sustained by my successor.

Memories of an outing we organised for the diplomatic corps to show them what we had achieved gives me satisfaction to this day. This took quite some logistical planning, as we had deliberately chosen a remote location, but the regional commissioner there, Nsa-Kaisi, organised this

---

142 Minister Agriculture 1972–1975 and 1981–1982; Minister for Education and Culture 2000–2005; Minister for Agriculture Food Security and Cooperatives 2005–2006; Minister for Home Affairs 2007–2008.

well. We took them by plane to Mtwara, then by helicopter to Newala District, from where the diplomatic corps travelled on buses via different routes that would pass through several villages before we all met up for a small celebration of the PEDP programme at one school. We had used differing bus routes so that the diplomats would not suspect that we were taking them only to schools which had done particularly well. The development partners were surprised and impressed and I was gratified to be able to demonstrate to our guests that we could achieve something generated from our own idea and implement it by ourselves.

One of the things that gave me satisfaction as I left office was that we were reaching the point where there would be at the worst situation one textbook for every three students; we were getting close to one textbook per student at the primary school level. Though there is still much to be done, more than ten years on from my leaving office I am disappointed that this country still does not have sufficient teachers and textbooks.

I wish I had been as successful when it came to the water sector. I tried to privatise the Dar es Salaam water supply system, but the World Bank people stipulated conditions which we couldn't agree with. The company would have made money, but we wouldn't see the probability of receiving a reliable supply of water. Eventually, we had to break the contract with Biwater Gauff (Tanzania) Ltd, just twenty-two months into the ten-year contract. Biwater took us to the World Bank's International Centre for Settlement of Investment Disputes (ICSID) for breach of contract but failed in their claim for damages.

Can certain services such as water and power be privatised? The debate continues until this day. We laid the foundations for the privatisation or the break-up, if you like, of TANESCO into power generation, transmission, distribution and sales, but I didn't get around to it in my time. Certainly water was an area which was frustrating to me. Perhaps this proves the point that certain services should be left to the government to deliver, although I am not persuaded on this. I wanted to have an efficient water delivery system that people would be prepared to pay for; not free, but cheaper than it is nowadays; there are some suburbs in Dar es Salaam where the water points are so few and far between that the people have to buy water and the cost is too high, particularly for the poor. Providing access to safe water is one area where I was disappointed, I could not make a marked improvement.

We did launch a water project from Lake Victoria to Shinyanga and Kahama financed from our own revenue[143]; though built by the Chinese, they did not finance it. The plan to do this was not well-received in the beginning. I recalled that the Germans had considered this during their time of rule in the previous century, so I decided to commission a survey. This showed it could be done, so we began this project in 2004 and it was completed during my successor's time and I understand there are plans to extend this further.

Of course, there were more reforms I would have liked to have implemented and there were improvements I could have achieved if we had still been operating under the one-party system during my time. Then again, I am yet to meet a leader who says they successfully achieved all they desired during their term in office.

---

143   This water project was launched in 2004 and completed in 2009.

CHAPTER 13

Internal and Foreign Relations

Relations with Zanzibar were somewhat sensitive during my time and I am thankful that we were able to settle differences which arose, as I am a great believer in the Union, as we call it. It is important for both the Mainland and Zanzibar, as our economic relationship is strongly interconnected with our lands so close; while another factor is protecting the security of both territories. Furthermore, the cost of maintaining a modern state that is truly independent would be prohibitive for a small place such as Zanzibar; it would set them back economically. Though I do wonder whether I could have been more proactive in strengthening the Union, as some Zanzibaris continue to regard us Mainlanders as oppressing them and matters of sovereignty continue to arise as a sore point now and then. Regrettably relations have been delicate for decades, I think it was Hassan Nassor Moyo and Salim Said Rashid, members of the first cabinet of the revolutionary council, who told me that towards the end of Sheikh Abeid Amani Karume's life relations were strained between Mwalimu and him. Fundamentally the underlying issue in Zanzibar is the almost antipathy between the ruling party and the opposition party; irrespective of whether this animosity is rooted in misbelief or history, it was and continues to be a matter of concern to me.

I was very tense when the president of Zanzibar, Salmin Amour[144] sought to extend his presidency to an unconstitutional third term. This was a difficult time for me because I didn't want to appear to be dictating to the Zanzibaris, yet at that same time I had the principle of the two-term limit to uphold; I was also conscious of history, when Mwalimu had removed the second president of Zanzibar, the late Aboud Jumbe. Although I had received several delegations of elders from Zanzibar pressing for the extension to a third term, I knew deep down that there was enough talent in Zanzibar to find a new candidate for the presidency; there was no extraordinary reason why Amour should extend his term in office. Really, he had no basis for his argument for a third term. As the president of the Union and chairman of the ruling party it fell to me to be tough and I was determined not to have our constitution changed, so I made necessary preparations for what I feared would be my showdown meeting with Amour at the CCM national executive committee meeting during early March, 2000. The final decision was made by the national executive committee, the decision was not mine to determine, though of course I was the chair. I explained the arguments on both sides, I allowed discussion and so on. I knew that if I failed it would have been truly catastrophic for Tanzania. We didn't even get to that point at the meeting, as Amour took the wind completely out of our sails by assuring us that he was not seeking a third term. I think Amour and his supporters realised I was determined to defend the two-term limit for the presidency of Zanzibar using all means at my disposal; I don't think he was prepared to push me to the limit. I was truly relieved, and everyone was surprised when we both emerged from this meeting in good spirits. I am proud that I managed to maintain the unity of my country this way.

Zanzibar had had no national flag since the union in 1964 and I was happy that a national flag for Zanzibar was adopted during my time, though their having a twenty-one-gun salute on Revolution Day elevates the president of Zanzibar to the same status of the president of the Union; which is not an issue as the powers of each leader are spelt out

---

144   President of Zanzibar October 1990–November 2000.

in our constitution. In any case these are all trappings we have inherited from the West. Why do we Africans put so much store in them? What is important is sound governance and positive development for the people. I ensured that the celebrations of the 40th anniversary of the Union of Tanganyika with Zanzibar were held in Zanzibar, which had never happened before and was well-received. I also tried to ensure that Zanzibar was not forgotten when it came to public works, even though highways are not a Union matter. I determined that we should make provision for some road work in Zanzibar to show that the bad roads in Zanzibar were also a concern to the Union government.

However, in late January 2001 a tragedy occurred which shook me to my core: the police shooting dead twenty-two people on Pemba. I was attending the World Economic Forum in Davos, so the Vice President of Tanzania, the late Omar Ali Juma was in charge, who incidentally came from Pemba, was in charge as well as the newly elected President of Zanzibar, Amani Abeid Karume, though of course as president of the republic I accept full responsibility for what happened. I acknowledge that this will always be a black spot on my presidency, even though I wasn't here when this calamity happened. These deaths were tragic, though I did feel strongly during the subsequent reporting that no-one considered the pressures which the police were under when they chose to fire. The opposition party, CUF, is predominant in Pemba and their supporters were riled up because they hadn't won the election, although they had done well in Pemba. The protestors said they were just demonstrating against the results; however, they beheaded a policeman and then set off for a police station, chanting, "We are going to collect weapons". This police station had an armoury, you can imagine the consequences if these angry protestors had managed to take over the armoury? The ensuing violence would have been an even greater catastrophe, with many more deaths. The protestors clashed with the small contingent of police there, who responded with force when reinforcements arrived. This dreadful event shocked me because usually coastal people don't like violence. This was not an isolated event either, though the worst. There is a summary of events as an appendix to a speech I gave concerning this tragedy.[145]

The CUF were understandably furious and, being more adept than my government in communicating with human rights bodies and other governments, they speedily sought outside support. We were weak in this area, I suppose it was the complacency of office, having ruled for so long as a one-party state we didn't feel the need to be propped up by outside support. This terrible event became a global story and I was interviewed by BBC's Tim Sebastian for the HARDtalk television series[146]. I found his interview style provocative, he pushed that the government had deliberately ordered the killing of the protestors. I asked him, "What do you know about my country that you can judge the interaction and the conditions of the police and the government in such a manner? What right do you have to pass a judgement like that?" I was criticised for being forthright, that it was bad taste to rebuke the journalist. In those days we African presidents were not accustomed to being spoken to by anybody in this manner; nowadays this combative interview style is commonplace. The opposition party used the interview to say that this proved I did not feel sorry for these deaths and this interview was another example of my usual arrogance. Indubitably, I regretted these deaths, I do to this day. But I still feel that there is a false presumption by the West that all societies are alike – which we are not. In Britain someone can understand what the rule of law is, but here – what is the rule of law? Here it is often the fear of authority, this is a big difference between our societies.

I returned to Tanzania and worked to smooth relations with the opposition and seek a constructive way forward, but then the West exacerbated the situation. There was a general tendency of the diplomatic corps to simply believe the opposition's allegations, rather than objectively take our statements into account as well. Some diplomats who disbelieved what government said about the tragedy hired a plane and flew

---

145 '*Appendix: A Chronology of Events which were the Cause of Deaths.*' '*Address to the Nation on the Events of 26–28 January 2001 in Zanzibar 2001*'. Speech (pages 30–44) and appendix (pages 45–47) included in Volume 3, Part One, Cluster 1 of '*The Mkapa Years Collected Speeches*'. Dar es Salaam: Mkuki na Nyota.

146 Regrettably the BBC would not make a copy of this programme available for readers of this book to watch the interview.

into Pemba to find the mass grave the opposition claimed existed. It is established practice to inform the ministry of foreign affairs when diplomats travel outside the capital, but they undertook this journey in secret. Naturally there was no mass grave, the bodies of the casualties had been given to their families for burial and there were not the number of deaths as had been claimed by the opposition. I was furious at this presumption by these diplomats that this government would deliberately commit mass murder and then try to hide the many bodies in a mass grave. The diplomats had acted with blatant disdain of the ruling government's authority and conduct. I called in the diplomatic community to State House on the first day of February[147], which I followed with an address to the nation two days later[148]. I did not mince my words; that was the toughest speech I have ever given to diplomats. I was serious as I saw the need to place this shocking event in Zanzibar within the larger context of restoring confidence and trust once more with those within the diplomatic community, with whom we had steadily built a productive and strong relationship since I took office in 1995. I also needed to show that our government upheld the rule of law and accountability within this multi-party atmosphere; as I said in my speech to the diplomats: "We want, and we will build, a democratic but civilised political dispensation". I was told that later when discussing this amongst themselves, one diplomat said to another, "You know I really thought that some of us would be declared persona non-grata and told to go back home".

I set up a multi party-commission[149] under the late Brigadier General (Rtd.) Hashim Mbita to investigate the matter; which helped to settle matters a little. The team produced a good report and the sensible

---

147 'Meeting With Heads of Diplomatic Missions Based in Dar es Salaam on the Situation in Zanzibar, 2001.' Speech (pages 23–29) included in Volume 3, Part One, Cluster 1 of 'The Mkapa Years Collected Speeches'. Dar es Salaam: Mkuki na Nyota.

148 'Address to the Nation on the Events of 26–28 January 2001 in Zanzibar 2001'. Speech (pages 30–44) included in Volume 3, Part One, Cluster 1 of 'The Mkapa Years Collected Speeches'. Dar es Salaam: Mkuki na Nyota.

149 Commission team members included Masauni Yusuf Masauni, Ali Abdullah Suleiman, Salama Kombo Ahmed, Hassa Mlawa, Bruno Mpangala and Kassim Ali and Phillip Mkamanga. The report can be found at: https://www.hrw.org/reports/2002/tanzania/index.htm#TopOfPage

composition of the team commanded the confidence of the government, opposition and diplomatic community. The commission recommended compensation for the families of those who died, which the government provided. This whole incident was a great shock to me: the violence, deaths and subsequent furore. It attracted a lot of criticism here and abroad, some of which I accept, absolutely; though I honestly don't know how I could have handled it differently. My actions were curtailed to some extent because the Zanzibaris have their own president, who is also the vice-chairman of CCM, the ruling party. If I had had a direct interaction with political developments on Zanzibar, then perhaps I could have done more.

This deeply traumatic episode was so unnecessary. I simply cannot see how one can feel so indispensable that you are prepared that people should die in a quarrel so you can maintain your authority. On the other side of the coin, how can people feel so strongly that they feel they must resort to such violence in order to remove someone in office? Especially if the constitution is democratic and there are ways in which you can get leaders out of office or make your representations. Why resort to ways that will lead to a loss of life? Violence should be absolutely the last resort, and I don't think this was such an occasion where it was justifiable.

This painful experience taught me to reach out more to the opposition, converse and listen to them. If there is a bit of a battle, then let it be a battle of ideas, not of physical might. We are a free country, everyone has equal rights. I also learnt that you can be so removed from some people that they can get angry, thinking you are dismissing them, you don't want to listen to them as they don't count. Hence I subsequently met with the opposition more often and was more disposed towards them. For instance, in the lead-up to the next general election, which saw me leaving office, I made time during the campaign to meet with leaders of the opposition in Zanzibar and talk about the campaign conditions there, though some of the comments they made were somewhat negated by the president of Zanzibar and my intelligence services; probably because Zanzibar is made up of islands and in such a small environments rumours can easily grow and seem to be facts.

Perhaps this is the way democracy is evolving on our continent, even where you have peaceful elections people who voted for the opposition say their votes were stolen; it's as if unless they win it is not fair, yet it is not fair when you suggest things that could cause chaos in a country. If asked what would help democracy in any African environment I would like to see: the right to form a political party; the freedom to operate, canvass, or mobilise membership; the opportunity to meet safely and promote a party's manifesto during a campaign. There should also be the same time available on television and national radio for the opposition as for the ruling party. There should not be many restrictions on political meetings, but the government must ensure that the public can meet safely. This is essential for the evolution of democracy on our continent; far too often in Africa we see ruling parties trying to win by restricting the canvassing capacity of the opposition; while on the other hand opposition parties strive to impose their will as a right.

An objective and fair electoral commission, which is acceptable to all parties is an essential pillar in the evolving democratic culture on the African continent. The composition of the electoral commission is often disputed in African countries, yet someone must appoint them. Then you must have an open process of counting votes and you must allow for the political parties to have representatives there to observe the counting. These measures can silence opposition and build confidence in the democratic process. From my experience in Tanzania, I think the opposition had confidence in the electoral commission generally; it was led by judges of good character, though the opposition did question about how much freedom they had to hold rallies. The other complaint was that the ruling party had the advantage of the use of the government's communication structures and processes – national radio and national television, and the national information services through the ministry of information and culture; these being used as tools or weapons of the ruling party. How you achieve a healthy balance is one of the questions in the evolution of democracy in our continent, certainly in our country. I think there is little reason to complain about the voting process; during my time, no-one was prevented from voting. There were some complaints about the counting stage, until we provided that every political party is entitled to have an election agent at the counting points.

Inclusivity should be a major concern of the leadership of all political parties if you want to really hold on to the trust and confidence of your followers. I regard inclusiveness as a vital element of democracy because we are so multi-ethnic in sub-Saharan Africa and it's easy to build grievances based on ethnicity. Maintaining national unity is the biggest challenge in all nations of sub-Saharan Africa. I find any form of racism abhorrent, and we should all be grateful to Mwalimu for his strong stand against racism and tribalism; I believe this honourable legacy from him is one of my nation's greatest strengths. My own family is an example of the absence of tribalism, I am a Makua from the South, my wife Anna is a Chagga from the North, what are our two sons? Tanzanians! Incidentally, I come from a matriarchal tribe, and once when my mother visited us and saw our sons being naughty, as children will be, she said to me, "You know you have given them the surname of Mkapa, which is wrong, you can see from their conduct that these are Chaggas"*!*

It is equally as important to have as inclusive a government as possible, otherwise there is likely to be quarrelling amongst the majority party's leaders about the composition of government; which can divert attention away from nation-building or project implementation. Having a government where some leaders are prepared to fight amongst themselves as if it is a matter of life or death is not healthy for society. When there were state visits or visiting delegations, I would ensure that opposition leaders were invited to state dinners and left it to the delegations to arrange to meet with opposition members. Opposition members will probably say that I breathed too hard down their necks, perhaps they are right. Maybe I was too harsh with these nascent political parties or maybe I ignored them too much; it might have helped the democratic process if opposition leaders were seen with me from time to time, their criticism of me for not including them is probably justifiable.

Overall, I think that diplomats during my time showed preference for the opposition, though to be fair this may have originated from their interest in the evolution of democracy in our country, especially since the first multi-party election was held in 1995. The diplomatic community tended to be more sympathetic to the opposition parties and interact with them more often; maybe the diplomatic community thought their support of the opposition would keep the ruling party on its toes. I was often preoccupied with what kind of context, and to serve what end, communications were between the diplomatic community and the opposition parties. I didn't mind the funding and support the opposition received, although when it reaches a high level then you must ask what this is about, because there could be a danger that certain countries might be working with the opposition against the government, which disturbed me.

I don't think there were attempts at direct intervention, though we did have a dispute with the residential representative of the European Union (EU) leading up to the general election in 2000 because he wanted to dictate the firm which would print the ballot papers. We refused, saying we would look at the EU's tender and shortlist, but the ultimate choice would be ours. At first they thought we were not serious, but we were, because otherwise the European Union would have been directly interfering in our process. In 2015 it was twenty years since the first multiparty election in Tanzania, yet this political system is still in a state of evolution.

Certainly there were representatives from certain nations who believed they deserved preferential treatment from us, the British obviously; though they were cautious around me because they knew I had been politically educated by Mwalimu who was very sensitive to paternalism. Some members of the diplomatic community tried to be quite overbearing with ministers at times, I remember my Minister of Works, John Magufuli, coming under pressure from the American ambassador, Robert Royall, when he tried to implement a cabinet decision to change vehicle number plates in order to easily identify those vehicles which had been purchased with donor funds. We had taken this measure to restrain the misuse of these vehicles, many of which were used by the government. The Americans didn't like this at all as in their case these vehicles were used by some American aid workers to drive about while on holiday in the country. Royall was furious, he told Magufuli that this was unacceptable. Magufuli replied, "There is no way in which you can change our decision and if necessary, I am prepared to help you load your vehicles and take them back or to wherever you want to take them". Royall was surprised, Magufuli added, "I am serious, this is a sovereign country. What is wrong with recognising that a vehicle is a donor project vehicle?" The change went ahead.

Returning to relationships within this country, I became used to being criticised by the newspapers which thought I was dictatorial, but I was only firm. I had thought and read about the issue in question more than the media usually had, I also had more background information than them. Of course, when I took the media to task their natural reaction was to say this was my arrogance showing. Though I did find that reading the letters to the editor could sometimes be helpful in assessing people's reactions. Frankly I do not like interacting with the local media nowadays, as so often they come ill-prepared; which was certainly not the way journalists conducted themselves during the time I worked in the media. News does not seem news, rather opinion, or utterances; this one has said this and in reply this one has said that. Why are only their words news? Very seldom do you get the story behind the news. News requires analysis; regardless of how important a person may be, news is not simply that person's utterances. What is regarded nowadays as investigative reporting is usually superficial and sensational, with minimal analysis and no follow-up. I recall the days of serious morning conferences between the editors and reporters where we discussed a rival paper's stories, considered how our own stories could have been improved upon, what stories to pursue further, new angles to the same story, or when we should revisit an issue. I don't know if this kind of serious evaluation is still held each day, I suspect not, which disappoints me. How can news today be a driver for change?

A free media is one of the key pillars necessary for good governance; I tried to foster positive and professional relationships between the government and the media during my time, including installing communication officers in ministries, independent departments, agencies and regional secretariats[150]. I learnt this from South Africa, where the leaders were using the ministry responsible for information as a channel for telling the people what was happening in government. Senior civil servants were placed in various ministries whose role was to keep up-to-date with what was happening at that ministry that could affect the people

---

150   You may be interested to read my speech at a workshop geared towards improving government communication: 'Improving Public Communication of Government Policies and Enhancing Media Relations'. 'The Mkapa Years Collected Speeches' Volume 3, Part One, Cluster I, pages 86–98. Dar es Salaam, Mkuki na Nyota.

and then relay this. My idea for instigating information officers was that they should explain to the people but should also give feedback to the central government on people's reactions. The citizenry must know that you are working in their interest, though this should not be used as a promotional tool. I wish I had done more on improving the information framework which I started; I should have insisted that these information officers were more productive.

I was very conscious of the need to sell policies; particularly during my second term, when we were deep in implementation. I knew that it was important to explain the background to my actions, as without that I could be regarded as making arbitrary decisions, which was not true. A good friend from my journalism days, the late Abdallah Ngororo, said, "You know it is not enough that we have a ministry of information and so on, you should try to establish a person to person rapport, why don't you start a monthly address to the nation on any topic of current interest?" I was a bit sceptical to start with, but they proved to be popular, especially in the rural areas. The broadcasts offered a deeper dimension to what I wanted to convey than a mere press release. At that time radio was the best way to reach the maximum number of people, especially those in the rural areas and the illiterate. The monthly broadcasts helped me to show that I was aware of the many problems our people faced, which I hoped would bring me closer to the people I was serving. My broadcasts were not always about a crisis, sometimes it was an international issue, though usually it was an issue of local interest. I also took the opportunity to share the rationale behind decisions I had taken and convey that I was in charge.

I relied upon meetings of my party to get a sense of people's reactions to our country's progress and their pressing concerns. The members came from across the country and we met regularly – the central committee every month and the national executive committee four times a year. I also tried to meet with differing representative groups, such as elders or youth, when I travelled around the country. I valued my regional tours, for I was able to consult extensively; this was particularly useful when trying to gauge the mood of the people. There were also a few occasions when I found that I had made a presumption about a situation or had been misinformed and subsequently overreacted.

My principal anchor for receiving and giving out thoughts and information was CCM, my party, and its structures such as the central committee, national executive committee, and regional committees. However, I became unpopular with some within my party for admonishing some colleagues on aspects of their conduct. First, there was an element of mercenaryism creeping into the party which I didn't like at all; you shouldn't buy votes. Secondly, there were some party members who felt they were untouchable due to being well-established within the party, either because of their long history of membership, or because of their wealth. These members felt self-important and above criticism by others; some were egocentric. When it came to selections within the party of those members who would stand for parliament in the 2005 general election I rejected several rich applicants who I suspected would use their office for self-aggrandisement. As I was beginning to think who was going to succeed me, I thought it was time to set out guidelines on what the party expected from members serving as members of parliament or higher; these guidelines would also serve as an admonition to potential new members of parliament.

I did this publicly in my speech to the CCM National Executive Committee during mid 2004, the general election was scheduled for late 2005. In this speech, *'The Courage of Leadership'*[151], I raised the state of the party, the need to focus on policy and implementation and the kind of leadership required to honour our pledges to the people as set out in the CCM election manifesto. I admonished my fellow party members for their lack of courage in standing up for our values, to defy the emerging perception of "…a race to enter government driven by determined guile, trickery and corruption, rather than a discernible courage to lead the nation". Later stating: "It used to be the case that nothing could be more demeaning for a party member than for it to be known that he had been bought. Being bought was slavery in our eyes; it was selling your humanity. For in that case one does not decide by God-given powers of reasoning anymore, but in accordance to the wishes of the buyer". I described the courage of leadership as having four main qualities:

---

[151] *'The Courage of Leadership, 2004'. 'The Mkapa Years Collected Speeches'* Volume 3, Part One, Cluster I, pages 122–139. Dar es Salaam, Mkuki na Nyota.

1. Ability to develop a clear vision of goals and direction;
2. Ability to provide dependable leadership towards the vision;
3. Tenacity of purpose as well as refusal to be driven off course; unless there are compelling reasons, and,
4. Courage to stand up for, and defend, the values that we hold dear.

Reflecting on this now, I wish I had advanced this more, regardless of the reaction I received. The Arusha Declaration states: *'Leaders must set a good example to the rest of the people in their lives and all their activities'*. This still holds true today.

The civil society was growing during my time, they certainly have blossomed now; there seem to be a myriad of non-governmental organisations (NGOs) and civil society organisations (CSOs) with many receiving a considerable amount of foreign aid. Unfortunately some NGOs were overzealous in their criticism of government, some even seemed totally anti-government and did not recognise that the governing party has rights and that people within government also have their human rights. It upsets me when there is little sympathy for a policeman killed in the line of duty, for example, that policeman had human rights as well. We talk so much about rights, yet we don't talk about obligations beyond those of the government. Every child has a right to education, but how can a government in a developing country provide this to every child, and what should every citizen do to help the situation? Constructive criticism would be more helpful.

Perhaps the simplistic approach of some NGOs and CSOs to merely criticise reflects the weak or immature state of many civil society organisations in Tanzania; Kenya has a dynamic NGO and CSO community which is thoughtful and presents alternatives. It could be a by-product of our reliance on Mwalimu making decisions for this nation for so long, coupled with the fact that it took so long for new political parties to form. Perhaps this resulted in the development of a society where constructive criticism was stunted, thus a populist and headline seeking approach of criticism, rather than suggesting helpful alternatives, became the easier route.

The army has an important role in development, as well as in the defence of the country. I suspect my relationship with the army was helped because I had volunteered to do national service, so was familiar with their environment. I was, and still am, an advocate for national service. I refused its planned phaseout during my time and insisted that the national service be brought back directly under the Tanzania Peoples' Defence Force's (TPDF) management, as it had come to be led by a separate cadre of officers, which I believed had downgraded its profile with TPDF members and the public.

I remember the first guard of honour I inspected as president and commander-in-chief, I think it was on Independence Day, 9 December 1995. The army uniforms were supposed to be green, but the uniforms were so faded and well-worn that there were many shades of green; and several of those in parade wore boots that were so old. The meagre defence budget had meant that the soldiers had suffered. During a visit to the army's Lugalo barracks in Dar es Salaam I saw the inadequate accommodation some of the lower ranks lived in, the structures dated back to the colonial times. We held a general meeting and as usual I took questions from the soldiers, encouraging anyone to ask, regardless of their rank. One soldier explained the hard situation they were living in and their small entitlements. I sympathised with their plight; but explained the situation about the state's poor finances, how much we received and how much we could allocate, adding:

> It would be easy to favour one or two ministries, but then other ministries would have to wait. It would be easy to give in to all requests, but this would mean, for instance, that medicines in the health centres are not there, or even in the referral hospitals. This is where your relatives go for treatment – your father, mother, brothers. So, do I make your lot happier and the situation more difficult for the rural population, the others? No. So, we will try to have a balance as we go on.

I was told that the soldiers commented, "Eeh, this fellow talks bluntly". We worked to improve the soldiers' situation and with increasing revenues and support from others I left them in much better shape.

I also sought to improve the conditions for the police and worked well with my second Inspector General of Police, Omar Mahita, an intelligent man who, besides being good at his job, also argued the case well for improving the living and workplace environment for his staff. Unfortunately, when it came to the Tanzania Intelligence and Security Service there was controversy concerning the troubling death of the former director general, Lieutenant General (Rtd.) Imran Kombe, who had retired. He was shot by two policemen who had mistaken him for a criminal. There was much suspicion that this had been arranged by me and the government, something I assure you is nonsense, and these policemen were convicted for the crime. The person who had taken over the position proved to be able and solid, Cornel Apson Mwang'onda. I feel good that I maintained the professionalism of the uniformed services.

Conscious of the importance of unity within our nation and sensitive to the criticism that Mwalimu had been pro-Christian, which was unjust in my opinion, I tried to foster Muslim – Christian relationships and ensure that there was a balance within the government. Certainly for the top echelon of the political leadership once the president is elected then there is a consideration of the religion of the prime minister, though not enshrined in legislation, a balance is necessary. In Tanzania there is quiet and accepted recognition that there must be a balance to avoid any fear of one religion or tribe dominating the running of the country or the ownership of the economy. There certainly should not be any rumour-mongering over the dominance of, or favouritism, to a certain faith; this desire for a balance between the major religions in Tanzania is something I appreciate, it is something special if you look at so many other nations around the world. I like people of my faith, Catholicism, to be religiously respectful of people of other faiths, and I hope the same from those who follow other forms of worship. I cannot stand groups which start running down other religions; I believe that one's faith is a very personal matter. I am pleased I was able to sustain the relations between religions in this country, encouraging harmony and co-operation.

Perhaps my largest achievement in this endeavour was my help in getting the central mosque built in Dodoma. I knew Muammar Gaddafi had helped Ugandans to build a mosque in Kampala, so I sought out a colleague from my days as Minister of Foreign Affairs, the late Ali

Treki[152], who had been Libya's foreign minister and had come to fetch the Libyan soldiers we had captured in Entebbe and Kampala during the war with Idi Amin's Uganda. I explained that Dodoma, our national capital, had Anglican, Catholic and Lutheran cathedrals, but lacked a central mosque and I would like to have a mosque as part of my legacy to the Muslim community, could Gaddafi help? I was asked to lay the foundation stone, but thought it more appropriate that my Vice President, Dr Ali Mohamed Shein do so, which he did in 2005. The mosque, the second largest in East Africa, was completed in 2010; it is a beautiful sight when you fly into Dodoma.

There is a conscious effort to provide open opportunity for all, especially in education. When the Christians asked for some government schools which had been mission schools beforehand to be given back to them to turn into university colleges, I arranged for schools in Dar es Salaam, Dodoma, Lushoto and Iringa to be returned[153]; which was followed by the Muslim community asking to be included as well, whereupon they were granted the former TANESCO training college which became the Muslim University of Morogoro. There were people who complained about my doing this, especially providing the land and infrastructure of this former college to the Muslim community for free. But it was the education and enrolment policies which mattered, not that they received the infrastructure gratis. I attended religious occasions such as the consecration of a bishop and meetings of the National Muslim Council, BAKWATA. I think I had reasonably good relations with all around, particularly with Chief Sheikh Mufti Hemed bin Jumaa bin Hemed, who was a very wise and learned man.

I am impressed by the Aga Khan IV, the Imam of the Nizari Ismailis. As well as being a spiritual leader who is respected across the world, he is heavily involved in development, with a positive interest in social welfare and the media. I enhanced the diplomatic status of the Aga Khan Devel-

---

152 Libya: Foreign Minister 1976–1982; Ambassador 1995–2001; UN representative 2003–2009; President UN General Assembly 2009–2010.

153 The Catholic church affiliated St Joseph's Millennium Primary School and the St Joseph's Cathedral High School in Dar es Salaam, the Anglican church affiliated St John University in Dodoma, the Lutheran church affiliated Sebastian Kolowa Memorial University in Lushoto and the Ruaha Catholic University in Iringa.

opment Network, which he appreciated. I also facilitated the beginning of his Nation Media Group owned *'The Citizen'* and *'Mwananchi'* newspapers in Tanzania. There had been hesitation by others about bringing in new competition for the media; while I thought it was good to introduce variety and competition into the media field. After I left office I served on the board of the Aga Khan University; and after board meetings we would often meet with the Aga Khan. I had no idea of his extreme wealth until I saw his residence at Aiglemont estate near Paris; he doesn't flaunt it and has done much to help others. I had the privilege of meeting Pope Benedict in the Vatican in 2005, with Anna and my younger son, Nicholas, his spouse Foster Mbuna and their first born, Nigel Benedict Alexander. I could feel Pope Benedict's piety when I met him.

A construction project which I was proud to be involved with was the 'Unity Bridge' which links Mozambique with Tanzania across the Ruvuma river. Mwalimu and Samora Machel had always talked about that as they were 'brothers'; considering their shared liberation struggle and had countries bordering each other, that they should build a bridge to link the two countries, but were unable to do so. Joaquim Chissano, who succeeded Machel, was my friend since when we were both foreign ministers. As presidents, the two of us were conscious of our countries' historical connections. Unknown to me, President Chissano had broached the subject of funding a bridge with the Japanese, who had turned him down; the Japanese prime minister had queried its worth, describing it as a bridge from nowhere to nowhere. I subsequently raised this with the Japanese prime minister during a state visit and was also refused. I accepted this but explained to him that the reason there was not much activity across the river was precisely because there was no bridge. I said it was a national commitment for us to honour our founding presidents who had envisage a unity bridge that would bring our countries together and promote trade and movement across the border. I told him:

> Mr Prime Minister: One, I want to tell you that we are going to build this bridge with our own funds. Two, I want an assurance, more, I plead with you not stop your aid programmes with us because you think we are spending up what we earn ourselves badly

because of this bridge, so please continue your aid programme. Now Mwalimu is gone, Samora is gone. I don't know who are going to be our successors, but the longer the time the more the idea of this bridge will fade into the background. Chissano was the foreign minister in Samora's time; I was the foreign minister in Mwalimu's time. We have decided that this must be the legacy, a joint legacy of our two leaders, so we are going to build it.

He said he understood, though I think that the Japanese did not believe that we would proceed. I got in touch with Chissano, who said, "Oh you did? I asked the Japanese too and got the same answer. Well, for that reason let us make sure that we build this bridge before you leave and before I leave". We agreed to split costs 50/50 and laid the foundation stone during 2005, the last year of our presidencies. To be fair to the Japanese once they learnt the project was going ahead they contributed towards tarmacking part of the road to it. This bridge means more to me than the national stadium, a construction project which also began during my time, which was partly funded by the Chinese.

Relations between Tanzania and China, particularly under Mwalimu, have been exceptional, though they had temporarily abated prior to my taking up the presidency. After I became president I had received this message from Mwalimu via Charles Sanga, his personal assistant: "We have many friends in this world, but we have one genuine friend, and that's China." I appointed Charles Sanga as Ambassador to China in 2000 and attended the first Forum on China–Africa Cooperation (FOCAC) that same year; actually I broke off from campaigning for the 2000 general elections to attend this forum. I was one of the four presidents who attended and I think this helped to revitalise the friendship between our nations. I don't like what the West says about the relationship between China and African countries, I suspect it is because they feel that they own us still and should have priority before anyone else; which is wrong. As independent African countries we should be able to determine what it is we want out of China and what it is that the Chinese want out of us, then see how these interests can be reconciled. I am proud that the national stadium was built in partnership with the Chinese. I had made it clear to His Excellency Hu Jintao that I didn't want a grant of

100%; instead I sought a commercial partnership; with Tanzania contributing just under half of the construction cost. This truly was a joint effort; a departure from our previous total dependence.

I know the West did not like my attitude towards Robert Mugabe, I was especially unpopular for this with the British when I was foreign minister. During 2002, I attended a Commonwealth Heads of Government Meeting in Australia where the forthcoming election in Zimbabwe was a very contentious issue, with some calling for Zimbabwe's immediate suspension from the Commonwealth. When it was my turn to speak I said I was surprised that the Commonwealth wanted to send a such a negative message to Zimbabwe and the world. I asked, what had the Commonwealth done in the past to aid the independence struggle of Zimbabwe? Why couldn't we allow Zimbabweans to evolve their own electoral system in their own way, in the way best suited for their nation? Zimbabweans had spilled their own blood to gain independence, they had earned their right to determine their own future. I added:

> We have really absolutely no right to tell them what to do. Even I, whose country has given its sons and daughters in battle with the racist regime that time, even I dare not instruct Zimbabweans about how they should go about governing themselves. No, you can't do that, I for one will not sign on that. Also, they haven't even held the election, we don't know the way they are going to vote, how political parties will fare. How can you judge them before they even vote? That will not be fair.

At the end of the session we had a small reception during which some African and Caribbean country leaders thanked me for having spoken up. Zimbabwean leaders have not forgotten my defence of them at that Commonwealth meeting. I was pleased to appoint the late Brigadier General (Rtd.) Hashim Mbita as High Commissioner[154] there, as I knew

---

154 High Commissioner to Zimbabwe 2003–2006. Longest serving executive secretary of the coordinating committee which became the Organisation of African Unity Liberation Committee. Among the many awards received were Zimbabwe's highest honour for a foreigner, the Royal Order of Munhumutapa, African Union's 'Son of Africa' and SADC's Sir Seretse Khama medal.

how high their esteem was for him as he had played a leading role in the liberation movement.

It is one thing to commend the Western style of governance, but it is unreasonable and unfeasible to expect us developing nations to almost replicate Western governance structures and processes. It has taken the West centuries to reach this stage, while for many African countries we have marked only around fifty years of independence. The West must make allowance that we are feeling our way, evolving our own systems of governance. It doesn't necessarily mean that democracy will take centuries to become embedded, as it did in their countries, but they should take into account that it is a different environment. Tanzania is a developing country of over 120 different tribes and two distinct culturally different religions after all. I don't think these considerations are recognised by those advocating a 'one-size fits all' democracy.

Furthermore, there must be some allowance for democracy to evolve, especially in countries where the military has overthrown a civilian government. When returning to civilian government the opportunity must be taken to reflect upon what led to the coup and how to avoid a recurrence that led to a faction becoming so estranged and angry. Even where you have had continuous civilian government, there can be events or situations which mean a nation should rethink its system, such as whether to choose from a party list or from a constituency. Each approach is influenced by history and circumstance. Should one approach be regarded as more democratic?

This reminds me of the first Commonwealth Heads of Government Meeting I attended, this was in Edinburgh during October 1997. In my innocence and with my socialist leanings when it came to development, I said: "There are certain basic needs, which if they are met, increases the dignity and the quality of life of the people. Water, education and health – three basic needs. Why can't we concentrate aid in these areas so that people can really look like people, talk like people?" Some delegates and staff people looked at me in surprise, thinking I was naive. Mwalimu always said development is about people. It is not about construction and modernity. I regard Cuba as a good example, it has universal healthcare and education, and free access to water – that to me is a developed country. Then you see homeless people sleeping on the streets four blocks from the White House in Washington DC. How can the United States of America be regarded as the most developed country in the world? I care deeply about this, a country such as Tanzania must make sure that there is free access to education – primary education at least, water and health care. Then you will notice the difference in the people. These basic needs are what we must focus on as a priority for development.

Overall I appreciated the Commonwealth meetings, it was good to have those surveys of world politics every two years, how the world has changed, what is changing, what kind of threats there are, what we should anticipate. Though I think there were more benefits at the ministerial level meetings, where ministers of particular portfolios share experiences and discuss ideas. The Commonwealth also provides good scholarships, although there are fewer available nowadays.

I suppose the Southern African Development Community (SADC) has in a small way similar value to that provided by the Commonwealth. They always remember me at the SADC headquarters in Botswana, Gaborone; as there had been inertia year after year over building a headquarters. In August 2004 while passing on the baton of the chairmanship[155] of SADC to the Mauritian Prime Minister, Paul Bérenger[156], I declared I was fed up with waiting for a development partner to help build a headquarters for SADC; SADC was our organisation, why couldn't we manage to construct our headquarters? How could other countries respect SADC members when we couldn't even organise ourselves to build a headquarters? I was firm to my fellow SADC leaders, stating that we must start contributing immediately to a fund for the construction of the headquarters. I pledged to open an account for the construction of the headquarters in Gaborone, in which I would deposit USD 500,000 from Tanzania. Mugabe quickly pledged USD 500,000 as well, which led to all the members pledging the same amount. We were able to lay the foundation stone on the land donated by Botswana during the following year's summit.

There was a logic to founding SADC in 1992 because we cooperated

---

155   I was chair of SADC from August 2003 to August 2004.
156   Prime Minister of Mauritius September 2003–July 2005.

well on our common cause of political liberation. But there has been a tardiness in agreeing on the economic aspect of cooperation. One problem was the Southern African Customs Union (SACU), which was already in existence as part of the overall coordination of customs within South Africa, Swaziland, Lesotho and Namibia. The second problem was the fear that since the end of apartheid member states would be inundated by the more developed South Africans. Many worried that by opening up the gates we would lose our own economies and be replaced by a South African economy from Limpopo to Dar es Salaam. Like it or not, the South African economy was a stronger economy, even if we had defeated it politically. Now there was a fear that we third world economies would be totally inundated by South Africa. Another issue was that our members had observed sanctions against South Africa for decades, even fought them, yet now they were supposed to allow South Africans to do business in their own countries. Nevertheless, we said no, the political coordination and unity we used in ensuring the end of apartheid should drive us to integrate economically. The momentum for greater economic coordination overcame these considerations. Thankfully, the reluctance of people to accept that new relationship with South Africans has dissipated.

I think it is in my blood to foster relations and alliances within African countries. My first job was working on the African desk of the ministry of foreign affairs where I saw first-hand Mwalimu's commitment to the region of southern Africa. I then served twice as foreign minister before becoming president. Relations are very much part of my heart and sentiment, cooperation means a lot to me. I believe in sorting out differences in trade, borders and so on, by talking. The readiness to sacrifice so we can have greater unity or strength, is important.

The progress of the East African Community has similarly been hampered by an element of fear on the part of Tanzanians that they will be inundated by Kenyans who are more commercial-minded, and Ugandans because they are better educated. The apprehension is that both countries have more professionals, who will come here and deprive Tanzanians of jobs and business opportunities. I think this is the underlying reason for the slowness of integration. There was integration under the British colonial rulers, why can we not achieve this when we are now independent countries? My predecessor had initiated the renewal of the East African Community and I took this up very willingly because we are pan-Africanist. I really believe in regional integration and see now that I should have pursued this more vigorously. It disappoints me that it is moving so slowly now; this is taking far too long. Though it is hard to persuade some leaders to 'give up' national control. Museveni always asks, "What is wrong with you Tanzanians? You are holding us back".

It is not only the lack of substantial progress of the East African Community which disappoints me. I held the first International Conference of the Great Lakes Region (ICGLR) in 2004 in Dar es Salaam. The Dar es Salaam Declaration on Peace, Security, Democracy and Development in the Great Lakes Region[157] which we agreed upon was supposed to avert such unrest as we have since seen in Burundi and eastern Democratic Republic of the Congo (DRC). If we had been really proactive in applying the principles in this declaration we could have averted, or at least minimised, many of the events of instability in our region. I wish I had achieved more here; the ethos and commitments of this declaration are something I believe in.

I was often frustrated in my dealings with development partners and the World Bank and IMF. Essentially, I wanted help for my nation to reduce poverty and stimulate economic growth, but like so many African countries, our nation had grown tired of having initiatives forced down our throats by others. We encountered a range of attitudes from development partners, ranging from an arrogant 'we know best' attitude, to an almost evangelical eagerness to help. This often resulted in matters being pushed through, and/or decisions made without sufficient background information feeding into the decision making process. From our side it was vital that our nation, as with other developing nations, retained ownership of our national vision and strategies for development. I acknowledge that our perspective may have been coloured by our African socialist backgrounds, and we did not have sufficient technical expertise and experience of some issues, particularly the free market economy. But, we Africans had strived for independence for our

---

157 Downloadable from: http://www.icglr.org/images/Dar_Es_Salaam_Declaration_on_Peace_Security_Democracy_and_Development.pdf

nations, had great pride in our nations and were determined to make our own path.

Parties on both sides had suffered from communication breakdowns during the years and I wanted to help to improve aid relationships, for Tanzania as well as other developing nations in the South. My early work for Mwalimu when he was involved with the liberation movements had taught me the importance of seeking to keep communication between parties proactive and productive. Thus, I undertook to improve these relationships whenever I, and, honouring Mwalimu's example, tried to do this as an internationalist.

The Swedish government hosted a workshop in 1999 on improving relationships between development partners and those nations they were trying to assist. I appreciated being asked to share my thoughts at this meeting and was open and frank with the attendees. I have been told that this meeting was a turning point, creating a new awareness of the concerns of developing countries, and causing development partners to review how they interacted with us African nations.

I was pleased with the outcome of a two-day meeting in Dar es Salaam in early 2001 of the heads of twelve southern and eastern African states with the heads of the World Bank, Jim Wolfensohn, and IMF, Horst Köhler. Such an event has not been repeated since. It was quite an achievement to bring these leaders together, as the past conduct of these two international institutions had alienated many African leaders, especially Robert Mugabe. Many of these leaders held a negative or ambivalent attitude towards the World Bank and IMF, and vice versa. So in order to put to rest the suspicions and lack of confidence in each other, I suggested that we gather together and listen to each other's perspectives. It fell to me to persuade my fellow leaders to come, which was not an easy task. Perhaps I succeeded because African leaders knew of my record of real friction with the World Bank and IMF! I wanted to open the path of communication between these parties, and while there was a lot of plain speaking, I was pleased to say that we broke down barriers during this meeting. I think it was a watershed moment. This team of Wolfensohn and Köhler really redeemed the relationship between those two financial institutions and developing African countries; they should be recognised for this. Of course the reality was that both parties needed each other. Though, I made a point of stressing at this meeting that the responsibility for our continent's development rested with us Africans.

The British Prime Minister, Tony Blair, asked me to be a member of The Commission for Africa[158]. When the leader of a major development partner like Britain asks you, you cannot say no, especially on a matter which is very close to my heart as African development. Tony Blair was a clever man to work with and a smooth operator. Perhaps the most famous member of that commission was the pop star Bob Geldof; he provided a popular aspect and helped to sell the idea to the public that Africa needed help. He organised ten Live 8 concerts around the world to help raise public pressure on the leaders who would attend the G8 Summit in Gleneagles, Scotland, that year. I was invited to attend a lunch with six other African leaders at the G8 Summit in Scotland, I think Blair needed to have some African leaders there to emphasise the importance of the Commission's report. Blair seemed committed, though George Bush acted as if this was just one of those 'feel-good' meetings about helping Africa. The G8 summit pledged an increase of USD 25 billion in aid to Africa. This was my second time at Gleneagles, I had been there before during a weekend break of the first Commonwealth meeting I attended, which was in 1997. Gleneagles is an impressive place, I realised then that there are people who are so wealthy that they can stay in places like that to play golf and relax. I asked myself whether Tanzanians would ever reach that level of wealth.

The World Economic Forum at Davos is like a jamboree, everybody is there. I'll concede that it does give you an opportunity to meet colleagues, those with whom you have shared projects, or would like to collaborate with. If you prepare ahead, you can do a lot of business and sort out matters while on the side-lines; which is helpful. Otherwise it is really for the developed economies, rather than for a country like Tanzania. Though I appreciate that there is a certain creative energy which provides stimulus for learning about differing perspectives and approaches. It does give your country's profile a boost of course; especially if you are on a panel in the assembly. I became known as a voice for Africa, especially

---

158 Report *'Our Common Interest'* available from: http://www.commissionforafrica.info/2005-report

about HIV and AIDS, which gave impetus to development assistance, I am glad to say. There was the incident popular with the media when the actress Sharon Stone was so impressed by my arguments about the need to address malaria that she stood up during a panel discussion,[159] offered USD 10,000 to the Global Fund to Fight AIDS, Tuberculosis and Malaria and encouraged others in the audience to donate for the purchase of bed nets. As it turned out later, much of the money pledged did not eventuate; thankfully UNICEF made up the balance.

Recalling some regional affairs which occurred during my presidency, the most unexpected was the almost simultaneous bombings of the American embassies in Tanzania and Kenya. I was standing by the window in my office in State House when I heard this big boom. I exclaimed, "What the bloody hell is that?" Shortly after I received a phone call to tell me that the USA embassy in Dar es Salaam had been bombed. Kenya suffered far worse, with 213 killed and an estimated 4,000 wounded; while we suffered 11 deaths and 85 wounded; though the loss of just one life is a tragedy in itself. As I said to the press at the time, "We were very angry at the inhuman, evil and despicable act", describing the act as, "completely alien to our history, alien to our political culture". These dual events were the first al-Qaeda bombings and brought the profile of the fiendish Osama bin Laden and al-Qaeda to the attention of the world.

We were involved as peacemakers in the Burundian civil war, which had commenced in 1993, though we took on a peace mediating role from 1996, with Mwalimu as leader. It is not that I sought this, but they had approached Mwalimu, and I couldn't say no. Not only because they are our neighbours, but also if they thought that Mwalimu could help, then I would facilitate it. This is just as it is now, while I may be approached to help other countries due to my political influence and contacts, I don't have the organisational capacity and have to rely on my president to facilitate that. I saw that being good neighbours we must be part of reconciliation efforts, though to be frank I was hesitant to embark on this at the time. These peace-making efforts consumed a lot of time.

---

159 You can watch this Davos panel discussion at: https://www.youtube.com/watch?v=R8CF4E0XjD0.

After Mwalimu's untimely death we approached Mandela, who agreed to conclude what Mwalimu had started. It was very tough, the mutual suspicion between the two ethnic groups of the Hutus and Tutsis was incredible, and regrettably is continuing as I write these memoirs. The meetings and negotiations dragged on and on until it almost seemed like these people were turning the negotiations into their job. Mandela was furious and threatened to cut their per diem allowances. Thankfully the peace accord was signed in Arusha in 2000, with Museveni, Bizimungu[160], Moi, Kengo wa Dondo[161] and Zenawi and me contributing to the document. Despite the diversity of the nations we led, we were united in seeking an end to this long-standing conflict which left an estimated three hundred thousand people dead.

I am proud of how I sustained Tanzania's profile on the international scene. Sometimes it is forgotten how a president's, especially an African president's, responsibilities can extend beyond the nation they serve, but we leaders are always conscious of this.

---

160 Pasteur Bizimungu: President of Rwanda July 1994–March 2000.

161 Léon Kengo wa Dondo: Prime Minister of Zaire November 1982–October 1986, November 1988–May 1990, and July 1994–April 1997; President of the Senate of Congo since May 2007.

Chapter 14

"There's no art to find the mind's construction in the face."

–Shakespeare's 'Macbeth'

Being a leader can be quite lonely, most of the time the burden is on your shoulders alone. It is vital to know the people who are loyal, the loyalty you seek from friends and colleagues is based on principles, not on flattery of you, or their self-interest. You are isolated as president and must be wary of potential ulterior motives of others. Mwalimu was not hypocritical, and he could not abide hypocrisy in others. I dislike hypocrisy as well, though I just keep quiet, rather than speak out against hypocrisy as Mwalimu did.

I value sincerity in people, as well as straight talking. I desire openness and do not like it when people hesitate to state a different view for fear I will take offence. That someone may hold a differing view does not bother me at all, I am ready to listen to them. Allowing the opportunity for others to state their view is important. Though I stress the necessity of stating differences politely, one should not forget the weight and dignity of the position of the person. This current trend of attacking the person rather than the issue at hand is not constructive and can have negative after-effects. The actual issue might end up being discounted or overshadowed by the personal criticism. A leader's personal faults are not necessarily inherent to the office you are holding. How far does your personal life affect your performance as a leader? This is something to consider.

I always presume that a person is not trying to trick me or take advantage; though this does happen. When someone's insincerity or duplicity does emerge I never respond, rather let them talk on. When they have said what they want to say I tell them to go and forget about our encounter. If they ask to see me again I don't see them, as they would waste my time.

There has always been a political section that felt I was too arrogant; too self-opinionated, too self-assured. This perception may have emerged when I was editor of the party and government newspapers, as my editorials were firm and direct. I don't mind a good discussion, but I am not interested in social repartee. If I attended a meeting and found unsound or wild talk then I would just not say anything. Others would then complain: "You see? He is illustrating again his disdain for us". This makes some people think that I am an arrogant man, but it's simply the way I am. I have been told that Mwalimu said of me: "You know, Ben is intellectual, you have to qualify that – he is intellectually arrogant. He doesn't entertain stupidity and when some people just want to chat, Ben doesn't have time for that". This criticism of me probably also stemmed from the quality of the opposition leadership during my time in office; as I so often found the intellectual substance of their argument wanting when they criticised me, so I just dismissed it. However, I was not dictatorial and could agree to disagree and move on if necessary. There was free discussion at party meetings and if necessary we would seek to agree on a team which would be tasked with coming up with an acceptable resolution and party statement.

Before I became president I had not considered the responsibility of the president to provide solace. I had experienced some foretaste of this aspect of the role, having been press secretary to Mwalimu; but I didn't realise that this personal aspect of leadership would take so much of my time, nor how this was an important aspect of a good leader. When a crisis or a tragedy occurs, you must determine when to issue a statement of sympathy, whether it merits you putting everything aside to go and express sympathy directly to the people affected; and whether it was necessary to raise the event to the level of a national tragedy.

Tragedies were a time when I realised that it meant something to these suffering people to see me visit them, I learnt that leadership includes being there at the time of crisis to offer comfort and hope. One of my shortcomings is that I am not very demonstrative about my feelings; I was not accustomed to this, while my successor, President Kikwete is very good at this. Two tragedies so soon into my first term showed me starkly of my social responsibility to others. During my first year in office there were excessive rains which caused much flooding and washed away a lot of the railway line. We didn't possess any helicopters then, which forced us to seek help from South Africa to get to the affected areas. Only a few years before we had been at loggerheads with the racist regime, now it was a different regime and their air force came forward to help. I did feel uncomfortable that it was our former enemies helping our army, but we needed to see the full extent of the damage. This reliance on another country brought me down to earth about the realities of power in a poor country such as Tanzania and taught me that I must work on making our armed services mobile so they could respond to such emergencies. We flew from Dar es Salaam over the regions of Tabora, Singida, Dodoma and Morogoro, the extent of the flooding was horrific; so many people were suffering. The sinking of the ferry, the MV Bukoba, in Lake Victoria in May 1996, which resulted in the drowning of at least 894 people, was even more shocking. The loss of so much life was just terrible; at the time I wondered whether the boat had been adequately serviced, how this could have happened. The ferry was overloaded, but it was also an eyeopener to realise that we were so broke that the maintenance had not been done, resulting in the deterioration of the vessel. I would visit the memorial to those drowned and missing during my regional tours to Mwanza.

There was the dreadful crash on the Mwanza–Musoma road during my 2000 campaign; with eighteen killed and thirty-nine injured. I visited the injured and paid my respects at the mortuary; I will never forget that. Then the horrific accident when a passenger train rolled backwards into a goods train in Igandu in 2002, killing 281 people.

This also ties in with a misconception that as president you can resolve any problem, this may be a delusion experienced by many leaders across the world, though I think this problem is exacerbated in a developing country. The peasantry sees you as the one person who can fix everything, yet in reality you are part of a system of government. You may be at the apex of that system, but you are not isolated from the system. This belief in your complete power as president could be frustrating at times, other times a burden. I felt this keenly when there were incidents of peasants and pastoralists fighting over the land and killing each other, for in a way the peasantry was relying on me to keep them safe, yet there was only so much I could do.

I was also very upset about the death of seventeen prisoners at Mbarali police station, a small police post in Mbeya[162]. They had been locked in a small room with insufficient ventilation, the prisoners shouted for help, but no-one heard them, so they suffocated. Such a senseless death of these prisoners on remand, they should not have been confined in this thoughtless way. Then came the question as to whether I should hold the regional police commander, Said Ali Mwema, accountable; the pros and cons were presented by my advisors, the ministry and the police. To what extent should I punish the man who was not directly responsible, how could I regard Mwema as accountable? Eventually, I decided I would not sack him, though he was transferred, and five police officers were dismissed and charged with murder. Mwema later rose to become inspector general of police. Accountability is another tough issue for leaders to face. You must be practical and a little humane, but you must think of those who have suffered the loss of a loved one. How to balance your reaction between sympathy and punishment, is a troubling challenge that leaders grapple with, you cannot be prescriptive, you must carefully evaluate the issues of each incident.

Another time when you feel the weight of office is when you must decide on the prerogative of mercy for someone who has been sentenced to death for the crime of murder or treason. There is a prerogative of mercy council, which looks at the condemned's circumstances and

---

162 Mbarali police station, Mbeya, November 2002.

record to decide whether they should hang, or the sentence should be commuted to imprisonment for a certain term. This council is advisory, the final decision rests with the president, who is the chair of this council. This was literally a matter of life or death I was considering, during those days I felt really low, I couldn't even enjoy my food. I exercised mercy throughout my ten years, which I know many found very odd, as my predecessor had not done this, the last hanging being carried out in 1994. I commuted one hundred death sentences to life imprisonment in April 2003.

The president has much power, though not as much as in the early days, when our founding president could detain you for any length of time. Nowadays you must state in court that you are holding someone for a reason and the judiciary will judge whether this detention is appropriate or not. I endorse such restraining influences on power. I also value the separation of the powers: legislative, executive and judiciary; this is vital, especially for developing nations. This was one of my concerns when we were undertaking the review of Tanzania's constitution during 2015. There must be a structure which can mitigate a president's power, or at least provide for time for a president to rethink. Perhaps this is where a second parliamentary chamber could be useful, it could offer the opportunity for those who have had substantial experience to review bills. It need not necessarily be composed of elected officials, it could be an advisory council who could at least warn quietly of any potential for a negative impact from a proposed bill. At the very least this would spare the president from total opprobrium if he signed an unwise bill into law.

Secrecy, the need to keep some matters confidential has been and will always be an issue for a leader. Then there's a question of how open a government can be and the period before secret papers can be made available to the public. Britain had a thirty-year rule for the declassification of government papers, which is being progressively reduced to twenty years. Tanzania still has a thirty-year period. Some of Mwalimu's papers can be seen, particularly those from the 1960s and 1970s. Mwalimu's personal assistant, Joan Wicken, faithfully kept a diary during the thirty years she worked for Mwalimu. She stipulated that her diaries could not be made public until thirty years after her death, which is a shame. I would have loved to read her recollections but will be long gone by the time these become available to the public.

I believe more information should be made available, that our government papers should be available after twenty years. History does not necessarily always repeat itself, but it is important, though unfortunately many of us are not ready to learn from the past and hence make decisions without enough background information. One justification for not releasing information is that as we are a young country then those who are affected by decisions might feel like seeking retribution. I don't think the potential for retribution is worth the silence. Though one should always bear in mind that a leader may have made a decision in good conscience and based on the information available at the time; which often isn't considered years later when people subsequently criticise historical decisions with the benefit of hindsight.

Though there is the other side of the coin, I do not think it right that nowadays little is kept secret, you can even read minuted instructions by the president in a newspaper; I don't think this is right. How can this happen, what kind of environment is it when matters that are discussed in cabinet are made public knowledge? Sometimes you must be able to hold a discussion where people can be open about a matter, but if there is a fear that something will be leaked to the media then it would make people bottle up, which is not good for leadership. Some secrecy is necessary; otherwise you will not have room to operate. It is not appropriate to think aloud on everything, but it is important to know what you discuss with a colleague will be in confidence. During my time we did not release information on sensitive or delicate issues. Though looking back now I think there was a tendency to stamp everything as secret. I should have made the civil servants make more information available.

The national interest does not mean the interest of the public at all times; however, the Tanzanian parliament now says they want everything in the open. For example, if the government is negotiating a major contract then these negotiations must be shared in parliament so the members of parliament can discuss and give their consent. This doesn't happen in other countries and should not happen here. Naturally the government must act responsibly and follow governance rules and processes, but there are times when it is not appropriate to have a negotiation scrutinised in the public arena of parliament. There can also be the potential of the opposition using a national issue to try to settle scores, which could derail the negotiations. The key is achieving the right balance in transparency, coupled with a clear demarcation on the limitation of the powers of the three organs of governance: the judiciary, the legislature, the executive. These days there is a tendency for parliamentary committees to over-stretch their role; occasionally they even want to take the role of the minister and issue orders as if they have statutory power – which they don't have.

Continuing with the respect for statutory power, I firmly believe that one must make legal and statutory arrangements to ensure real independence of the judiciary. The appointment is one thing, but after appointment you must let them become truly independent and self-regulated, well apart from any political considerations. Again, I learned this from Mwalimu, who held strong views and possessed great honour and integrity. When there were lapses in the judiciary he always insisted that they use their own rules and processes to discipline each other. Naturally judges must be well-educated and observe very closely indeed the law and procedures, this is their grounds for maintaining their independence. Naturally their integrity must be absolutely beyond reproach.

Moving on to matters I know some will be keen to read about, the allegations made against me. It is the personal criticism that hurt, political criticism I don't mind at all. There is a perception that excess by presidents happens in all sub-Saharan African countries, that we are all alike in our desire to embezzle money. There is a presumption in Tanzania that once you get into State House you start amassing private wealth. This was not me, I sought office very purposefully, and I would like to be judged by the purpose for which I sought office and what I achieved for my fellow citizens.

For example, the allegation that I favoured my son's father-in-law with the sale of the Kiwira coal mine made me feel very bad. This allegation is absolute nonsense. As far as I know everything was done above board, including the registration. I asked what other proposition there was and was told there was nothing else, so I said, "I am not going to stop privatisation because this proposer is a fellow parent-in-law; that is his problem. If this is an economic proposition which the government will gain from, then fine". I know he had done the homework, talking with the East African Development Bank and travelling to India and China at his own expense to seek funding to rehabilitate the setup and result in generating 200 additional megawatts of power for the national grid. But we were both bad-mouthed and regrettably he became unwell and died before he could progress the project. The government took the property back in 2008 due to political pressure, it was returned to the State Mining Corporation (STAMICO), and nothing has since happened. It annoys me that in this country which suffers from an insufficient electricity supply no electricity has been generated; the mine remains idle.

Another incident which hurt was the unjust accusations made when my brother-in-law was involved with searching for a company to run TANESCO, the Tanzania Electric Supply Company. He was involved with the company NETGroup Solutions Ltd, which I did not know about at that time, nor do I know now what he received from his work for them. I knew that some members of cabinet were hesitant about bringing in NETGroup Solutions to manage TANESCO, but I thought this hesitancy was due to the fact that TANESCO was a large public service institution and our decision to use the services of a South African company would be unpopular amongst the public. As far as I was concerned this company was the best choice to improve the performance of TANESCO, no-one said directly to me that they were reluctant because of my bother-in-law's involvement with NETGroup Solutions.

There is no doubt that corruption was a major election issue during 1995 because it was so noticeable in our declining economy; this affliction was everywhere. I decided to set up a commission to investigate this pernicious problem; I thought this was the best way to address the scourge fairly and objectively and did not want to end up with a kangaroo court. The Presidential Commission of Inquiry Against Corruption was well constituted; chaired by Joseph Warioba[163], and they produced a good report[164]. There was an addendum which set out instances which could be justiciable, which we reviewed with the Attorney General. We did not want to appear that we were going after people simply because

---

163 Prime Minister 1985–1990; Attorney General 1976–1985; Minister of Justice 1983–1985.

164 'The Report of the Presidential Commission of Inquiry Against Corruption'. 1996.

they are former leaders, in fairness we really had to satisfy ourselves that the evidence would hold in a court of law.

Eventually, we had only two major cases, one was with a former Minister of Works, Communications and Transport, Nalaila Kiula. This aroused a lot of ire among politicians because they began wondering whether they were on the 'hit list' or not, so I was bad-mouthed a lot. I did not take this senior leader to court to show that I was fighting corruption; but chose to act because the prosecuting officials assured me that they had a strong case, and to let matters lie would not have been a responsible decision on my part. Kiula was acquitted and I was criticised again for taking him to court; though I take the criticism of me in this instance in stride, because at the end of the day the final decision whether to proceed with charging this former minister with corruption was mine. The second case was because many from the ministry for lands and human settlement development were also extremely corrupt, enabling some Tanzanian Indians to buy plots which they then quickly resold at a profit. We took the Indian fellow, whose name I cannot recall, who was a kingpin of that network to court and he was sentenced, I believe it was for at least two years.

The political establishment, particularly the opposition and certainly the diplomatic corps had expected a longer list of fellows being taken to court. Since we didn't do that people said we were covering up because many were friends, or we were afraid because the people involved in corruption held senior positions. I can assure you that there was no instance where the evidence could have stood in a court of law, but we decided not to go ahead out of personal consideration, or fear of political effect. As with the death sentence the final decision was mine, and I acted on the basis of whether the evidence was sufficiently strong to stand in court. So from the point of view of court cases the impact was not as dramatic as expected, though as a result of the commission I removed twenty thousand ghost workers from the public service payroll, dismissed eight hundred revenue collection officials, retired the following senior officers: forty-three magistrates, forty-one from the ministry of works, ten from the police, nine from the immigration department, six from the prime minister's office, and five parastatal chief executives. Furthermore, I dismissed three magistrates, as well as revoked the licences of five court brokers.

Another consequence of the commission's report was that we established the Prevention of Corruption Bureau (PCB), a body like this had not existed before in Tanzania. However, there were some teething problems with this organisation, as the director, Major General (Rtd), Anatory Kamazima, a stiff upper lip military man, and his deputy, Edward Hoseah, turned out to be almost incompatible with each other in character, attitude and personality. This meant that the bureau got to a slow start and then struggled somewhat. The resulting criticism that not enough was achieved is valid, but at least I laid the foundation stone for the bureau; which is now called the Preventing and Combating of Corruption Bureau, (PCCB).

After I left office I featured in an investigation by the PCCB when Ambassador Costa Mahalu was accused of corruption when purchasing Tanzania's chancery in Rome. As the economy was improving, we had decided to buy properties in capitals where Tanzania would always maintain a mission to reduce the country's expensive long-term rental commitments. We acquired a property in London, though we had to borrow some funds for its purchase, which created controversy at the time. We built a chancery in New Delhi; as Tanzania has a long connection with India and we couldn't find a suitable building to buy.

We decided to buy a property in Rome because the Food and Agricultural Organisation (FAO) is headquartered there. After quite a search we found a property which several other countries also wanted to purchase, though the female owner preferred Tanzania. She framed it quite bluntly that she would gain a higher price from the Libyans or the other African and Latin American countries who were interested, but she liked Tanzania and would sell to us provided that the sale price was split in a certain way. The vendor desired that part of the total price be paid into an Italian bank and the other part be paid offshore; she was very direct about this, I was told it was not an uncommon practice in Italy.

Ambassador Mahalu, who is a lawyer, tried to negotiate but subsequently advised the ministry of foreign affairs that the owner was immovable on this method of payment. I think our civil service was apprehensive of making the purchase in this fashion, so my permission was sought, which I gave. Hence the purchase was made by two separate payments, though the evidence is clear that the total sum came from the treasury in Tanzania, the total sum was paid to the bank account of the embassy, from where it was divided and paid into bank accounts in Italy and Monaco.

The PCCB learnt about this transaction as someone, who was not identified then or subsequently, called in on a radio programme, saying they were from Kibaha, and that they knew for a fact that this money had been stolen and people were being protected. I tried to explain privately to the PCCB that charging the ambassador with theft was unwarranted, their response was that I should publicly admit that this is what happened and attest that he had my permission to proceed in this manner. I was shocked when they took Mahalu to court. It was inconceivable that this transaction could have been done without my knowledge; ministers and civil servants always referred to me if there was any difficulty. It was ridiculous to think that no-one would seek my permission. Perhaps there was an underlying political motive, whether to show that the administration under the new president was more prudent, or give a warning to others, I don't know, but I said I was prepared to appear in court as a witness. Many politicians didn't like that I was going to do this, because I was setting a precedent which might impact on them later. But as the bureau was questioning my decision to buy this property and to authorise this method of payment, and, as far as I knew, the full payments were transacted in this manner, then why shouldn't I appear in court to give evidence as a witness for the defence? The issue that someone was being wrongly accused of diverting funds was more important to me than the precedent of a former head of state appearing in court. I was respectful in court; there was one time when the prosecution corrected me for asking a question in response, the young man said to me, "I am the one who is asking the questions", to which I apologised, which surprised those present. I am told that President Kikwete could not believe it when he was told I had appeared in court that day. But I had no ego in this matter, justice is what I wanted. If you are going to set the precedent of allowing the challenging of your predecessor, then you must be prepared to have him attest in his own favour.

I do not believe that past presidents should be taken to court for transgressions during their presidency. Certainly, if they have stolen something then there must be a way to recoup this, but to take a former president to court could undermine the whole concept of government. You must be careful not to lower the dignity of the office, it is necessary to preserve the aura and integrity of the highest office in the land; I regard this as part of the evolution of democracy. Though I add that there must be a way of removing someone who doesn't prove worthy of the office, and that way should be entrenched in the constitution and clearly spelt out. However, any course of action would depend on the strength of political parties in that country. Nevertheless, no president should be allowed to use his impunity to misbehave.

Returning to the case regarding the property in Rome, of course Mahalu was acquitted; there was no evidence of the diversion of funds for personal use by him. He never asked for compensation after the verdict, he said, "No, I just want my name cleared. It has been cleared that's it." The issue had become a cause célèbre, particularly fostered by the late Reginald Mengi and his IPP Media Group, but as the case progressed and the ambassador's innocence became clear, coverage abated. Once more Mahalu was decent, saying, "Let bygones be bygones."; this shows his professionalism.

Later Mahalu was appointed as chairman of the drafting committee of the Tanzanian Constitutional Review Commission, where he played a leading role in helping the government to produce a draft new constitution. You would expect him to be bitter about how he had been treated, but he was still willing to serve the government; I was told he worked well to harmonise positions so a draft could be agreed upon. Public service can be a thankless task, but there are many who continue to try their best, despite the criticisms or unfounded accusations of malfeasance they suffer. On the other side, no organisation has 100% perfect employees, which is the same within the public service.

A major issue which emerged once I had left office was the furore over the External Payments Account, often called EPA. My understanding is that my presidency was not the first one to allow debt purchase, this even occurred during Mwalimu's time. It was a common practice of international businesses which had earned Tanzanian Shillings but found that it was not favourable for them to transfer their money out of the country because of the poor foreign exchange rate. The foreign business would sell the amount or debt they held at a discount in return for the foreign currency they desired. They would receive a discounted proportion of their foreign exchange in return for that foreign exchange holder receiving 100% of the Tanzanian shillings or the debt.

I was initially very hesitant when I was advised that some people wanted to do this, until the Governor of the Bank of Tanzania, Daudi Ballali, came to me and explained the proposal to ease the substantial import-related external debts, known as the external payments arrears. He said those who wanted to buy the debts at a discount were prepared to give some money to CCM election campaign funds. He added, "Look, the pressure is on me to allow this to happen". The fraudsters exploited my loyalty to my party to persuade me to agree. I didn't see harm in doing something that had been done by others before and I had been told that everything would be properly transacted.

Should I have allowed this to happen? Could I have prevented it? I don't know if I could have prevented it. This was supposed to be a common business practice, yet I later learnt it was not and this malpractice occurred during my presidency and for that I should bear responsibility, but only to that extent. I'm not an accountant and did not manage the transactions, I really thought it was one or two transactions, I did not know it was on such a large scale. Apparently the total amount was 133 billion Tanzanian shillings, approximately USD 100 million; some people obviously sensed an opportunity to make some money fast! It never entered my head that people would forge documents of the external payments which stated that we authorised this fellow to own this debt of ours because he has purchased the debt for such an amount. I was shocked to later learn about this forgery, no-one told me about that at the time, I would have dealt with that if I had known.

In retrospect, I have to say that I feel I was used. *'There's no art to find the mind's construction in the face. He was a gentleman on whom I built an absolute trust.'* – from Shakespeare's *'Macbeth'*. I kept thinking of this quote; it does happen that people in whom you have confidence can betray you, this happened to me. People were just making money for themselves, it was not really in the interests of my party. I am not bitter, to what end would that serve? I do feel for the late Daudi Ballali because I knew him well enough to affirm that he would not have done such an evil thing as allowing those forged documents. We had worked very well together in putting the economy back on its feet before this happened. It was frustrating that I couldn't speak out about this when it became public, particularly as there was this persecution of Ballali, but in the end I decided that the best course of action was just to shut up, because what would my speaking out solve? It wouldn't have exonerated anybody. It was a very difficult situation for me and this was not helped by the presumption that I must have taken my cut, which is wrong, I didn't receive any money. I know that people have said that this EPA saga was arranged to benefit me, but I didn't have any foreign exchange of my own here which I could have converted anyway; I received nothing.

During this difficult time I often recalled from the Bible: *'Because the foolishness of God is wiser than men; and the weakness of God is stronger than men';* (Corinthians 1:25). This helped me then and still does today, it keeps my faith strong. My family remained very firm and loyal in their belief in me. Certainly my friends and those who had worked closely with me had trust in me, they knew I had behaved above board, and hadn't taken any money. It also gave me comfort that the people I worked with from the World Bank and IMF did not believe I was involved, the development partners as well; after you have worked with foreign governments for ten years they establish a record about what kind of person you are. This support for me helped to assuage my pain a little. But it is disconcerting, traumatic even, to wind up with such accusations against you after ten years of sacrifice to your nation.

Another unfounded criticism was that I gave my address as being State House when I borrowed money from NBC bank, which they claimed was a misuse of power. In fact this was a standard loan made at the usual interest rates, which I duly paid, and there is no restriction on a leader providing for their future income, as long as this is not done in a dishonest manner. Despite knowing that I would receive a retirement benefit as a former president, I was concerned that a new government might change the terms of retirement. Accordingly, I sought to arrange a steady and proven source of income for after I left office. Initially I thought of investing in farming, but an investment consultant advised against this due to the length of time it can take to see a return; he recommended that I should invest in a house instead, as the value usually holds, if not rises, and rental income can be at a good rate. The consultant suggested a property in Seaview, Dar es Salaam. I agreed and sought a loan from NBC bank of USD 500,000 to help with the purchase. When completing the application form for the loan I gave my address as State House, where I was living. The loan was provided at a commercial interest rate and there was a schedule of payments for the interest and principal which I complied with. During those first few years the rent was sufficient to pay the instalments to the bank. As I drew near to the end of my presidency, I reflected whether it was good to have an incumbent president with a loan, as this could be misinterpreted in the media. I determined to clear the debt before I left State House, which I managed with my final salary and benefits; all my obligations were met and we received the title to our property from the bank.

Then came a furore in the newspapers that I had misused the office of the presidency to get a personal loan which I had obtained at favourable rates; I had turned State House into a place for my own business, despite that Mwalimu had said the State House is a sacred place. This didn't upset me that much because it was all nonsense; however, Anna was angry, she stormed into the bank and complained:

> What kind of bank are you? I thought you were supposed to observe customer privacy? Where did these journalists get these details about dates and amounts, unless they got them from here? This is a commercial bank and you are not supposed to give particulars about customer loans and stuff like that.

I didn't know she had complained to the bank in this forthright manner until long afterwards. I understand that those employees of the bank who had dealt with my loan were eventually fired from the bank for breaching confidentiality.

So that's the story about my personal loan from NBC. I used the address as State House because that's where I was living and the loan was at a commercial interest rate, I did nothing wrong. I suspect this fuss was created because I was responsible for the privatisation of the NBC bank and there were those who were unhappy with this privatisation, so they sought to show that I had benefitted from this. Fortunately some of the more perceptive newspapers investigated the matter and realised there was no real story there and the issue faded away. I am grateful that I was able to obtain this loan to purchase the rental property, because if the state were to withdraw my pension I think the revenue would be enough to enable us to maintain our household.

I am curious about the media's assessment of my personal benefit whilst I was president, especially if you think of how the media attacked me about the bank loan to purchase the property in Seaview. I gave farewell addresses in several regions before stepping down, where I thanked the people for their past support of me and encouraged them to vote for the party's candidates. I was given gifts during these farewell rallies: chairs, walking sticks, two tractors with attachments, a small lorry, cattle and goats. I had thought that the media would be interested in how I put these gifts to use, whether I used them on my farm – which I did, or sold the items for personal gain, which I did not. But no, the media has no interest, yet they still occasionally come back to this legitimate bank loan, which has been paid off long ago.

I believe that parliamentarians should declare their assets each year, I did. I declared my assets before I was elected and when I was elected. I hoped that my ministers and other senior officials I appointed would follow my precedent, but no one followed suit, no one. They couldn't criticise me for being so open because my action was warmly welcomed by the people; but they decided not to follow my lead and I regret that this reticence has remained. Later I was peeved over this nonsense about the bank loan and decided that I would cease declaring my assets now I was retired. Of course I was criticised for this as well. Perhaps my not declaring my assets after I retired may have compounded those accusations of EPA earnings and the housing loan; though I doubt it. If you are a serious investigative journalist all you need to do is to pay 10,000 shillings to the registrar of land titles or registrar of businesses to ascertain what I own.

Our choice of a radar for the Julius Nyerere International Airport in Dar es Salaam became a controversy covered by local and international press. We had no functioning radar at this airport, the main air travel hub for the country, which meant some airlines were reluctant to fly there and some threatened to cease flying to this destination. KLM kept flying in, for which I respect them to this day. The ministry of defence suggested purchasing a radar which would cover Dar es Salaam and surrounding areas for civilian and military aircraft. Being able to serve both purposes was attractive so I said go right ahead with the purchase from BAE, (British Aerospace plc). Then the trouble started. Clare Short, the United Kingdom secretary of state for international development, she's a real socialist, thought we were outrageous in spending this money on a 'war machine'. She said that the UK was helping us in the economic recovery process, why did we want to spend GBP 28 million on a radar? Clare said she wanted to come to Tanzania to talk this over, I said please do come. She flew to Dodoma, where parliament was in session. I explained to her that it was a question of security and in delicate countries like ours you don't want to give an excuse for the military to say *'he has left us exposed; he doesn't care about our requirements'*. Furthermore it was unwise to have Dar es Salaam, the country's commercial capital if not the best part of the political capital, uncovered, while Zanzibar needed coverage as well and that the coverage should be for both civilian and military. The next morning we took Clare Short to a development project and a women's project then returned to Dar es Salaam together. When we landed at the airport the media was massing round; I said to her, "You take care of them because I have no interest in that". The media were surprised at how she had changed her view. Clare Short said that what I had explained to her made sense, she made it clear that any misunderstanding was over between us. The media were furious, they had really wanted to get at me. I understand that Tony Blair advised that the sale of the radar by BAE to the Tanzania should go ahead.

Much later it emerged that the radar system had been overpriced at USD 40 million and a Tanzanian who holds a British passport, Shailesh Vithlani, a marketing advisor to BAE, had received a 30% commission of over USD 12 million; I didn't know that this man was negotiating as a go-between between British Aerospace, the Tanzanian army, and ministries of defence and communications. This unfortunate issue then dragged on until the media realised that BAE had also sold overpriced jets to Saudi Arabia, which was a greater scandal. Also, the media finally realised that I hadn't taken any money on the purchase. There is always the presumption that the big man is getting his money, but I certainly didn't. Though I can't swear that the 'big man' in the ministry of communications, ministry of defence or the attorney general did not get something, I don't know; frankly I just don't want to know now. The exposure of the BAE Saudi Arabia deal raised questions in the United Kingdom parliament, with Tanzania's purchase coming under the umbrella of the exposé. The UK government demanded that British Aerospace recompense Tanzania, resulting in compensation of GBP 29.5 million which was allocated to education in Tanzania, to buy textbooks and desks, as well as teaching aids for the teachers.

Governing is difficult; there are so many things happening at the same time within twenty or so ministries; how do you know of everything which is going on? You can't micromanage. We have had a tradition with military purchases, such as that radar system, that once the case has been made for the purchase then you left it to the military to make the transaction. One of my recommendations to my successor was that while this may have been good practice in the past under Julius Nyerere's leadership when we were building up the army, purchases for the military had now grown to become expensive, therefore, the president may want to seek verification about the necessity for some of the expenditures, particularly regarding procurement of the large cost items and that the transactions are above board.

After sharing with you these unpleasant and unfounded allegations made against me, I will share a little on my home life whilst president, though not much, as I am a private man. One criticism of me was that I was not very sociable, which is true. Many's the time I would rather read a book than have hours of polite social conversation. Also, I had to be on guard at social occasions, for having visited me at State House could be a useful weapon either for self-promotion or for dealing with opponents. *'I've just had a talk with the President you know, we were having dinner the other day'*, that kind of using me for their self-interest, I do not like at all.

Furthermore, as you will now know from earlier in this book, I am shy; most of the strong friendships I have were formed when I was young and have carried on throughout my life and this small, yet strong circle of friends would drop by to visit me while I was president. I have appreciated my journalist friends throughout the years, including David

Martin[165], who had worked for *'The Tanganyika Standard'* since 1964. He led an interesting life, he was versatile and hardworking, with a tremendous sense of humour. He could be a little disrespectful as sometimes I was; I regard this as part of being a journalist. It was a moving moment for me when I paid my respects at his grave in Zimbabwe.

I did not appreciate it when people revered me as president and still don't like it when it happens now. Self-aggrandisement is not my style; I dislike glorification. I was the first Tanzanian president not to have my face portrayed on our currency. Asides for not wanting to show myself as 'the big man', I took into account the unnecessary cost of changing the currency. I insisted that I should not be addressed by the usual honorific title of *Mtukufu* (Glorious President); preferring the title of *Mheshimiwa* (Honourable), which is used for government ministers, members of parliament and regional commissioners. I regarded these two actions as a unifying factor in our newly multi-party nation. Furthermore, using the title of *Mtukufu* could be a divisive factor in newly independent and tribal countries.

I think modesty helps people to feel that you are just one of them – as undoubtably you are. I believe in moderation in all things. Mwalimu provided a good role model with his modest lifestyle, my faith and religious education has influenced me as well. A leader is human like anyone else, they can and do make mistakes. As president you are just carrying additional responsibilities for a limited period of time. The real challenge is not to be swayed by your surroundings and the many flatterers. Regrettably many African leaders portray themselves almost as if they are emperors. This offends me because it contravenes the basic principle that we are all equal. A leader must exercise caution on how they perceive their self-worth; your utterances are not proclamations.

The constant protection was a nuisance; many people think it must be fun to have these entourages made up of motorcycle outriders, escorts and more. I know there can be security concerns, but you must avoid excessive grandeur such as large entourages and shows of force. You are

---

165 Further information on David Martin's involvement with Tanzania and the liberation movement: http://www.sardc.net/en/david-martin-40-years-of-service-to-african-liberation/

the commander-in-chief, which means everywhere you go there will be some members of the uniformed services, especially on regional tours; but if there is an excessive show of eminence of office then you are distancing yourself from the people. For example, I missed that I could not go to my club for a beer and to talk to friends, which I had done most Saturdays beforehand. I understand that there are heightened security risks for all leaders nowadays, although, the level of protection must be justifiable. Protection measures must be controlled, otherwise they can be threatening to the people. A leader may end up being feared rather than respected. Moderation is called for, rather than a show of force. I often requested my bodyguards to keep their distance.

During my presidency I had surgery in Switzerland on my hip. In hindsight probably this wasn't conveyed well to the public, yet how much of your life must be public? The public think they own you. I was confident that my assistants, particularly the vice president, a very able person, and the prime minister could run the country while I was recuperating, and the party was in the hands of the Secretary General, Philip Mangula[166], a man of great integrity. I wasn't concerned. I kept working, of course, even producing my monthly broadcast, as I wanted to reassure the people that I was recovering well. Though I realise now that we did not give out enough information about the progress of my treatment, particularly as I had not warned the nation that I would be undergoing surgery. Perhaps the political parties were beginning to be interested if I should pass away, as then they would have an election!

I prayed before and after the operation, just as I pray every day now; I am sure that many people prayed for me then, for which I was grateful. I continued to attend church each Sunday and Feast day while I was president. I keep my faith to myself, I don't proselytise at all; I go to my Catholic church while Anna goes to her Lutheran church. I know any religion has its shortcomings, but overall, I regard religion a useful support to life. My faith provided me with strength during my time as president, still does.

I seldom worked on public holidays, unless there was an official engagement. I didn't take much by way of holiday; my only regular holi-

---

166 Secretary General of CCM 1997–2007.

day was Christmas when I would go to my house in my home village of Lupaso. I also have a house in Lushoto, where I appreciate the peace and nature, though I couldn't go there as often as I would have liked. It is quiet and cool up there in the Usambara mountains, with a calm atmosphere. You do need time to relax when you are president, but I was under such pressure to reform, to get the economy right, that I took little time off. One of the recommendations in my handing over notes to my successor was to make sure he took time off, that he shouldn't be as I was. Thankfully I slept soundly, the stress didn't get to me.

My favourite hobby was and still is reading. Mostly non-fiction, such as Hernando de Soto or Noreena Hertz and biographies. I also found British journals such as *'The Economist'*, *'The Spectator'*, the *'New Statesman'* helpful to keep abreast of global events. When I travelled abroad I always wanted to spend a little time in a bookshop, still do. Sadly the culture of reading has diminished markedly, so few people read nowadays. I don't think we read enough about what is happening in other countries in similar circumstances as ours with the same aspirations, how they are undertaking development. Study tours have become popular now, rather than reading, though perhaps this is because many members of parliament see this as an opportunity to collect travel allowances.

Anna was extremely supportive, she has been throughout our marriage. She is a very strong character and always has taken care of the worldly matters for our family, which I thank her for. She is down to earth, while I sit reading and thinking. At the State House everything is taken care of – food, transport, etc but she still was the one on hand to continue to take care of the family. When I got into office she was very helpful indeed, despite our tradition that the wife of the president cannot work in a paid position and that there was no constitutional position of first lady. This meant she had to give up her paid employment, which frustrated her as she wanted to use her skills. Hence she initiated The Equal Opportunities for All Trust Fund (EOTF) to supplement my efforts at raising the lot of women, particularly those in the rural districts. The fund's work includes teaching women basic entrepreneurship and value-add business skills, providing education on mother and child health issues and reproductive health to nurses and women, providing access to education for orphaned and street children, and assisting those with disabilities to set up small business, as well as providing some wheelchairs and ambulances. Each year before the Dar es Salaam international trade fair, commonly known in Tanzania as *Saba Saba*, Anna brings together women from the Mainland and Zanzibar to attend a three or four-day business development seminar. Afterwards they participate in the *Saba Saba* exhibition at the EOTF's stall, where Anna's involvement guarantees that the stall is visited by the president and other dignitaries, thus bringing good exposure for their small businesses. Through this fund Anna has done much to support some thousands of women in poverty, as well as some vulnerable children and disabled persons. Despite her advancing age she continues her commitment to the fund as I write this chapter. I am proud that she has been recognised for her work by being awarded the 'Order of the Smile' from the Polish government. Anna is the second African to win this award, the first being the late Nelson Mandela.

My family has been an important anchor in my life. Both as a son, but also as a parent. It was the anchor of my parents that saw me through to adulthood and Anna and my children have helped to keep our family together. I often wonder what kind of world I will leave to my children and their children, they have been born into a fast-changing world. My sons, Stephan and Nicholas, have been supportive as well, though they would ask me, "When are you going to settle down and rest? This country will always be here". Unusually for many African leaders my sons are not actively involved in political issues or processes. They have sworn not to enter active politics; maybe I deterred them because that is what I have done most of my life. Their standpoint, especially the younger son, who is a lawyer, is: "Listen you have sacrificed enough from this family for the country; you don't need others to sacrifice as you have done". They do follow what is going on and have strong views about the performance of people in politics, current and past; though I encourage them to keep their criticism to themselves. It did not disappoint me at all that they chose not to enter politics; I never considered pushing my sons into politics, as some other leaders around the world have done. I think temperamentally they would be very unsuited to the rigours of this career. I may well be intellectually arrogant, but I have to say that my sons are strong-minded and opinionated and these character traits are not good in politics

Under Tanzania's constitution I was permitted to be president for two five-year terms; I had no desire whatsoever to ask parliament to allow me to increase the term of office. I was tired, I had done enough for my nation and the media had started getting to me. I think a limitation on the number of terms a president may consecutively serve is good, two terms are an absolutely necessity to bring about change, then it is time for someone else to take over. It is helpful if the one who takes over knows the processes, structures, operations, and intra-relationships of government, in the sense that they have worked in or have advised government. If a leader comes in who has had minimal interaction with government then they spend the first three to four years trying to understand how government works in order to get their policies implemented. This can mean that ten years is not enough for that leader to achieve what they wanted to. I have talked about this with Joaquim Chissano, who had the opportunity of serving a third five-year term but turned it down. He told me that he felt that the people were beginning to feel that he had been president long enough, though he added that for the first five years you are reorganising government so that you can start implementation of your programme. Implementation commences during the second term, while the third term should be concerned with conclusion of the policies you implemented. This would leave the nation in a strong state to move forward. I appreciated what he said, especially if you are unfamiliar with government when you take the helm and of course you are an honourable leader. There is another side to this issue, we are now getting younger and younger leaders, what do they do after their ten years' service as president?

Looking at neighbouring countries we have seen leaders trying to retain power beyond their allotted term. If you have served well, yet choose to remain beyond your term, which results in a threat of unrest and violence, why do you, the leader, want to see that violence erupt? Why spoil your record of leadership and create a crisis; why? If such a leader does continue then they will almost be forced into a more autocratic rule. Some people appear to be messianic in their approach to power and leadership.

I ended up serving just over ten years, from 23 Nov 95 to 21 Dec 2005, when I handed over to my successor, Jakaya Kikwete. The election had been scheduled for 30 October 2005, but on 27 October the National Electoral Commission announced that the election was postponed to 14 December because of the death on the day before of opposition vice-presidential candidate Jumbe Rajab Jumbe, the running mate of Freeman Mbowe, the presidential candidate for the opposition CHADEMA (*Chama cha Demokrasia na Maendeleo* – Party for Democracy and Progress). Under electoral law an election must be postponed for at least twenty-one days if a presidential or vice-presidential candidate dies, hence my stay was extended.

I was upset because I had attuned myself to leaving, I had even moved most of my things out of State House into my home at Seaview. I had just held a farewell rally in Arusha and the next morning I was to fly to Tabora for another farewell rally. On returning from church the chief of presidential security came to me and said, "I am afraid we have bad news for you". He told me about Jumbe's death and that it meant that the election could not be held in three days' time. 'Good Lord why do you want to do this to me?' I muttered to myself, then said to my colleague, "Is there no way we can get around it?" and asked him to request the speaker of the National Assembly, Pius Msekwa, as well as the chairman of the National Electoral Commission to investigate this matter, but their responses were that we had no option but to postpone the election.

The general election was peacefully conducted, and I gratefully handed over to Jakaya Kikwete. There is a photo of me turning to the crowd saying, 'thank you, it's all over now, it's someone else's turn'. So many people noticed my relief, saying to me: "You really had felt it, this load on your shoulders".

"Yes, it was tough", I would respond. I had done what I had set out to do all those years ago when I spoke to Mwalimu about putting myself forward as a candidate. I felt that I had done my best under great pressure, at times it was almost a thankless task. Abraham Lincoln said: "Nearly all men can stand adversity, but if you want to test a man's character, give him power". I assure you I have no regrets about my conduct as president. Well, to the extent that I have any regret, it is that perhaps I should have been tougher in my conditions for passing on this important role to my successor.

Chapter 15

Pseudo Retirement

I felt such absolute relief that I no longer held the taxing roles of president and commander-in-chief and the alleviation of my tiredness increased when I relinquished the position of chairman of my party. It had been custom for the past president to retain the role of party chairman for the remainder of his term, though my predecessor, President Ali Hassan Mwinyi, had set a precedent by asking to hand over to me as soon as possible when I was appointed president. I declared to President Jakaya Kikwete: "I am not waiting for you to ask me to do so, I am telling you that I am going to leave. I am going to hold an extraordinary congress of the party and I want you to take over the chairmanship".

He responded, "Well, if that is your wish, fine". Thus I retired from the presidency and chairmanship of the party. There is a council of elders within the party, comprising former chairmen and vice-chairmen of CCM, but we rarely meet. Other than that, I hold no formal position within the party, other than being merely a member. People did try to involve me in the politicking of the 2015 general election, especially in the nominations for candidates, which I didn't like one bit.

While former heads of state are provided with retirement benefits, I was conscious that these could be altered at some time in the future which might place Anna and myself on an unsure financial footing. I wasn't concerned for my sons, we had provided them with a good education and it was now their responsibility to make their own way in the world. The house we had purchased in Dar es Salaam would provide a rental income and we also had a home in Lupaso, the village I grew up in. Throughout our married life prudent Anna had acquired parcels of land: some land in Kigamboni, as well as a small livestock farm in Bunju, both properties are not far from Dar es Salaam. Then there is my peaceful retreat, our property in Lushoto, where I go to rest, think and write, though I can only type on my laptop using three fingers and don't know if I could write poetry nowadays. I have a whole library of books there; when I travel I always seek to visit bookshops. I like to read a lot, especially biographies. Other people's lives fascinate me, particularly political biographies because they give you an insight to the psychology during the span of a leader's life. I also find books by colonial fellows who worked in Tanganyika interesting, what their impressions were and what the country was like in those days. For relaxed reading I like detective stories – Henning Mankell, Agatha Christie and Edmund Bentley are favourites; I enjoy the wit of PG Wodehouse as well. Reading provides me with solitude, which I cherish; I do not watch many movies, and particularly abhor war movies.

I had seen this dilapidated place in Lushoto whilst visiting one of my ministers there and was told that the house had belonged to a leader from the independence movement, but since his death his children couldn't agree on who should inherit the property, so had left it to run down, and had recently decided to sell it. I was able to acquire the property using my savings and eventually renovate it. I later purchased a farm in Morogoro through a connection from years before I became president, when I had served on the board of a private, predominantly Indian secondary school in Dar es Salaam, the Shaaban Robert Secondary School. The secretary to that board was an Indian lawyer, who always insisted that if we had a board meeting it must be between Monday and Thursday, because on Friday he would travel to his farm in Morogoro. His children inherited the property, all of whom were absentee bar one son, who was now anxious to also leave Tanzania, hence was trying to sell the farm which was a participant in the Mtibwa Sugarcane Outgrowers Scheme. The Mtibwa Outgrowers Association preferred that the property was acquired by one person, rather than a partnership. When the son learnt that it was me who was interested in buying the farm, he said: "Oh, my father used to speak so well of him, so this is the one I want to sell it to". The farm doesn't provide much income, but I enjoy spending time there.

It's funny how life goes on after completing one's presidency. I had not planned to do anything, however, it became clear quite soon that I was going to continue to be involved in leadership, though on an international rather than national stage. I enjoy this work, it is stimulating and rewarding to interact with peers and work together to improve the conditions of the poor, oppressed and marginalised throughout the world, though I confess I do not like the associated requirement for travel.

Requests for me to serve on international bodies started pouring in, the first came within a very short time of leaving office, when Dr Patrick Bergin from The African Wildlife Foundation came to see me to plead that I join his board. Sir Quett Ketumile Masire[167] was already on the board, but they wanted me to join because of the wealth of wildlife in Tanzania and my interest in taking care of the wildlife. I agreed, having been on the board of the Tanzania National Parks Authority (TANAPA) when I was editor of the party newspapers. Tanzanians value the revenue from tourism, and there is a perennial question of how much park revenue should be devolved to the immediate local population as an incentive for their respecting the park and its wildlife. Disappointingly, I do not see much real appreciation of the wildlife itself; nor do many Tanzanians seem to cherish how beautiful their country is. This is a challenge for the minister of natural resources and tourism, particularly in educating the younger generation about the land, its flora and fauna, so they learn to value it. The Kenyans appreciate their land and wildlife more than us Tanzanians.

I enjoy visiting our parks and wish I had the time and resources to visit more often, there is so much to see, including the beaches, especially Kilwa on the coast. During Mwalimu's and my time we made an effort to take visiting foreign dignitaries to see a national park. I established Kitulo National Park in the Southern Highlands as Tanzania's fourteenth

---

167 President of Botswana, July 1980–March 1998; Vice-President September 1966–July 1980.

national park. One of the things I said to my successor was, "Look there is a lot of work here, but you must find time to relax". This was something I had failed to do, and I am glad President Kikwete took the time to visit the parks.

I was happy to be approached by the Club de Madrid as I was impressed by the calibre of the former national and international leaders who were members, and there was a diverse representation from all continents. I appreciate that the Club de Madrid seeks to look at international affairs and current issues and offer a democratic assessment of possible solutions. I thought I could help by offering an African view of international affairs and issues; as well as offering my own thoughts. I find it refreshing to work with my peers and appreciate the worthy scholars and practitioners from various fields who join us at our meetings to present a paper; this helps you see things from a different perspective. The Club de Madrid aids leaders who are still in office to gain another viewpoint of what is happening around the world. When I look back at my time in office, I have to admit I missed this learned input from others a lot; unfortunately I often did not receive a rich range of ideas and a broad perspective of views from which to make a decision.

Once I joined the Club de Madrid, I was told about a particular programme where I could help: The Shared Societies Project, which is concerned with how to build unity in newly independent countries that are multi-racial and multi-religious. The concept of shared society is important in these unstable times and appropriate for Africa because we Africans are so multi-faceted on religious, racial and tribal grounds. I am pleased to be part of this project and regret that while during the independence struggle there was a movement towards unity and to forget about these differences, we Africans who fought for independence haven't been able to sustain this unity these days as well as we should. Tanzania is one of the few countries which has managed to safeguard unity. Regrettably, very few sub-Saharan countries have managed to maintain this precious sense post-independence.

I was asked to be co-chair of the Investment Climate Facility for Africa (ICF) with the internationally known Irish businessman, Niall FitzGerald. I was pleased to receive this request as I had been a member of the Commission for Africa which recommended the establishment of this body in its 2005 report *'Our Common Interest.'* This is a furtherance of the concept that there is a lot you can do by yourselves, particularly in identifying problems, bringing people together to discuss and decide on the way to tackle them, determining how much effort you can manage yourselves and when to seek the help of others. The ICF reflected my personal philosophy of how development should operate: development being in your own hands, to think, plan, consult and/or obtain help from other parties; you will note the similarity to Tanzania's TASAF. A country identified the problem, recognised there was something they could do about it, though with extra assistance from ICF, whether by providing knowledge, professional experience and/or finance. The implementation process had to be supervised by the country itself, thus ensuring that ownership of the project was embedded with the country, rather than being the ICF's responsibility. The ICF contributed up to 30%, though sometimes the costs were shared 50/50. To my immense disappointment ICF struggled to obtain sufficient funding and ceased operations at the end of 2016. I would like to see ICF operate once more, as there are still many matters which it could help with.

The ICF assisted governments to improve their investment climate, for example an issue brought to us was the too lengthy and/or costly registration of companies, whether local or international. We introduced systems and procedures to reduce these barriers to business. In some countries it can take five years to settle a business dispute, which can deter foreign investment. ICF reviewed the judicial system, particularly the commercial codes; trained staff and initiated the digitising of court documentation. An added benefit to introducing electronic records is that it reduces corruption because everyone can access the evidence and judgement. The ICF also aided the speeding up of the process of cargo handling in ports, record keeping of land suitable for industrial use and registration for taxation by new businesses.

It pains me to say that the ICF was not successful in Tanzania, even though ICF was headquartered here. It is very disappointing that we were unable to instigate the land rights and land registration programme in Tanzania. There was a time when the government was trying to advance the notion of public-private partnerships, and one way to attract foreign enterprises to enter in a partnership is to ensure that if an investor wanted to build a factory then the investor could be assured that the land they want to utilise will be properly demarcated and appropriate compensation paid for acquired land. We have often seen land bought or acquired, yet the enterprise does not commence operations due to a dispute over the ownership of the land or compensation dues. The poor should have their land rights enshrined, but we also need a commercial court system through which you can negotiate, explain the long-term benefits to the poor, and make appropriate final compensation.

This reticence by Tanzania to embrace pro-investment initiatives gives an insight into our cultural perspective of economic development; there remains a hangover from our socialist background. We are behind in our understanding of business, we don't know enough about banking and investment. This was brought home to me when, as co-chair of the Investment Climate Facility, I experienced such difficulty trying to persuade my country to change procedures, processes and rules. The ICF had more success with improving the investment climate in Rwanda, for example with the litigation processes for investors, than in Tanzania. It was a bitter irony that I could not help my own country improve such commercially related legal processes; but could help other countries.

I was asked to be involved with the pilot programme for the United Nations initiative 'Delivering as One'. Eight developing countries from around the world worked on a project during 2007 to 2008 to harmonise the delivery of differing UN organisations. The aim was to shape coherent programmes, reduce transaction costs for governments and lower the UN's overhead costs. There was quite some resistance by the UN organisations because they preferred to keep their independence. I enjoyed working with Oscar Fernandez-Taranco of the United Nations Development Programme (UNDP) in Tanzania; he was very enthusiastic and worked hard to make the pilot a success here.

My biggest limitation to being involved in these international bodies is lacking an assured source of funding, especially because you must travel a lot. I cannot travel alone, as I am required to be accompanied by my chief bodyguard and two additional security personnel and I prefer to travel with my personal assistant to help me with my work, which continues wherever I am. I don't understand our government's requirements that I must travel with a protocol officer, though. Hence accepting international requests becomes expensive to the government of Tanzania. Double standards exist though, when an international organisation or conference calls upon someone like Tony Blair or Bill Clinton they are paid an appearance fee for their speech, whilst often us Africans are expected to give our views and assessment for free. I find this unbecoming really, I have a foundation which I need to earn money for. Yet I can't say no to these invitations because they do need a sub-Saharan Africa perspective from someone who has experience and has felt the impact of development aid. So I go, though I do ask for my travel and accommodation costs to be paid for.

It was late December 2007, I had been out of office for some years so was not up to date with all political activity in the region when the crisis in Kenya burst on the scene. Joaquim Chissano, under the umbrella of the African Forum of Former Heads of State, called Ketumile Masire, Kenneth Kaunda and I, saying let's rush there before things get very bad. We met with the Orange Democratic Movement (ODM)[168], Raila Odinga's party, President Mwai Kibaki[169] and others. Unfortunately we struggled without the necessary financial resources with which to effectively carry out a programme of reconciliation or help, until John Kufuor, then Chairman of the African Union, came in early January, as well as Jan Eliasson from the UN. They proposed a three-person mediation team led by the late Kofi Annan, with Graça Machel[170] and me, which would be financed by the African Union. Yoweri Museveni came later in January in his capacity as chairman of the Heads of State Summit of the East African Community, though he made some statements which made some think he was pro one side.

Thankfully our presence calmed matters down, particularly when we visited the internally displaced persons to tell them we were trying our best to resolve the situation, we wanted to give them some hope. This phenomenon of the internally displaced persons and those injured and killed much saddened me. We went to the soccer stadium at Eldoret

---

168 Since 2012 known as the Coalition for Reforms and Democracy CORD.

169 President of Kenya December 2002–April 2013.

170 First Lady of South Africa July 1988–June 1999, First Lady of Mozambique November 1975–October 1986.

which was full of these poor people who had fled for their lives. We saw the remains of the church in Eldoret which had been set on fire on New Year's day, killing over forty women and children who had sought refuge there. Those poor innocent little children who were killed or injured, so sad. What did *uhuru*/independence mean to these suffering people who had lost loved ones, or been injured and/or had to flee their homes? How could any leader condone this? It was tragic, I hope this never happens in my country.

Negotiations began, though we found both sides very intransigent. We would meet each team separately, then together; when together they would have fierce arguments. Sometimes I thought they would literally go for each other's throat. At first it was a question of who won the general election until we said, "Look, it is now a fait accompli, you can't continue this argument, unless you want more violence. So let us talk about how the country can be governed in fairness with representation of both sides". This was not easy for both parties to agree upon, particularly as each side wanted exclusive power. Ironically though, if matters got very heated we would adjourn to have a cup of coffee and stroll outside together, where they would mix as if they were compatriots or even friends, conversing easily and sometimes laughing! With the combinations and permutations of Kenyan politics one of them had been in the same party as the other at some point so they knew each other well.

It was especially difficult to persuade the ODM that they had to accept Kibaki as president. Eventually, we did agree on the issues that would have to be tackled by the new government, as well as the size of its cabinet, which was going to be huge at forty-four ministers. My president then came to help in his capacity as new chair of the African Union. He decided that the mediation team would meet the two leaders, Kibaki and Odinga accompanied only by their lawyers: Attorney General Amos Wako and James Orengo. We would 'lock ourselves in' until we finally resolved the outstanding issues. We stressed to the two leaders that what mattered was mutual respect and establishing a working relationship as it was high time for them to be pragmatic. Fortunately by then they had realised that the stalemate could not continue, they had to find a solution. What's more the effect on major businesses such as tourism and flower export were beginning to be felt by many wealthy Kenyan business people. Eventually, Kibaki and Odinga reached an agreement and we decided not to call in the negotiating team; rather we would present that team with a fait accompli. This was because the negotiators, Martha Karua, who was Minister of Justice, and ODM's William Ruto were the most difficult to deal with, having exacerbated tension during the mediation process. The atmosphere changed when we got Kibaki and Odinga together without Karua and Ruto present. When these two heard that they were being invited to witness the signing of the agreement[171] they were furious, saying there had been a conspiracy to persuade Kibaki to agree.

As mediator you must clearly spell out the pluses and minuses of each side's position to both parties. Of course there are pluses and minuses on both sides, but what would be the consequences? You must be frank and transparent about the consequences of failure, then appeal to their consciences because deep down they are human beings. You tell them what you have seen as well as the likely further suffering of the people should the problem continue, in the hope that the disputing leaders will soften a little. I think it was appealing to their conscience, "Look, we have come to the edge of the precipice and it's up to you now", which brought Kibaki and Odinga to reach an agreement. I ask the leaders to work with the mediator(s) to find the common denominator that can hold them together. This was my toughest mediation assignment outside of Tanzania; the toughest assignment I have faced throughout my working life was the Zanzibar issue concerning a third term for their president. That situation had been more challenging personally as I was the leader, while in this Kenyan crisis we were only the mediators, although failure would have been a bad reflection on the mediation team. I am proud of my role as a mediator on this difficult Kenyan assignment.

This was the only time I worked with Kofi Annan. He listened, he asked questions, he was very good at consulting with the affected parties. My sole complaint was that at times he seemed too media conscious, often his comment was, "What do the media say?" Though to be fair maybe it was his people pushing this, rather than him. This is the United

---

171   The power-sharing agreement, the Nation Accord and Reconciliation Act 2008 was signed on February 28, 2008. It is estimated that up to 1,400 people died during the fifty-nine days, while up to 600,000 were forced to flee from their homes.

Nations: let's have a picture, who is going to talk, what shall we say? In very difficult negotiations you must be sparse with disclosure. I know the newspapers want their headline, but you should limit yourself to saying: "Today we made some progress", that's it.

Assisting the South Sudan independence referendum, held in January 2011, was a painfully slow-moving undertaking for me. The Republic of Sudan was not keen on it, though it could not obstruct the proposed referendum because the government had committed to the referendum in the 2005 Naivasha Agreement (also known as the Comprehensive Peace Agreement) between the government of Sudan and the Sudanese People's Liberation Movement. I was asked to be a member on the UN Secretary-General's Panel on the Referenda in the Sudan, along with former Portuguese Foreign Minister António Monteiro and Nepalese public servant Bhojraj Pokharel. We were ably supported by the accomplished Eritrean diplomat, Haile Menkerios[172], who was the special representative and head of the UN mission in Sudan. I was impressed by the attitude of the then Vice President, Ali Osman Taha[173]; you could see he was a hard-liner, but he was a good listener and gracious, receiving us whenever we wanted to meet with him. It was a good venture in the sense that what we were really doing was monitoring the progress of preparations and quietly counselling to minimise potential hitches, especially at the political level. The Sudanese government officials moved very tardily indeed on voter registration and delivery of the ballot papers, which made us sceptical. There was also a problem with the disputed territory of Abyei. We were there to monitor on voting day, which went surprisingly well. It was very difficult to challenge the result of the referendum, as the vote was overwhelmingly for independence. Working on this gave me great satisfaction, especially that we managed to conclude the exercise without making enemies of the South or the North. So, I

---

172 UN Special representative and head of mission in Sudan March 2010–July 2011; UN Special representative and head of office to the African Union as under-secretary-general from July 2013.

173 Foreign Minister of Sudan 1995–1998; Second Vice President of Sudan January 2005–July 2011; First Vice President July 2011–December 2013.

was involved in the birth of a nation, South Sudan becoming the newest country in the world on 9 July 2011.

Whilst working on this I realised the bureaucracy of the UN and its size; this is a huge organisation. But should we Africans be asking ourselves: why do we need the UN? Isn't it a testament of failure on our part? Why can't we Africans avoid such conflict? Such strife is a diminution of the independence of a country; a reflection of the poor decisions we make that cause uproar.

The continuing problems in the Eastern Congo of the Democratic Republic of the Congo consumed a lot of my time after I left office; in fact this situation continues to be a cause of concern. Olusegun Obasanjo and I were appointed UN special envoys in late 2008 to work on the negotiations between the Congolese government and the National Congress for the Defence of the People (CNDP), trying to bring Presidents Paul Kagame[174] and Joseph Kabila[175] to work together to subdue the armed rebel groups. We found it impossible to deal with the ragtag political parties; they would sign agreements and agree on repatriations, then within weeks they were quarrelling about what the signed agreement meant. When negotiating I would look at those leaders and say to myself, what are these people fighting for? The cost of deprivation of the women and children – murder, rape, child soldiers, the migration of people fleeing from their homes and livelihoods, is this suffering worth what these leaders are fighting for? Our fruitless efforts at mediation were a disappointment to us; after we had officially presented our input Obasanjo said, "This is the last time they will see me involved in this". Obasanjo and I wondered how long the negotiated agreement would hold; I recall he estimated three years, and he was right as during 2012 we were called upon by the International Conference of the Great Lakes Region to mediate once more. I believe that as long as the Democratic Forces for the Liberation of Rwanda (FDLR) exists as an armed group in the Democratic Republic of the Congo we will not see any substantial changes. The process of disarming must go ahead; it was a crucial obstacle to the

---

174   President of Rwanda since April 2000.

175   President of the Democratic Republic of Congo since January 2001.

peace process that Obasanjo and I tried to help with and continues to be. Disarmament might lead to loss of life, but it would be worth it for the majority of the people, who have been suffering for such a long time.

The meeting of the Panel of Eminent Persons organised by the UN Conference on Trade and Development (UNCTAD) was another UN initiative I was involved in, along with Gro Harlem Brundtland[176], my colleague Joaquim Chissano and others. It was chaired by Fernando Henrique Cardoso[177], a fellow member of the Club de Madrid. Frankly, I don't think our report changed the outlook or the thinking within UNCTAD. It is hard to bring change within a conservative institution you know, and when UNCTAD tried to get into the meat of a problem they were told that this was an area for the World Trade Organization (WTO).

My favourite UN project is the UN Commission on the Legal Empowerment of the Poor. I worked on this with Gordon Brown[178], the co-chairs were Madeleine Albright[179] and Hernando de Soto, a man whose writing I admire; the executive director, Naresh Singh, was good as well. Our report is called: *'Making the Law Work for Everyone*[180]*'*. The right to economic participation is to me of equal, if not greater importance than ensuring the right to democratic participation. I liked working on this commission because we addressed real problems challenging the poor which I will summarise. There are four components, or pillars, of legal empowerment of the poor. Access to justice and the rule of law is the first component. To ensure that everyone has the fundamental right to legal identity and is registered at birth. How many impoverished citizens across the world are registered on a national identity database and/

---

176 Prime Minister of Norway February 1981–October 1981, May 1986–October 1989 and November 1990–October 1996. Secretary General World Health Organisation July 1998–July 2003.

177 President of Brazil January 1995–January 2003.

178 Prime Minister of UK June 2007–May 2010.

179 USA Ambassador to the UN January 1993–January 1997; USA Secretary of State January 1997–January 2001.

180 http://www.undp.org/content/dam/aplaws/publication/en/publications/democratic-governance/legal-empowerment/reports-of-the-commission-on-legal-empowerment-of-the-poor/making-the-law-work-for-everyone---vol-ii---english-only/making_the_law_work_II.pdf. Published 2008.

or have a birth certificate? We must repeal or modify laws and regulations that are biased against the rights, interests and livelihoods of poor people. We must facilitate the creation of state and civil society organisations and coalitions who work in the interest of the excluded, and the voice and representation of the working poor should be strengthened in social and political dialogue.

Governments must have a formal judicial system, land administration system and relevant public institutions which are accessible to the poor by recognising and integrating customary and informal legal procedures with which the poor are already familiar. Their access to legal services should be institutionalised so that the poor can learn about laws that affect them and be able to take advantage of them. Concrete measures should be taken for the legal empowerment of women, minorities, refugees and internally displaced persons, with support mechanisms for alternative dispute resolution. You can see the parallels of this project to the Investment Climate Facility.

The second pillar relates to property rights for the poor and oppressed, including how to establish an operating legal framework and how to address the problematic issue of inheritance. Labour rights is the third pillar, especially important for women and children, who are so often oppressed; the issue of slavery comes under labour rights. It is vital to create synergy between the protection and the productivity of the poor, through improving the quality of labour regulation and the functioning of labour market institutions; and ensuring a minimum package of labour rights for workers and enterprises in the informal economy. Governments should seek to increase access to employment opportunities, expand social protection for poor workers, promoting measures that will guarantee access to medical care, health insurance and pensions. As women are a major force of poverty reduction in poor communities it is important that legal empowerment drives gender equality. The fourth pillar relates to the informal business sector. A 2005 study[181] by Hernando de Soto's Institute for Liberty and Democracy found that it was difficult for 90% of Tanzanians to enter the legal economy and in

---

181 'Program to Formalize the Assets of the Poor in Tanzania and Strengthen the Rule of Law: Diagnosis Progress Report. Vol 1'. Institute for Liberty and Democracy (ILD) Lima 2005.

fact 98% of all businesses were operating extralegally. All of these are worthy recommendations. How to get them implemented is the crux of the matter.

Boutros Boutros-Ghali[182] approached me and said:

> Look as you can see, I'm getting on in age. The South Centre is one of the international legacies of Nyerere, (founding chairman from 1995 to 1999). We had two other chairmen after that, (Luis Fernando Jaramillo from Colombia and Gamani Corea from Sri Lanka), then I took over. But I'm getting on and I think it is time I passed this on to someone else. I have settled on you to take this over. Not only because you are from the South, but you have worked with Mwalimu, you know what his ideas were, therefore you can protect them well.

I regard the South Centre as a good cause and have been their chair since 2006. I also appreciate the opportunity to continue to project the profile of Mwalimu on the international scene. Incidentally this involvement turned out to be a blessing in disguise because it got me away from the country at a time when there was this nonsense of allegations in the media about my service to this country as president.

Although we meet only twice a year it is quite demanding to keep track of the activities of the centre. When Mwalimu was the chair, he could spend two or three weeks at the centre trying to get up to date with what was happening and initiating activities. He would travel there with his entourage, but I do not have the means to travel there with an entourage and stay for a long time. Thankfully we have a good executive director, Martin Khor, who served on the South Commission, the precursor to this centre, so he understands well the origin and aims of the South Centre.

My work with the South Centre provides me with great satisfaction. We undertake research on all aspects, for example global governance,

---

182   Secretary-General of the United Nations January 1992–December 1996; Chair of the South Centre 2003–2006.

economic matters, relationships between countries, intellectual property rights and health issues. Though I regret that many African countries do not take advantage of our information. For example, the South Centre's work has helped me argue the case against the economic partnership agreements between Europe and Africa. Why should we have all these international organisations? These are all funded by the developed countries and isn't this a way of preserving the status quo? This is something that has been troubling me since my involvement with the Commission for Africa. I recall we were having a working breakfast where there were some journalists with us. I said:

> If the Africans don't move fast enough they will just be a market for the developed countries, nothing will be made in African countries, even for their own use.

A journalist asked:

> Why are you complaining about that?

I replied:

> Because some of the business rights we are defending will ensure that you will have oligopolies with only large multi-nationals. Tell me a good reason why there shouldn't be a businessman in Tanzania who produces enough toothpaste for the country? Why we should Tanzanians use Colgate toothpaste which is produced in another country? I know there are economies of scale, but there are also economies of dignity too.

Another example is cornflakes; Anna puts out cornflakes for breakfast which are produced in America. Is this what the free trade market is about? Doesn't Tanzania produce enough maize, why don't we help Tanzania make cornflakes for our own consumption? I don't mind getting something special, like wine from France, but cornflakes? Yet again I raise the necessity of a change of attitude or mindset amongst us Africans to self-realisation and self-assertion.

Anyway, the journalist I spoke with during that breakfast meeting differed very much with my view. Yet the more I have served on these missions the more I realise how skewed in favour of the developed countries of the West the structures are, not only of the economy, but also of politics. Which is why now when China is making inroads into Africa we hear the West saying, 'Watch out for the Chinese, they will take all your land'. The Chinese have been here since independence and haven't taken our land. They helped us to build the 1,860 kilometre railway line which links landlocked Zambia to the port of Dar es Salaam. Built during 1970 to 1975, it was China's largest single aid project at the time, costing USD 406 million, yet they didn't take our land.

Because of my interest in education I was happy to be asked to be a trustee for the new Aga Khan University in Arusha. The Aga Khan has great resources, so it will be a notable university for East Africans. I helped to remove some misgivings of people from Arusha and government, especially since the Aga Khan's administrators of the project took so long for the initial preparations. They say that building this new university will be a fifteen-year USD 450 million project.

"I cease to be a person dealing with my nation, I am more of an international leader now", was a complaint of Mwalimu after stepping down as president. I find this as well, I receive more requests for my input from the international community than from my fellow citizens. Outsiders can see my worth in contributing to the thinking of the world on issues relating to development for the people and I still want to contribute. I suppose you could call me an internationalist. I appreciate that I am still needed, but it does seem odd that I seem to be appreciated internationally rather than in Tanzania. Some colleagues have said this is because in Tanzania people don't respect intellectuals, they are not thought of as an asset to the nation, and there is a certain laxity, a certain inertia in Tanzania. We past leaders are regarded as fine for social occasions, but definitely not wanted for really serious work in our own countries. I am usually called upon to go to dinners at the State House a mere six hours before they are due to be held, to be used as a 'flower on the wall'. They expect me to attend state ceremonies such as Independence Day or Union Day; if I don't show up they say what has made him mad that he has absented himself?

It is an irony that I seem to be recognised for my post-presidency involvement in leadership not by my own countrymen, but by those outside of Tanzania. Perhaps some people are worried I would meddle in Tanzanian affairs if I was more used here. I know that some were concerned I was competing with my successor, trying to take the shine off him. Yet us former leaders can be of help to current leaders as we have the benefit of experience and hindsight. Also, being one step removed means that sometimes we may raise issues which those closer to the current leader may feel unable to do. I regret that such private interaction does not occur between current and past leaders, generally across Africa. I think this is a serious omission or shortcoming in Africa, a real loss to our people. I consulted with my predecessor about Zanzibar, as he had been president of Zanzibar. He also helped me with historical matters, and of course he contributed at party meetings. Festus Mogae told me that he consulted with his predecessor, yet he is the only other African leader I know who did this. For example I don't think Jacob Zuma is on talking terms with Thabo Mbeki, who has much to offer. Of course, the extreme is how Frederick Chiluba[183] treated his predecessor Kenneth Kaunda[184], Zambia's first president. I quietly told Chiluba, "Look, you don't build on the sins of your predecessor, you build on the good foundations he laid, or the good things he did do. That is what will give you support; no-one praises you for knocking down your predecessor". It was tough talking to Chiluba about this, but it needed to be said.

When I was approached for my thoughts on a new constitution for Tanzania one of the recommendations I made was that it would be helpful if we could have a small second chamber in parliament as a kind of hibernation point before implementation of legislation, where the proposed legislation could be reviewed by people of substance and experience. For example, there has been a demand by the legislature that mining contracts that are entered into with foreign entities should be scrutinised by parliament, as well as approved or ratified by parliament. With great respect, I don't think most parliamentarians would understand half of

---

183   President of Zambia November 1991–January 2002.
184   President of Zambia October 1964–November 1991.

what is in such contracts. But if you had another sphere where people could take their time to review such contracts and then refer them back to the house, then this would be more helpful. This would provide an opportunity for learned and impartial checks and balances, providing some governance review. This should counteract inadequate, inappropriate or partisan legislation, including that with a bias towards central government over local government. The members of this second chamber would be retired professionals who are prepared to give expert and impartial advice, such as chiefs of staff, former chief secretaries and business leaders, though this group could not include past presidents, as this might colour recommendations that go to the incumbent.

I am proud of our Benjamin William Mkapa Foundation. It grew from a seed planted by Bill Clinton when he visited me during my last year of office; he had come to review progress of the Clinton Foundation HIV and AIDS programme in Zanzibar. He asked me what I was going to do after concluding my term later that year. I said, "Oh I am going to retire, I don't know yet what to do".

"Why don't you start a foundation" he suggested, to which I responded that I did not have the money to start a foundation. Bill Clinton advised that as the cause I was interested in, HIV and AIDS, was such an important problem he was sure I would be able to attract funding. I was a little doubtful, but he kindly offered to ask his staff to look into the possibility of receiving funding. I am grateful to Bill Clinton for this initial encouragement and subsequent financial support.

The first phase of five years, which was funded by the government of Norway and the Clinton Health Access Initiative, concentrated on hiring, training and placing 'Mkapa Fellows'. These employees were posted to outlying stations in neglected areas of the country where most professionals ordinarily don't like to live and work. It was important to me that the foundation provided practical on the ground assistance to those who were much in need and often overlooked. Our fellows know that they will work in under-served areas, and we provide incentives such as a housing allowance, mobile phone and communication allowance, as well as a slightly increased salary. We provide a laptop if there is electricity available so they can study and improve their knowledge. This first phase proceeded well, and we were gratified at our high staff retention rate. Most of those who left did so because they were attracted by the higher salaries offered by international agencies; staff retention is a common problem for developing nations.

The second phase expanded to include nurses, then pharmacists. There was no competition with the Tanzanian government's TACAIDS, which I had established during my term in office. We communicated clearly that the foundation was there to supplement and help TACAIDS in the fight against this scourge, rather than compete with it. Our training programmes are of such good quality that government asked us to train and recruit nurses and pharmacists for their programme. The Global Fund to Fight AIDS, Tuberculosis and Malaria (commonly known as The Global Fund) became our new major donor, and the foundation also received support from Irish Aid, the Abbott Fund and the United Nations Population Fund. Frustratingly, because the foundation carried my name it was difficult for Tanzanians to understand during the foundation's infancy that this was not my money and the foundation was not my foundation. Some people assumed I was in charge and that I had a lot of money, so could give them some. Eventually, the time came when I felt my foundation should seek funds from within the country in keeping with my ethos of self-help. I have been pleasantly surprised to find that our internal fundraising efforts have been successful, I think it has helped that the foundation is now well-known for its work. The foundation has grown so well that we now have a plot of land in Dar es Salaam on which we will construct a building, partly for our own offices and the balance of the building we will lease to bring in income to help meet the running costs of the foundation.

Taking part in these organisations provides me with the opportunity to interact with many fine minds around the world. Many I knew from my time as president and I appreciate now being able to have a relationship which is not based on national interests. The names of people I have enjoyed or currently enjoy working with follow, though not all are listed. From Canada, the former Prime Minister Jean Chrétien[185]. I am

---

185   Prime Minister of Canada November 1993–December 2003.

great friends with Martti Ahtisaari[186]; we first worked together throughout the liberation struggle in Southern Africa when he served as United Nations commissioner for Namibia, working to secure the independence of Namibia from the Republic of South Africa. We work together well, then and now; he has a strong connection to Tanzania. Martti introduced me to the phenomenon of the sauna, so I have a sauna in my home, though Anna describes my using the sauna as an excuse for me to sit and be lazy! I'm not sure if I will be popular for mentioning this leader: Sadiq al-Mahdi[187]. I like his intellect; his analysis of world events and development is extremely impressive. I think he is basically a democrat and he doesn't give up, he's still campaigning against dictatorship and army rule in Sudan. He is in and out of jail but remains very committed and constant. Kjell Bondevik[188], the former Prime Minister of Norway, is a leading person in the Shared Societies project. Others I appreciate working with are Horst Köhler[189], we worked well together and I like to make contact with him at international events; Alpha Konaré[190]; John Kufuor[191] who is a sterling person; Chandrika Kumaratunga[192] who is strong on democracy and always gives thoughtful contributions; Cassam Uteem[193] and Festus Mogae[194], with whom I worked very well. Oluse-

---

186 President of Finland March 1994–March 2000; Nobel Peace Prize laureate and United Nations diplomat and mediator; United Nations Commissioner for Namibia 1977–1981; founder of CMI Crisis Management Initiative.

187 Prime Minister of Sudan 1966–1967 and 1986–1989; Head of the National Umma Party and Imam of the Ansar.

188 Prime Minister of Norway 1997–2000 and 2001–2005.

189 President of Germany July 2004–May 2010; Managing Director of the International Monetary Fund May 2000–March 2004.

190 President of Mali June 1992–June 2002; Chairman of the Commission of the African Union September 2003–February 2008.

191 President of the Fourth Republic of Ghana January 2001–January 2009; Chairperson of the African Union January 2007–January 2008.

192 President of Sri Lanka November 1994–November 2005; Prime Minister August 1994–November 1994.

193 President of Mauritius June 1992–February 2002.

194 President of Botswana April 1998–April 2008.

Pseudo Retirement

gun Obasanjo[195] I get on well with; he is a true soldier statesman and I appreciate that he fearlessly tells you what he feels, he is open. This is helpful for someone in high office, because you receive so much flattery and misrepresentations that it can be difficult to know what people are actually feeling.

Sir (Quett) Ketumile Masire[196] is a leader I admire to this day. Modest, insightful, patient and with a common touch. He had age and wisdom but was also transparent like Obasanjo. He could be frank and fearless as well, telling you what he felt, and pointing out potential pitfalls of any route you wanted to take. I admired the way he nurtured the transition in his country from one administration to another when he left office. He was the first president of Botswana to retire early, thus ensuring a peaceful and democratic transition. Then there's Percival Noel James Patterson[197] from Jamaica, we were both foreign ministers, then he rose to be prime minister and I rose to be president and we got on well in the Commonwealth. He has a sharp mind, a great lawyer. Mary Robinson[198], the former Irish president; she's great. I like Dr Óscar Arias[199], he is for total disarmament, declaring that nations do not need armies. While I was in office he encouraged me to cut back on the size of our military, which I did not do, though he did argue his case well. Sir James Mitchell[200] comes from a small nation, yet he has much of value to say; I enjoy sitting next to him at meetings, he is a great man, a lawyer.

The Greek Prime Minister, Konstantinos Simitis[201], opened up my mind to the concept that a North-South relationship is not solely between the developed and the developing countries, but also within so-called

---

195 President of Nigeria May 1999 to May 2007; Head of State in Nigeria February 1976–September 1979.

196 President of Botswana July 1980–March 1998.

197 Prime Minister of Jamaica March 1992–March 2006.

198 President of Ireland December 1990–September 1997; United Nations High Commissioner for Human Rights September 1997–September 2002.

199 President of Costa Rica from May 1986–May 1990 and May 2006–May 2010; Received Nobel Peace Prize in 1987 for his efforts to resolve the Central American crisis.

200 Prime Minister of Saint Vincent and the Grenadines July 1984–October 2000.

201 Prime Minister of Greece January 1996–March 2004.

developed countries as well. He set me thinking on the perspective of the North-South relationship in Europe, with Greece, Spain, and Portugal in trouble; while Germany and other countries are strong. Sometimes you see a paternalistic attitude to the Southern countries of Europe as we African countries experience as well from the North. I enjoy working with Gro Harlem Brundtland, she is very good indeed. She worked well with Mwalimu and I also find it easy to work with her.

Despite all these important people I have met before, during and post-presidency, the person I am most grateful to have in my life is my wife Anna. I am not an easy person to get along with and Anna has stoically borne a lot during our marriage. She had to deal with our living apart because of my work, and my demanding job meant that she was largely responsible for rearing our sons Stephan and Nicholas. On 27 August 2016 we celebrated fifty years of marriage, a marriage I am truly thankful for.

In summary, I can honestly say that I am experiencing a full retirement.

CHAPTER 16

The Second *Chimurenga*: Africa's Struggle Continues

On the 9th of December 2011 Tanzania celebrated fifty years of independence. I was born pre-independence, began working for my country not long after independence, was now officially retired from work, though continue to serve when I am called upon. How did I feel at this momentous occasion? I was happy that we had maintained a united republic, as Mwalimu had set out to do over half a century ago and the celebrations were fabulous. Nevertheless, I harboured some disquiet for my country then and still do. Mwalimu had helped us to forge not only a sense of national unity, but also a strong sense of what kind of society we should be. He established structures that would foster our vison, yet we had to make changes, many of which I led when president. I knew we had no option but to make these reforms; however, the underlying issue is that we hadn't thought through what kind of 'creature' would emerge out of these changes.

Mwalimu's vision was very clear, but once we brought in reforms, what exactly became the vision for our nation? We defined Vision 2025 during my time as president, but I didn't see us thinking this through structurally, procedurally, and ideologically, which is a large regret of mine. Could I have led our nation through such a thought process? I wish that I had had the time to do this when I was president, though I had more than enough on my plate with all the reforms we were undertaking. Even so, I wish we had somehow found the time to think deeply about the future; even today I don't think we are thinking this through, which disappoints me.

There are relating issues to contend with: how do you consolidate a national vision of development which can outlive changes in administration? If every president is going to restructure ministries, can you really register development? How can we achieve an ordered progression in our development, despite a change in the government? It is a waste of precious time and resources when developing nations substantially change or do away with strategies, policies and programmes. Adapt and refine, certainly, as development programmes progress, but we should strive to maintain continuity. There is no need to completely remove all when a new governing administration takes over. It is arrogant of a new leader to drastically cast aside the work of their predecessor. Every leader should rise above their ego and consider the overall vision for the development of their nation and keep what is proving to be helpful to reaching this. All too often we see policies and programmes abandoned or downgraded at the beginning of a new leader's term, yet often that same leader later comes to realise that there was some value in what the predecessor had in place. I was open to continuing carrying on existing initiatives which my predecessor had begun, though I concede we came from the same party.

An incoming leader should review the programmes in place and quietly abandon those which are not working. They should have the integrity to continue the successful programmes. Anyway, in cynical terms, a practical politician should pick the 'low hanging fruit' to gain political kudos, so they should not cast successful programmes aside.

I believe there is a duty on the departing leader to publicise the successes of programmes, thus encouraging their continuation. Though then there is the problem of how to ensure that strategies and programmes are well-explained and well-understood. There is such a multitude of news media nowadays, which can lead to confusion.

China has and continues to undergo dramatic changes, yet the senior leaders in the party seem to deliberate deeply and analyse issues, which I don't see happening here. I see exchanges between individuals, and within a party, but not between parties. Even then, this is not the profound thinking which is needed to determine a configuration of the kind of society we should have. In Kiswahili they call it *tunu* – values, though this is not enough, they should be translated or realised within, embraced, and embodied in structures and procedures.

This is a deficiency and a gap in our nation's progress that I find worrying. For instance, look at any election manifesto and ask those from the political class, just how is this policy going to help the formation of this new society? You will not receive a uniform answer, a clearly held and unifying vision. Of course you will see health for everyone, education for everyone, but there must be something more binding and structurally visible and I don't see that.

I continue to press people to be a little more thoughtful than they are, we need to be forward thinking about our country. Where is the constructive debate about these core issues? It is not surprising that when I raise this issue I am often accused, yet again, of being arrogant. So the 50th anniversary left me a little perturbed; though I will celebrate our sense of national unity. I am glad that by-and-large we are politically stable, which is not common in our region.

I ask myself what kind of society my grandchildren will live in, what kind of Tanzania I will leave for them. We are being inundated by Western development from social media, television, movies, music, magazines and newspapers. How helpful is this in preparing us for development in real life? During 1999, I gave a speech *'The Quest for a Second Liberation in Africa*[202]*'* as a Herbert Chitepo[203] Memorial Lecture; I find it telling of our 'progress' that what I said then is still relevant, twenty years later. The first liberation was, of course, the political liberation, when "the struggle was relatively easy to conceptualise and organise. The enemy was clearly visible and identifiable". I described the three main components of the second liberation of Africa as: political, economic and cultural. Political

---

202 Pages 726–734, Volume 2, Cluster 7 of '*The Mkapa Years Collected Speeches.*' Dar es Salaam: Mkuki na Nyota.

203 First leader of Zimbabwe African National Union Zanu July 1963–March 1975. Robert Mugabe took over as leader after Chitepo's assassination.

liberation is "...whereby we will determine our own political dispensation and destiny that embraces universally accepted democratic norms, but with African characteristics, anchored in our African heritage". Economic liberation is "...the liberation from poverty that will enhance our dignity as people." I added, "The future generations in Africa cannot forgive us if we do not do our utmost to promote and protect continental interests on the international economic arena". Recapturing our self-esteem as a people is the cultural liberation: "We must not sacrifice our African heritage, our culture, our prism through which we look at, and understand, our own and the outside world". I concluded, "With vision and courage, we must prosecute a new chimurenga {this term meant a revolutionary struggle and in contemporary terms this struggle is in the political arena, for social justice and human rights} that will put strong foundations for a better Africa for our children. To that end, Africa must unite".

My greatest preoccupation is this abdication of responsibility for self-development. How can you have primary schools without toilets more than fifty years after independence? How can we say Tanzania is developing? I see members of parliament travelling all over the world to learn about how others are undertaking development. Do you really have to travel to learn from others how to build latrines for a school? What is the legacy of leaders who think development means that Tanzania can have primary schools or secondary schools without toilets? I read in newspapers that a corporation or embassy has helped a school to build latrines and we see this as development, which is ridiculous! Is there no shame that as a citizen you expect the government to do everything for you? How can you justify asking your government to dig simple pit latrines for the primary school in your village? Why doesn't the village collectively take on the responsibility to dig the latrines? Instead they complain that the government should do this. Is this development? What does self-reliance mean, fifty years after independence?

Continuing this theme of the need for us in the developing world to redefine development, we must also redefine the yardsticks by which we measure development, and an important yardstick is the continuance of a development. You may have a structure provided which is an achievement, an electricity supply system for example, but the real development is how you sustain it after that. Do you have the wherewithal, the resource base and technical competence to sustain it? Otherwise you will run it down or be totally dependent on foreign grants to maintain the so-called development.

On the other side, I do think the West is forgetful of the time it took their own countries to reach their current level of development. For example, if you think of the state Tanzania was at on 9 December 1961 and what we had achieved fifty years later, in comparison, it took the United Kingdom much longer to reach this stage, and they had a good resource base from the colonies to feed their nation's growth and development.

Another disappointment to me, though in a quite different category, is the slow pace of integration of the East African Community. I don't see any serious effort, I just see the politicking. People have become preoccupied with titles and roles, they have lost sight of the big picture. How different is poverty in Tanzania from poverty in Kenya? What is the difference in life in a slum in Dar es Salaam as compared to life in a slum in Nairobi? This is what people should have at the forefront of their minds, the East African Community should be a means towards growth for all. It is an irony that we were travelling and trading freely with each other when we were part of the British Empire, yet as independent brothers Tanzania, Kenya and Uganda cannot achieve this.

Good leadership is both a science and an art. A future leader could be born with natural leadership traits; yet even divinely bestowed qualities of leadership need nurturing and enhancement to make them relevant to contemporary challenges. I learnt that commitment to your role is vital, and you can continue to grow as a leader, even while in office, your learning should never cease. My understanding of the art of leadership has changed throughout my working life, and I believe the public's perception and expectations of leadership have changed as well. In the early days, the president was the unquestioned source of wisdom, initiative and professionalism. This was simply because there were scarcely any tertiary level educated Tanzanians. At independence, there were only 236 professionals who had received some form of tertiary education in a country of around ten million people; with an adult literacy rate of around 15%, with only 30.5% of the population having received any level of formal schooling. Furthermore, hardly any citizen had experienced a different kind of economic, political and social environment, only a few had been to South Africa, Britain or India. Hence the educated elite were given leadership positions by our founding president and became the major source of thought about strategies for development, with their strategies tending to be unquestioningly adopted and followed.

As horizons widened with more Tanzanians entering the workplace, education being broadened and more people travelling, the leaders started to become inclusive, seeking opinion and feedback. Previously people had simply been asked who they desired to be their member of parliament, but gradually parliament became competitive, with a formal system of nomination and a more rigorous review of prospective candidates by the party. If a leader had an idea, even Mwalimu, they were expected to share it for discussion within the party, and the consent and support of the members was extremely decisive on whether that idea would come to fruition.

This healthy pressure for consultation grew as Tanzania entered multi-partyism, heightened by the increasing number of graduates, the impact of basic universal education raising literacy, and increased interaction with other countries. Leaders learnt that they must take time to listen, to ferret out views from others. They realised that the opposition could force you to reconsider. This led to leaders becoming accommodating and inclusive, listening more, prepared to float ideas. This applied to the leader at the top as well, particularly since multi-partyism entered in 1992. I was the first person to campaign and then be president under multi-partyism. I had come up in the ranks in an environment which changed in context just as I reached the top. Certainly, the leader at the top may have the last word, but before they decide they must be satisfied that the decision will carry the day, be accepted and supported.

A leader is a primary example of work, service, and integrity, but nowadays they are more moderated because there are so many contesting positions in leadership. Should you like to read more on my thoughts of leadership in Africa, from the historical context until today, then I refer you to a paper I wrote for the World Bank Commission on Growth and

Development titled *'Leadership for Growth, Development, and Poverty Reduction: An African Viewpoint and Experience*[204]'.

I noticed some changes during my support for the 2015 general election campaign, ten years after I left office. I observed the impact of demographics, there were fewer elders about, with much more young people at the mass rallies. The youth will make a difference in forthcoming elections. In 2015 there were 16 million citizens in the 15 to 34 age group, twice as many than in the 35 to 50 age group. The voting age is 18 years in Tanzania and it is estimated that for the 2025 election there will be close to 23 million young people in the group of 15 to 34; out of a predicted total population of just over 67 million citizens. There is a growing number of high school and university graduates who expect to get desk jobs or factory jobs and we are not creating jobs fast enough. Population growth is a vital issue concerning development, yet so often ignored. If you don't talk of population policy – that you don't bring children into this world unless you can feed them, educate and care for their health–then you will have an implosion. The total population was 27.4 million when I took office in 1995; this grew to 36.1 million in 2005, a population increase of 31.7% during the ten-year period of my presidency. This meant that, as I struggled to reduce poverty and improve services in the education, health and water sectors, Though what I achieved would never be sufficient, as the need grew as the population grew. The number of idle youth I see hanging around on the streets is worrying, we are not developing fast enough to provide employment for these young people. This is a big problem with Africa, our economic growth is not matching our population growth. The growth of the number of citizens in a country is not a measure of development, in fact it can be a restraint to development. It is a failing of many African states that we don't have serious discussion about the potential consequences of the lack of population policy in our countries.

---

204 *'Leadership for Growth, Development, and Poverty Reduction: An African Viewpoint and Experience.'* Commission on Growth and Development working paper No. 8. 2008 Washington DC World Bank. Downloadable from http://documents.worldbank.org/curated/en/103131468008465788/Leadership-for-growth-development-and-poverty-reduction-an-African-viewpoint-and-experience

At the rallies I spoke at, I sensed that people were listening very carefully to what I was saying, and I felt their clapping was genuine. There were clear signs of the competitive atmosphere, when travelling by road I could see different party flags on individual houses. I was very much aware of the fact that there was political competition, which did affect the way I presented the case for my party and our candidates. I regarded this heightened competition during the 2015 general election as positive, though my only reservation was that on both sides there was a tendency to oversimplify. A lot of ad hominem attacks would take place, which is not what multi-partyism is about. If you concentrate on dealing with your competitor more than the issues, then what is the use of a party election manifesto if it is not a matter for discussion by the citizenry? Personal attacks are a weakness and distraction, it is best to leave those personal things aside unless they affect the record of integrity and service of the competing candidate.

I have seen a rise in populism in politics, which can be a distracting factor to a leader. I do not like the current weight given to populism, I believe it restrains action, which is not good; particularly if you are a least developed country. In the United Kingdom one can postpone legislation for years, but in a developing country such as ours postponing legislation can mean hindering development or action that could quickly transform lives. The other disadvantage to populism is that people tend to be influenced by crowds rather than ideas, which is not good. Crowds can be a measure of the strength of the ideas you are selling, but one shouldn't place too much emphasis on the volume of crowds. During the campaigns for the 2015 general election I was asked if I had seen how the opposition was drawing crowds at their mass rallies. I was not too disturbed because of two factors. First: the whole fun of opposing leadership, being critical of leadership and sometimes being even abusive, attracts crowds; people like to hear someone being 'shot down'. Then there is the curiosity of just who is this fellow who is seeking to replace the other? But that does not necessarily mean conviction by the members of that crowd that this is the person who will bring change and increase the pace of development. Observe the crowds, but don't be too influenced by them. It is true you should be popular, but it takes more than just crowds as evidence of popularity. Popularity must emanate from the ideas, programmes, implementation, likelihood of outcomes being achieved, but also ultimately upon the conviction that this person represents service and integrity.

CCM, which has been the ruling party in Tanzania since independence, still tends to behave as if we were a one-party state; they haven't absorbed the necessity of having to argue their case, present their record of achievement, and inspire others with their hopes for Tanzania. Yet now there is serious opposition which CCM needs to acknowledge, I think my party is only now waking up to the fact that we are a multi-party system. There should be more political interaction, not only to understand each other's views, but to educate one another about what you know about other countries, what others are doing, how they are going about development. I don't see enough of that; rather a lot of political posturing, such as, "We will liberate you". What do they mean by liberation more than fifty years after independence? What is lacking is political interaction which is constructive to a nation's development; there is a real shortage of serious engagement with issues. But this shortfall in political debate is not peculiar to Tanzania. Perhaps we have embraced Western democracy too much. Rather than making political parties a mechanism for tolerance and inclusion, which I believe would be more in keeping with the historical and traditional way of African leadership, we have followed the Western way of intolerance and exclusion. The concept of winner takes all has no African roots – our way is to be communal and inclusive.

So many political parties have sprung up in Tanzania, twenty-two political parties campaigned in the 2015 general election, some parties seemed so small, almost like a family affair. Only five parties secured sufficient votes to have a representative in parliament. Too many political parties seriously weaken democratic competition. I am disillusioned at the culture of wanting to become a politician because of the prospect of financial betterment, rather than the honourable ethos of providing a service to fellow citizens and your nation. Every country needs leaders who focus on serving their country. This going into politics for self-interest is not unique to Tanzania, and there is no doubt about its negative effect on society. Much earlier, business people preferred to be outside of political circles, but when we modified our leadership code to allow people to do a little business, some businessmen saw an opportunity to enter politics not to serve, but to protect and drive their business interest, while some academics saw a chance to travel and gain allowances. Let's not forget that the title of 'honourable member' is important to some to misuse this for their own betterment; human nature I suppose, but still a great disappointment. I wish people could find pride in advancing themselves in their chosen field, and if they decide to go into politics then do so for the right reasons. It seems to me that nowadays few members of parliament really care about their people and the development projects in their constituencies. I don't see as much interactive constituency work as in the United Kingdom, there isn't enough of this here in my opinion, and this growing gap between leaders and followers is not healthy for democracy and a nation's development. Of course this happens in developed countries as well, but this is a serious indictment in a developing country, for a leader should take time to listen to the people and learn of their woes. Mwalimu always undertook regional tours where he would meet the elders, not to lecture them, but to listen to their concerns. It is also helpful when citizens actually see their leader in their own environment; it reduces the distance created by a leader's education and entitlements. Instead, I often see members of parliament more willing to attend an international conference rather than be out in their constituencies; or they seek media coverage to gain populist support, rather than being with the people. This lowers the value of politics and produces a politics of personalities, which in turn will lead to more distance from, and disenchantment of, the citizenry.

Then there is the other aspect that nowadays elected governmental representatives are overly sensitive to how their constituents will react, which creates the danger that this focuses their view on local matters and the short-term, rather than considering the big picture and the long-term vision for the nation. What is missing is dynamic interaction by members of parliament on matters of policy and policy implementation. The then secretary general of the party, Abdulrahman Kinana, made a real effort to describe the party manifesto and its implementation during the 2015 campaign and this was good, but even then this was not sufficiently taken up by the candidates.

Above all, I worry about whether we will maintain a stable country. Tanzania has been stable for more than fifty years, I hope we remain stable, that our foundations stay strong. I am concerned about the argument which emerged during the 2015 election, about how many 'countries' there are in this union called the United Republic of Tanzania as there are a lot of ethnic groups in Zanzibar and the mainland. I also see the signs of some religious intolerance, which concerns me. We have been very fortunate that we Tanzanians have eschewed the idea of tribalism and ethnicity and I hope that the recent notion of regional differences which is creeping in does not take root. I think the phenomenon of ownership of the economy should be more broad-based, particularly with the number of large-scale agricultural and industrial production units often associated with Indian or Asian companies. I am a little concerned that in the future this may incite some jealousy; all political parties must be wary of this potential danger and be prepared to grapple with it. I worry about the future because poverty goes almost side-by-side with instability. If we do not register tangible success in fighting poverty, then it will emphasise the disparity between us, which will in turn gradually erase the sense of unity and stability. Our neighbours, Kenya, Uganda, Mozambique, Rwanda, Burundi and the Democratic Republic of the Congo have experienced instability, we Tanzanians can't just glibly accept that we are an exception; we must continually ask ourselves, are we rooting ourselves in stability?

Well, these are the problems of other leaders now. All I can do is offer counsel when asked and continue to remind leaders about the plight of the poor, marginalised and oppressed. I have had the *Desiderata* by Max Ehrmann hanging in my home office ever since I found it more than two decades ago. I read this whenever I feel low:

> *Desiderata*
> *Go placidly amid the noise and haste,*
> *and remember what peace there may be in silence.*
> *As far as possible without surrender*
> *be on good terms with all persons.*
> *Speak your truth quietly and clearly;*
> *and listen to others,*
> *even the dull and the ignorant;*
> *they too have their story.*

Avoid loud and aggressive persons,
they are vexations to the spirit.
If you compare yourself with others,
you may become vain and bitter;
for always there will be greater and lesser persons than yourself.
Enjoy your achievements as well as your plans.

Keep interested in your own career, however humble;
it is a real possession in the changing fortunes of time.
Exercise caution in your business affairs;
for the world is full of trickery.
But let this not blind you to what virtue there is;
many persons strive for high ideals;
and everywhere life is full of heroism.

Be yourself.
Especially, do not feign affection.
Neither be cynical about love;
for in the face of all aridity and disenchantment
it is as perennial as the grass.

Take kindly the counsel of the years,
gracefully surrendering the things of youth.
Nurture strength of spirit to shield you in sudden misfortune.
But do not distress yourself with dark imaginings.
Many fears are born of fatigue and loneliness.
Beyond a wholesome discipline,
be gentle with yourself.

You are a child of the universe,
no less than the trees and the stars;
you have a right to be here.
And whether or not it is clear to you,
no doubt the universe is unfolding as it should.

Therefore be at peace with God,
whatever you conceive Him to be.
And whatever your labors and aspirations,
in the noisy confusion of life keep peace with your soul.

With all its sham, drudgery, and broken dreams,
it is still a beautiful world.
Be cheerful.
Strive to be happy.

Let me move on to a more positive topic, the leaders of the future. I would like to share my suggestions for younger persons desiring to be leaders in their profession and hope that these are useful. Whatever your professional task, the first thing you have got to demonstrate is engagement in the chores you are given. You must demonstrate that your heart is in it and work hard. This behaviour indicates to your seniors that if they give you a higher position then you will work with the same ardency. I have talked about service and integrity, both are important. You must be able to demonstrate your readiness to learn more about your job and improve; this is part of engagement.

You must show a readiness to share your ideas, success, problems, as well as evaluation. To confidently think that you know everything about all the aspects of a task that is at hand is not good. This readiness builds your character to be more disposed to consultation when you rise in the ranks and assume higher positions. You must show from early on that you are ready to listen and ingrain this habit, for when you become a senior leader it is very easy to adopt the character of giving orders, and if you display a lot of that then others will not share their ideas with you or give you counsel. A leader nowadays must behave less monarchically than they did during my youth and middle age; they must consult more, and make sure there is respect for the law and procedures. It is crucial for a leader to avoid any element of arbitrariness. A readiness to listen is extremely important, the higher you rise the more critical this character trait is. If you are a leader who favours giving orders rather than consulting, then after a while those working for you get to know that you like a certain kind of report, so they will endlessly give you such reports. Then if you don't share thoughts for discussion or ask questions – the report, which will have been written to please you, will be all you have on which to base your decision. If your staff and colleagues are afraid of you because you are impatient, or do not listen, then they will not volunteer or share any views with you, hence you will not get the benefit of counsel, differing perspectives and recommendations. The readiness to listen cannot be underestimated, this is a crucial quality of a leader. You must take care that you exercise readiness to reflect on people's differing viewpoints, showing a generosity of thought, not rigidity, particularly when it is a controversial issue at hand.

You will have noticed that I have mentioned Mwalimu several times during these memoirs. Mwalimu Julius Nyerere, was undoubtedly the greatest influence on my personal growth as a leader and on my career. I encourage young aspiring leaders to seek a mentor or mentors who can offer you guidance and advice as your progress in your career. Furthermore, I urge you to read some of Mwalimu's writings and speeches, as I still do. Whether you agree or disagree with his socialist views, there is much about leadership that we can learn from him, even in today's altered world. Mwalimu was an iconic leader, a man of principle, intelligence and integrity. It takes strength to be a leader, Mwalimu was forceful when he needed to be, he was courageous and tenacious, totally committed to serving his people and the cause of the liberation of Southern Africa and the global South.

Young leaders, take up the challenge; the poor, marginalised and oppressed around the world need you to make a difference.

We have come to the end of these memoirs of my journey through life. I would like to thank those who made a positive and key contribution to my life. Above all is Mwalimu, Julius Nyerere, who had the greatest influence on my life – personally as well as politically. The two headmasters who encouraged me to advance my education: Fathers Gereon Schramm and James Lynch, they truly demonstrated how education can expand a young person's opportunities in life. Notable people from the international scene who provided food for thought and helpful connections are Joaquim Chissano, Martti Ahtisaari, Festus Mogae, James Wolfensohn, Horst Köhler and John Nagenda. It is difficult to mention all the worthy Tanzanians I have encountered without causing offence to others. Though I would like to mention Cornel Apson Mwang'onda, Ferdinand Ruhinda, Costa Kumalija, Kabenga Nsa-Kaisi and Walter Bgoya. Last, but by no means least, is my wife Anna, my sons and grandchildren; it gives me great joy to be a grandfather.

I would like to conclude with two quotes, the first from Mwalimu Julius Kambarage Nyerere:

> I am simply a believer…I believe in the equality and dignity of all human beings, and the duty to serve, their well-being as well as their freedom in a peaceful and cooperative society. I am an ardent believer in the freedom and welfare of the individual.

And from Rabbi Harold Kushner:

> Our souls are not hungry for fame, comfort, wealth, or power. Those rewards create almost as many problems as they solve. Our souls are hungry for meaning, for the sense that we have figured out how to live so that our lives matter, so the world will at least be a little bit different for our having passed through it.

I will leave it to my God and you to decide what difference I have made in this world.

My parents, Stephania Nambanga and William Matwani.

My father at the mission at Ndanda, he is third from left.

My class at Ndanda secondary school, 1954. I am in the front row, second from left.

As teaching assistants at Ndanda secondary school after completing St Francis College, Pugu. I am first on left, then John Kambona, next is Benno Nkane, with Philip Magani on the far right.

At Ndanda secondary school after completing studies at St. Francis College, Pugu. I am first on left, then Philip Magani, a student and John Kambona on the far right.

St. Francis College,
Pugu,
22nd March, 1955.

The Headmaster,
St. Francis College,
Pugu.

Dear Father Lynch,

I have considered the choice which you have given me, between my job at the school and my membership of T.A.N.U. and have come to the conclusion that I must resign from my post at the school.

But now I find myself presented with exactly the same choice. In so far as TANU is interfering with my work at the school, the problem is personal and sooner or later I would have had to reduce my activity in TANU or take the choice myself between TANU and the school. In that case the choice would have been real; and if I had found that I could not ~~had to learn~~ do both things sufficiently efficiently it is probable that I would have had to leave the school to organize TANU. But when resignation from TANU is given me as a condition of retaining my job the whole problem becomes one of principle. Who in Tanganyika is free to join and lead TANU? In theory all people outside government service. In practice I know that Native Authority employees are not free, or at least they are less free than mission teachers. But if the freedom of mission teachers were also to be doubted the position would become very gloomy for I cannot see any reason why every employer should not give the same conditions to his employees; and that possibility would be tragic. I must, therefore, resign as a protest.

I am sorry that my activity in TANU has actually affected the efficiency of my teaching; I am sorry about the inconveniencies that my resignation must temporarily cause you and my colleagues; I am sad about the economic consequences to my family.

If I were in your position, Father, I would probably have acted in the same way as you have; my only hope is that you will think it possible that had you been in my position you would probably have taken the same action as I have taken.

I thank you and other Fathers in the kind way in which you have always treated me. I shall need your prayers more than I have ever done before. Continue, Father, to pray for me.

Your loving son in Christ,

Julius Nyerere

JKN's resignation letter from St Francis College Pugu.
Source: Fabian Colonial Bureau, Oxford, UK.

Julius Nyerere's resignation letter from St Francis College, Pugu.

With Philip Magani at Makerere University College.

My family.
Front row, left to right: Avina Mkapa; Nicholas Mkapa; Stephan Mkapa.
Second row, left to right: Susan Mkapa; Hulda Bernard Mkapa; Stephania Nambanga; William Matwani; Anna Mkapa; Esta Maro.
Third row, left right: Me; Aquiline Mkapa; Bernard Mkapa; Blassius Mkapa.

With Anna at State House.

Celebrating our 50th wedding anniversary, August 2016.

Anna campaigning.

With our first grandson, Nigel Benedict Alexander.

My family.
Left to right: Stephan Mkapa; myself; Nathaniel Joseph (grandson) Anna and Nicholas Mkapa.
Standing: Nigel Benedict Alexander (grandson) and Mrs. Foster Mkapa (Nicholas' wife).

Farewelling Samora Machel as he left for Mozambique in 1975.

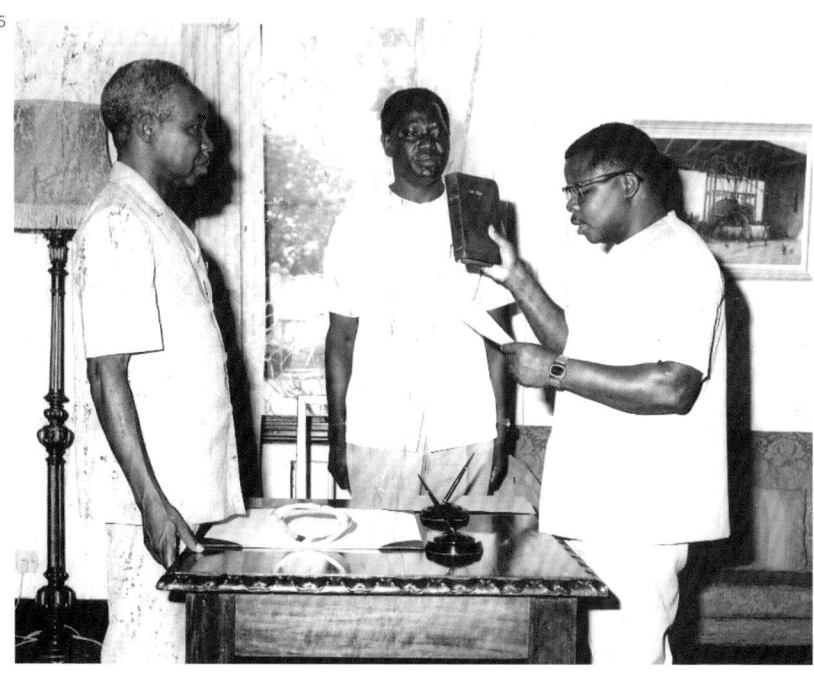

Being sworn in as high commissioner to Nigeria, October 1976.

Friday, February 3, 1967

THE NATIONALIST
First African owned English Daily in East Africa

Friday, February 3, 1967

No. 871
MWANANCHI PUBLISHING (1966) LIMITED
Habari House, Pugu Road, Dar es Salaam
Telephone 63206   P.O. Box 9221

EDUCATION OR ALIENATION?

WE REPRODUCE below questions which last year's candidates for the Higher School Certificate and G.C.E. were asked in the History Economic and Public Affairs Papers. Hundreds of Tanzanian boys and girls had to crack their heads answering these questions. It is worth noting that these questions were asked to sons and daughters of Tanzanian citizens FIVE years after independence!

- What safeguards has the individual in Great Britain against arbitrary actions by government?
- Do you agree that Parliamentary democracy in Britain works because the majority and the minority parties respect each other's rights?
- Do you agree that the results of post-war general elections in Great Britain strengthen the case for electoral reform?
- Is it true that Civil Servants in England play no part in the formulation of government policy?
- Comment on the status of the Prime Minister in Britain today. What dangers, if any, do you envisage as a result of a continued growth in his importance?
- What is the importance of question-time in the House of Commons?
- What are the advantages of having some leading Ministers in the House of Lords?
- Outline the structure and powers of local government in England. How efficiently do they meet the needs of the present day?
- What issues are raised in the selection and appointment of judges in Britain?
- What control has Parliament over nationalised industries?
- Compare the functions and powers of the Lord Chancellor and the Speaker as chairmen of their respective Houses of Parliament.
- 'The symbol of the free association of its independent member nations and as such the Head of the Commonwealth.' How strong is the monarchy as a Commonwealth link?

WE ASK:

- Can a youth who completes 14 years at school reading nothing but History books related to the above questions really be expected to know what obtains in Tanzania and Africa and the problems therein?
- Can such a youth be expected to know One Party Democracy?
- Can such a youth be expected to know socialism?
- Can he value, respect and pay attention to his leaders when all he is taught is about the leaders of other countries?
- Can he avoid his mind being tuned to the British way of life and completely forgetting his own?
- Can this youth be expected to become a politically conscious and active Tanzanian civil servant after school?
- Can he be expected to be conversant with what obtains in an independent, One Party Democratic socialist state as opposed to a Monarchial state?
- Can he know and appreciate his own country's Parliamentary system?
- Can he be proud of his own history and its values?
- Can he avoid growing up in a state of national alienation?
- And the BIG question is: WHAT IS THE MINISTRY OF EDUCATION DOING ABOUT THIS HUMILIATION?

My editorial in 'The Nationalist' which upset the minister of education, 3 February 1967.

Julius Nyerere with his press secretaries in front of State House. **From left:** Habib Halahala, Paul Sozigwa, Julius Nyerere, Hashim Mbita and me.

Minister of foreign affairs, 1979.

With Julius Nyerere when I was minister of foreign affairs.

With Olof Palme, Julius Nyerere and Salim Salim.

My president's cabinet, February 1977, after the merger of TANU and ASP to form CCM.

Front Row, seated left to right: Aboud Jumbe – Vice President; Julius Nyerere – President; Edward Sokoine - Prime Minister.

Second Row, left to right: Cleopa D Msuya - Industries; Benjamin W Mkapa – Foreign Affairs; Hassan Nassor Moyo – Home Affairs; Abdallah Said Natepe - Minister of State (President's Office); Alphonse Rulegura – Commerce; Ali Mzee Ali – Minister of State (Vice President's Office); Solomon ole Saibul – Natural Resources and Tourism; Rashidi Kawawa – Defence.

Third Row, left to right: Alfred C Tandau - Works; Leader Stirling – Health; Amir Jamal – Communications; Julie Manning – Justice; Hussein Shekilango – Minister of State (Prime Minister's Office); Crispin Tungaraza - Labour; Hasnu Makame – Capital Development; Tabitha Siwale – Lands.

Fourth Row, left to right: Isaac Sepetu – Information and Broadcasting; Mirisho Sarakikya – National Culture and Youth; Abel Mwanga - Civil Service; Nicholas Kuhanga - Education; Al Noor Kassum – Water, Energy and Minerals; Edwin Mtei - Finance.

Fifth Row: Daniel Machemba – Minister without portfolio

In the Cabinet but not in the picture: John S Malecela – Agriculture

Campaigning during 1995.

Campaigning with Ernest Nyanda (second from left) and Omar Ali Juma (third from left), 1995.

My office at State House.

With some ministers and deputy ministers in 1997.

Front Row, left to right: Aaron Chiduo - Health; Daniel Yona - Finance; William Shija - Industries and Trade; Omar Ali Juma – Vice President; Benjamin Mkapa – President; Frederick Sumaye - Prime Minister; Abdallah Kigoda – Minerals; Zakia Meghji – Natural Resources and Tourism.

Second Row, left to right: Monica Mbega - Deputy Minister, Finance; Nassor Malocho - Planning; Mudhihir M Mudhihir - Deputy Minister, Lands and Human Settlements; Bujiku Sakila - Deputy Minister, Education; Mohammed S Khatib - Minister of State (Prime Minister's Office).

Third Row, left to right: Bakari Mbonde - Minister of State (Vice President's Office); Ismail Ivwata - Deputy Minister - Water; Manju Msambya - Deputy Minister – Minerals; Pius Mbawala - Deputy Minister, Agriculture; Gladness Mziray - Deputy Minister – Health.

My second term cabinet in early 2002.

Front Row, left to right: Asha Rose Migiro - Community Development, Women Affairs and Children; Zakia Meghji - Natural Resources and Tourism; Ali Mohamed Shein - Vice President; Benjamin Mkapa – President; Frederick Sumaye - Prime Minister; Jakaya Kikwete - Foreign Affairs and International Cooperation; Mary Nagu - Central Establishment; Anna Abdallah - Health.

Second Row, left to right: George Kahama - Cooperatives and Marketing; Mohammed Seif Khatib – Home Affairs; Pius Ng'wandu - Science, Technology and Higher Education; Basil Mramba – Finance; Edgar Maokola - Majogo - Energy and Minerals; Juma Ngasongwa – Industry and Commerce; Juma Kapuya - Labour, Youth Development and Sports.

Third Row, left to right: Omar Ramadhani Mapuri – Prime Minister's Office; Andrew Chenge – Attorney-General; John Magufuli - Works; Wilson Massilingi - Good Governance; James Mungai - Education; Edward Lowassa - Water and Livestock Development; Philemon Sarungi – Defence; Arcado Ntagazwa – Vice President's Office, Union Affairs and Environment.

Fourth Row, left to right: William Lukuvi - Prime Minister's Office; Abdallah Kigoda - Planning and Privatisation; Charles Keenja - Food and Agriculture; Gideon Cheyo - Lands and Human Settlement Development; Bakari Mwapachu - Justice and Constitutional Affairs.

In the Cabinet but not in the picture: Hassan Ngwilizi - Regional Administration and Local Government; Mark Mwandosya - Transport and Communication; Daniel Yona - Vice President's Office.

Working on the monthly broadcast while in hospital.

With Chief Japhet Edward Wanzagi on the occasion of my being adopted into the clan.

Nelson Mandela arriving for the Burundi peace negotiations.

With Nelson Mandela, Bill Clinton and Yoweri Museveni at the Burundi peace talks, August 2000.

With Martti and Eeva Ahtisaari and Anna, Finland, August 1998.

With James Wolfensohn of the World Bank, 2001.

Addressing the opening session of the United Nations General Assembly, September 2004.

34

Photo 34–38: On regional tours within Tanzania during June 1998, October and December 2004.

35

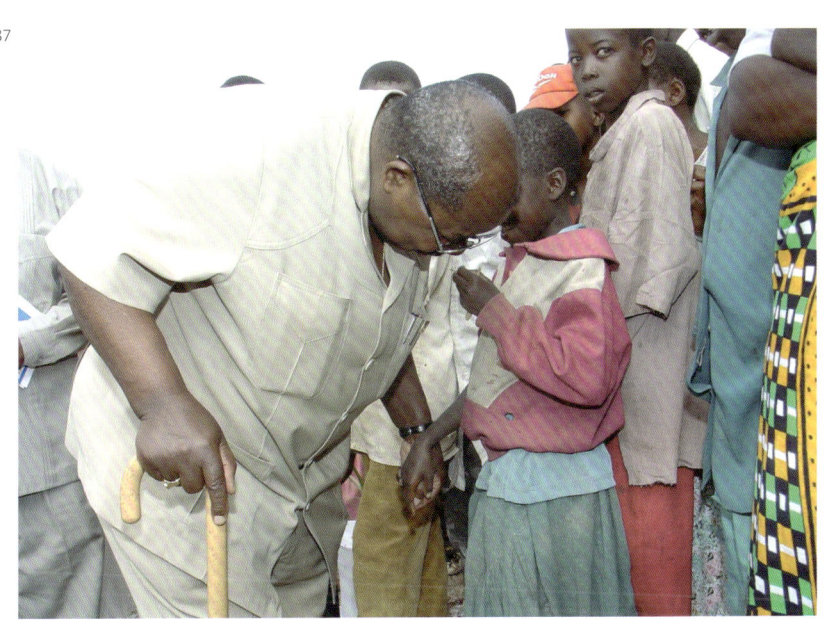

Meeting of 12 heads of state, World Bank and IMF chief executives, February 2001.

Front row, from left: James Wolfensohn (World Bank); Robert Mugabe (Zimbabwe); Daniel arap Moi (Kenya); Me; Yoweri Museveni (Uganda); Joaquim Chissano (Mozambique); Horst Köhler (IMF).

Second row, from left: Isaias Afwerki (Eritrea); Festus Mogae (Botswana); Bakili Muluzi (Malawi); Thabo Mbeki (South Africa); Frederick Chiluba (Zambia); Meles Zenawi (Ethiopia); Paul Kagame (Rwanda).

Commission for Africa, May 2004.

From left, front row: Linah Mohohlo (Botswana); Gordon Brown (UK); Sir Bob Geldof (UK); Tony Blair (UK); Me; Meles Zenawi (Ethiopia); Hilary Benn (UK).

Back row: Michel Camdessus (France); Anna Tibaijuka (UN), William Kalema (Uganda); Nancy Kassebaum Baker (USA); Tidjane Thiam (Côte d'Ivoire); Kingsley Amoako (UN); Foala Adeola (Nigeria); Ralph Goodale (Canada); Trevor Manuel (South Africa).

On the United Nations Security Council with Vladimir Putin, Tony Blair, George Bush and Abdelaziz Bouteflika, September 2005.

With Tony Blair and George Bush at the G8 Summit, July 2005, Gleneagles.

With Robert Mugabe, 2005.

With Olusegun Obasanjo at the Commonwealth Heads of Government Meeting, November 2005, Malta.

With His Highness Aga Khan.

Awarding Joaquim Chissano the Order of the Torch of Kilimanjaro First Class for his services to Mozambicans and Africans.

Inspecting the farewell parade of the Tanzania People's Defence Force, October 2005.

Recommending Jakaya Kikwete during the 2005 campaign.

At the inauguration of my successor, President Jakaya Mrisho Kikwete.

'It is all over'.

Tanzania's Four Presidents.

From left to right: Their Excellencies:

Ali Hassan Mwinyi (Tanzania's second president November 1985–November 1995);
John Joseph Pombe Magufuli (Tanzania's fifth president, incumbent from November 2015);
Jakaya Mrisho Kikwete (Tanzania's fourth president December 2005–November 2015);
Benjamin William Mkapa (Tanzania's third president November 1995–December 2005).

With Bill Clinton at the launch of the Benjamin William Mkapa Foundation, July 2005.

With my president, Jakaya Kikwete, and Kofi Annan watching the signing of the Kenyan power sharing deal by Mwai Kibaki (left) and Raila Odinga (right), February 2008.

APPENDIX I

The Arusha Declaration: Part One, The TANU Creed

The policy of TANU is to build a socialist state. The principles of socialism are laid down in the TANU Constitution and they are as follows:

WHEREAS TANU believes:

a) That all human beings are equal;
b) That every individual has a right to dignity and respect;
c) That every citizen is an integral part of the nation and has the right to take an equal part in Government at local, regional and national level;
d) That every citizen has the right to freedom of expression, of movement, of religious belief and of association within the context of the law;
e) That every individual has the right to receive from society protection of his life and of property held according to law;
f) That every individual has the right to receive a just return for his labour;
g) That all citizens together possess all the natural resources of the country in trust for their descendants;
h) That in order to ensure economic justice the state must have effective control over the principal means of production; and
i) That it is the responsibility of the state to intervene actively in the economic life of the nation so as to ensure the wellbeing of all citizens, and so as to prevent the exploitation of one person by another or one group by another, and so as to prevent the accumulation of wealth to an extent which is inconsistent with the existence of a classless society.

NOW, THEREFORE, the principal aims and objects of TANU shall be as follows:

a) To consolidate and maintain the independence of this country and the freedom of its people;

b) To safeguard the inherent dignity of the individual in accordance with the Universal Declaration of Human Rights;

c) To ensure that this country shall be governed by a democratic socialist government of the people;

d) To cooperate with all political parties in Africa engaged in the liberation of all Africa;

e) To see that the Government mobilizes all the resources of this country towards the elimination of poverty, ignorance and disease;

f) To see that the Government actively assists in the formation and maintenance of co-operative organisations;

g) To see that wherever possible the Government itself directly participates in the economic development of this country;

h) To see that the Government gives equal opportunity to all men and women irrespective of race, religion or status;

i) To see that the Government eradicates all types of exploitation, intimidation, discrimination, bribery and corruption;

j) To see that the Government exercises effective control over the principal means of production and pursues policies which facilitate the way to collective ownership of the resources of this country;

k) To see that the Government cooperates with other states in Africa in bringing about African unity;

l) To see that Government works tirelessly towards world peace and security through the United Nations Organization.

Appendix II

Socio-economic Achievements of the Third Phase Government of the United Republic of Tanzania

INTRODUCTION

Tanzania gained independence from Britain in 1961. The first phase government was led by President Julius Kambarage Nyerere from 1961 to 1985. Between 1967 and 1985 the Tanzanian economy was state controlled under the policy of socialism (*Ujamaa*) following the Arusha Declaration of 1967. Between 1980 and 1985 the Tanzanian economy experienced a sharp recession due to several factors including the negative consequences of the 1979 war with Uganda, declining cash crop prices, high oil prices and excessive and misguided state intervention in the economy.

After the retirement of President Nyerere in 1985, President Ali Hassan Mwinyi took over the leadership for the period 1985 to 1995. His main agenda was economic reform to revive the economy. During President Mwinyi's term the economy experienced the liberalisation of trade, interest rates, prices, exchange rate, the commencement of the privatisation of state owned enterprises and the introduction of a multi-party political system. However, these economic reforms did not yield sufficient growth and during his second term (1990–1995) the economy was in crisis and the growth rate declined. Furthermore, the provision of social services like education, health and infrastructure remained unsatisfactory (Muganda, 2004; Mwase and Ndulu, 2008).

President Benjamin William Mkapa's term was from 1995 to 2005; this is often called the third phase of government. President Mkapa undertook deeper economic reforms, established macro-economic stability, improved public finance management and restored donor confidence. During most of his period of leadership the country experienced sustained and high economic growth, single digit inflation, the revival of exports, high inward foreign investment, huge inflows of foreign aid, low budget deficit, improved collection of tax revenue, and a decline of grand corruption. Education, health and infrastructure started to improve (Muganda, 2004; Mwase and Ndulu, 2008; URT, 2008; Nord et al., 2009). However, there was a slight decline in the basic needs poverty rate from 38.6% (1991/92) to 35.7% (2000/01), then to 33.6% (2007) (NBS, 2009).

Table 1: Socio-economic Statistics of Tanzania in the Year of Independence, 1961

URBANISATION	POPULATION DENSITY
5.4% of the total population	11.7 people per sq. km of land area
HEALTH 122 hospitals with 16,226 hospital beds* 50 rural health centres with 1,801 beds* 1,362 dispensaries with 7,709 beds* Physicians per 1 million people: 39.5 Life expectancy: 43.9 years	EDUCATION 20 Secondary schools with 11,832 students 3,100 primary schools with 486,470 pupils Adult literacy: 15%
16 medical doctors	12 accountants One agricultural engineer One surveyor

Source: Nyerere (1973: 296-297); URT (1973); BEST (2012); World Bank data.
*1959

Given the above founding statistics, Table 2 below shows how Tanzania has accelerated over time as indicated by the stated socio-economic indicators. As we can see GDP per capita and indicators of health and education improved, with the population rising from 27.4 million in 1995 to 36.1 million in 2005.

Table 2: Socio economic Statistics from Independence up to the Completion of President Mkapa's Term

INDICATOR	1961	1985	1995	2005
Population (millions)	10.4	21.8	27.4	36.1
Urban population (% of total)	5.4	16.8	20.5	24.8
Population density (people per sq. km of land area)	11.7	24.7	33.8	44.1
GDP per capita (2001 prices USD)	217.94	279.25	289.56	380.41
GDP per capita (2001 prices TZS)	191,005	244,737	253,775	333,397
Exports (% of GDP)	27.6	6.8	24.1	20.8
Imports (% of GDP)	29.8	16.8	41.4	29.7
Gross Investment (% of GDP)	13*	18.6	19.8	25
Foreign Aid (% of GDP)	6.8	7.4	16.6	10.6
TZS/USD exchange rate	7.14	17.47	574.76	1,128.93
Life expectancy (years)	43.9	51	48.7	55.6
Infant mortality rate (per 1,000 live births)	143	106.4	95.8	58.7
Under five mortality rate (per 1,000 live births)	242	176.3	157.6	92.4
Total enrolment in public primary schools	486,470	3,160,145	3,872,473	7,476,650
Standard 7 leavers	11,732	429,194	386,584	493,946
Total enrolment in secondary school	11,832	83,098	196,375	524,325

Source: The author's calculations from IMF, World Bank, BOT and NBS statistics, and BEST.
*Gross Fixed Capital Formation (% of GDP).

ECONOMIC INDICATORS

Macroeconomic Indicators of GDP Growth and GDP per Capita Growth

Figure 1 shows that economic growth was volatile and declining during the 1970s, reaching a trough in 1983. During the first term (1985-1990) of President Mwinyi, economic growth rate was volatile and slightly rose, however, it fell during his second term (1990-1995). Under President Mkapa's government the economic growth rate was less volatile and rose sustainably. The mean GDP growth rate was 5.49% and the mean GDP per capita growth rate was 2.73%. Both of which were higher than the 2.95% and 0.36% respectively during Mwinyi's term.

Figure 1: Growth Rate of GDP and GDP Per Capita During President Mkapa's Term

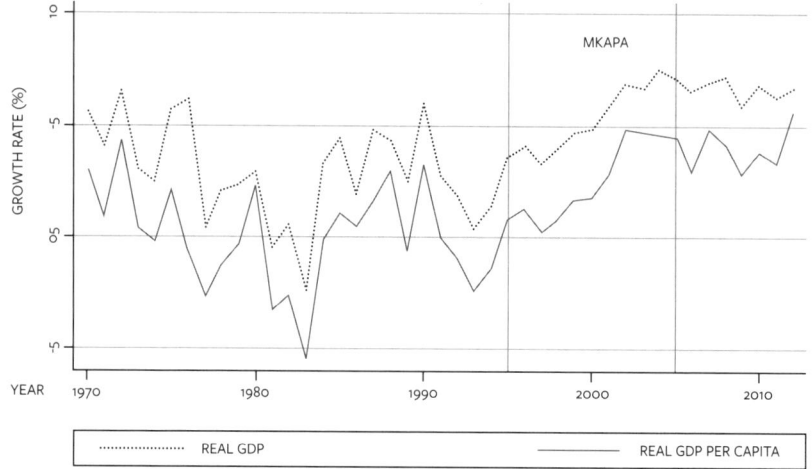

Source: The author's calculations from IMF, World Bank and NBS statistics

The main reasons for the positive and sustained growth rate during Mkapa's term were market friendly policies that encouraged domestic and foreign investment, prudent fiscal and monetary policies that led to macroeconomic stability, huge foreign aid inflows and debt relief that boosted investment and foreign exchange earnings, and more economic diversification. Other reasons were relatively high commodity prices due to high economic growth in Asia (mainly China and India) and relatively low international oil prices during most of this period. The Tanzania Development Vision (Vision 2025), the Tanzania Mini-Tiger Plan (2020), National Poverty Eradication Strategy, Poverty Reduction Strategy Paper and National Strategy for Growth and Reduction of Poverty were the major economic policy initiatives during this period (URT, 2005). Tanzania was also a signatory to the United Nations Millennium Development Goals.

Tanzania has been a major recipient of foreign aid, with foreign aid (% of GDP) rising to a climax of 29% in 1992. The volumes of foreign aid and exports rose significantly during Mkapa's term. Since GDP rose faster than the volume of foreign aid and exports, the shares of these variables as a percentage of GDP slightly declined (see Figure 2). The volume of foreign aid increased significantly due to increased donor confidence. While the volume of exports rose significantly mainly due to export diversification and the increase in mineral exports (particularly gold). The volume of imports also rose but imports as a percentage of GDP declined significantly.

Figure 2: Foreign Aid, Exports and Imports During President Mkapa's Term

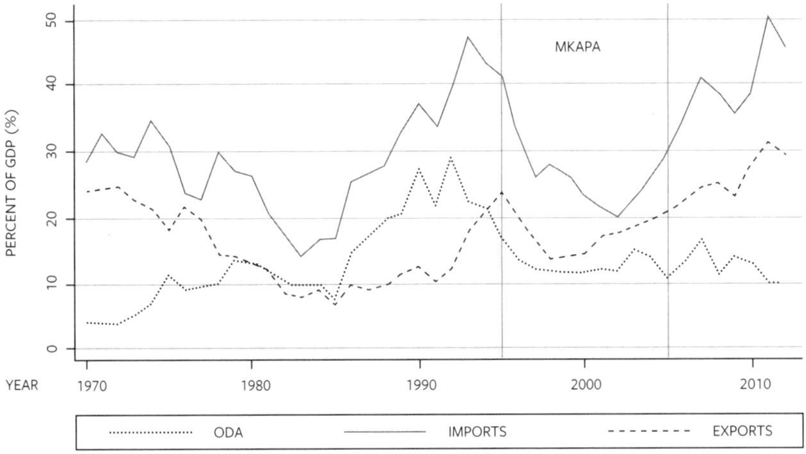

Source: The author's calculations from IMF, World Bank and NBS statistics

On average foreign aid (% of GDP) was lower during Mkapa's term, though it was more productive as the economy was more market oriented; the gap between exports and imports was narrower indicating a reduction in the current account deficit (Table 3).

Table 3: Average Foreign Aid, Exports and Imports

INDICATOR	MWINYI (1986–1995)	MKAPA (1996–2005)
Foreign aid (% of GDP)	21	12.4
Exports (% of GDP)	13.7	17.2
Imports (% of GDP)	35.5	25.5

Source: World Bank and BOT statistics.

Volumes of investment increased significantly, and after an initial dip from 19.8% (1995) to 14.9% (1997), investment (% of GDP) also rose to 25% (2005). Due to privatisation and economic restructuring this investment was more productive than that of the past when the state dominated the economy. During President Mkapa's term the volume of inward FDI rose significantly, and net inward FDI (% of GDP) also rose from 2.3% (1995) to 6.6% (2005). However, inward Foreign Direct Investment was mainly concentrated in the mining sector. The main reason for the significant increase in the volume of domestic and foreign investment was investment friendly policies and an investment friendly regulatory environment. For example privatisation of state owned enterprises and the establishment of the Capital Markets and Securities Authority (1996), the Dar es Salaam Stock Exchange (1996) and the Tanzania Investment Centre (1997). The 1998 Mining Act greatly encouraged foreign investment in the mining sector. Other reasons for the high volume of investment include huge foreign aid inflows and debt relief that allowed more resources to be channelled towards investment (Mwase and Ndulu, 2008; BOT, 2011).

On average inward FDI (% of GDP) was higher during Mkapa's term while investment (% of GDP) was lower. However, investment during Mkapa's term was more productive as the economy was more market oriented (Table 4).

Table 4: Average Investment and Net Inward FDI

INDICATOR	MWINYI (1986–1995)	MKAPA (1996–2005)
Investment (% of GDP)	22.6	18.2
Net inward FDI (% of GDP)	0.5*	3.5

Source: World Bank statistics.
(1988–1995)

The inflation rate significantly declined to single digit figures during most of Mkapa's term from 27.4% (1995) to 5% (2005). This was mainly due to the Government and Bank of Tanzania's efforts to control money supply and reduce the budget deficit. The current account deficit (% of GDP) also narrowed from 11.2% (1995) to 6.5% (2005). The inflation rate and the current account deficit (% of GDP) were on average lower during Mkapa's term (see Table 5).

Table 5: Average Inflation Rate and Current Account Deficit

INDICATOR	MWINYI (1986–1995)	MKAPA (1996–2005)
Annual inflation rate	29.3	8.9
Current account deficit (% of GDP)	13.1*	4.9

Source: World Bank and BOT statistics.
(1988–1995)

The broad money growth declined from 33% per annum in 1995 to 8.4% in 1996. This contributed to the drastic decline of inflation during Mkapa's term. Mkapa inherited from Mwinyi a fully liberalised exchange rate with no black market premium (Li and Rowe, 2007). So during Mkapa's term the Bank of Tanzania (BOT) managed the exchange rate in a market oriented manner. The BOT minimised exchange rate volatility and sometimes allowed smooth nominal depreciation so as to prevent the appreciation of the real exchange rate due to huge inflows of foreign aid and foreign investment (Li and Rowe, 2007). The nominal exchange rate growth rate was small during Mkapa's term.

Broad money growth rate and nominal exchange rate depreciation rate were on average lower during Mkapa's term; indicating tighter monetary policy and an already market aligned exchange rate (see Table 6).

Table 6: Average Broad Money Growth Rate and Nominal Exchange Rate Growth Rate

INDICATOR	MWINYI (1986–1995)	MKAPA (1996–2005)
Broad money growth rate	34.5	19.1
Nominal exchange rate growth rate	34.9	6.8

Source: World Bank statistics

President Mkapa's term is remembered for putting great effort on revenue collection. The Tanzania Revenue Authority was formed just prior to the general election in 1995 and Value Added Tax (VAT) was introduced in 1998. Revenue collection increased from 331,238 million Tanzania Shillings (612,587 USD) in the financial year ending June 95 to just over 2 trillion Tanzania Shillings in the year ending June 2006 (Just under USD 1.8 million). Budget discipline also improved due to the proper control of financial system. President Mkapa's government was even able to run a budget surplus (excluding grants from developmental partners) for the years 1995/96 and 1996/97. Deficit to GDP ratio (excluding grants) was high in years 2004/05 and 2005/06 due to an increase in development expenditure, the effects of a drought, pension payments and the general election (see Table 7). The Public Finance Management Reform Program (PFMRP I and II, 1998 and 2004) was an important public finance policy initiative during this period. The main aim of this policy was to reform and improve public finances and enable them to operate more efficiently in a market economy environment.

Table 7: Revenue and Budget Deficit During Mkapa's Term

INDICATOR	1994/95	1995/96	1996/97	1997/98	2004/05	2005/06
Revenue in TZS million	331,238	448,372.9	572,029.7	619,083.10	1,773,709.4	2,124,843.7
Revenue in USD*	612,587	772,775	952,176	967,453	1,626,137	1,796,862
Current revenue to GDP ratio	13.5	14.3	14.8	13.2	11.8	12.5
Deficit to GDP ratio (excluding grants)	-2.7	0.9	1.5	-2.4	-9.3	-10.3
Deficit to GDP ratio (including grants)	-0.3	2.4	3.6	0.2	-4.5	-4.4

Source: Bank of Tanzania, 2018. Current revenue is in millions of Tanzania shillings and the other figures (ratios) are in percentages.
*USD exchange rate obtained from the Bank of Tanzania, 2018

The overall lending interest rate declined significantly (36% (1995) to 15.2% (2005)) due to lower inflation, improvements in budget deficit, and the privatisation and restructuring of the banking sector. The savings deposit rate declined from 27% (1995) to 2.6% (2005) and the spread increased from 9% (1995) to 12.6% (2005). (see Figure 3)

Figure 3: Overall Lending Interest Rate, Savings Deposit Rate and Interest Rate Spread During President Mkapa's Term

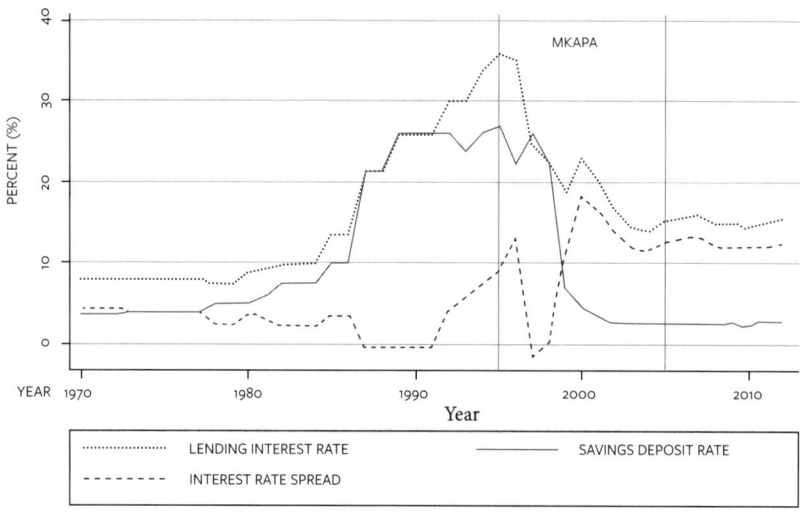

Source: The author's calculations from BOT and World Bank statistics

Thus, on average, nominal interest rates were lower during Mkapa's term while the spread was higher (see Table 8).

Table 8: Average Interest Rates and Average Spread

INDICATOR	MWINYI (1986–1995)	MKAPA (1996–2005)
Lending interest rate	26.3	20.4
Savings deposit rate	23.4	9.7
Spread	2.9	10.8

Source: BOT statistics.

One important phenomenon that characterised Mkapa's term was debt relief, which led to the cancellation of a large part of Tanzania's external debt. During his period Tanzania benefited greatly from the Heavily Indebted Poor Country (HPIC) initiative and the Multilateral Debt Relief Initiative (MDRI). As a result external debt stock (% of GNI) drastically declined from 143.7% (1995) to 60.7% (2005), total debt service (% of exports) significantly declined from 17.4% (1995) to 4.4% (2005) and total debt service (% of GNI) also declined from 4.4% (1995) to 0.8% (2005) (see Figure 4).

Figure 4: Total Debt Service and External Debt Stocks during President Mkapa's Term

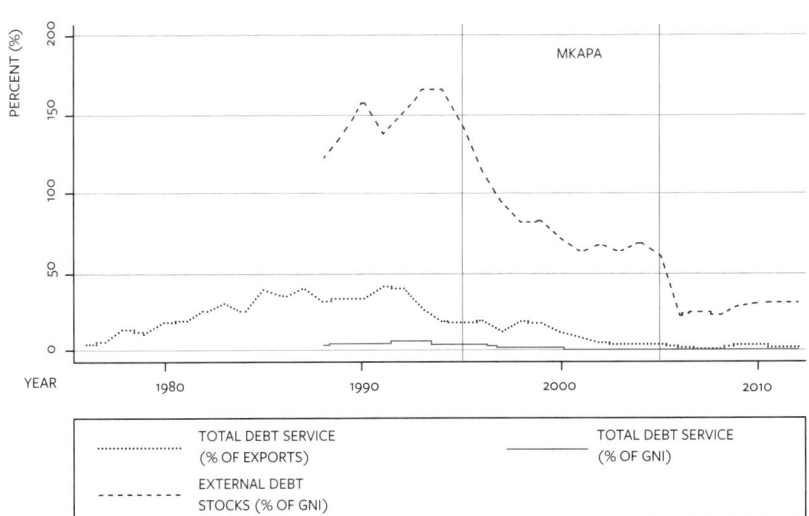

Source: IMF and World Bank statistics.

On average the debt indicators were better during Mkapa's term (see Table 9).

Table 9: Average Values of Debt Indicators

INDICATOR	MWINYI (1986–1995)	MKAPA (1996–2005)
External debt stock (% of GNI)	147.5*	76.5
Total debt service (% of exports)	31.5	10.6
Total debt service (% of GNI)	4.4*	1.8

Source: World Bank statistics.
*(1988–1995)

SOCIO-DEMOGRAPHIC AND GOVERNANCE INDICATORS

Demographics

When President Mkapa took office in 1995 the total population was 27.4 million. This had grown to 36.1 million by 2005; an increase in the population of about 31.7%. In 1995 the highest concentration of the population was in the age group between 15–19 years, being 20.1% of the total population, 5.6 million people. There was a slight increase in 2005 to 20.8%, being 7.5 million people.

Education

During Mkapa's term there were notable successes in primary education. The primary school Net Enrolment Ratio (NER) increased from 55.4% in 1995 to 94.8% in 2005. The Primary School Leaving Exams (PSLE) pass rate also increased from 21.3% in 1998 to 61.8% in 2005. The secondary school (Form I to VI) Gross Enrolment Ratio (GER) increased from 5.3% in 1995 to 11.7% in 2005. Form IV pass rates also increased (see Table 10). The tertiary education GER increased from 0.5% (1995) to 1.5% (2005). The major education policy initiatives during this period were the Education and Training Sector Development Programme (ESDP) (1997) and the Primary Education Development Programme I (PEDP I) (2001) (MoEC, 2001). These policies aimed to improve access to, as well as the quality of education, and in addition allowing more community and private sector participation in the education sector.

Table 10: Education Indicators During President Mkapa's Term

INDICATOR	1995	1996	1998	2001	2004	2005
Primary school NER	55.4	56.3	56.7	65.5	90.5	94.8
PSLE pass rates	*	*	21.30	28.60	48.70	61.80
Secondary school GER (Form I to VI)	5.3	5.2	*	*	9.4	11.7
Form IV pass rate (Division I-IV)	79.9	74.9	75.7	77.38	91.5	89.3
Form IV pass rate (Division I-III)	24.6	23.4	29	28.32	37.8	33.6
Tertiary education GER	0.5	0.5	0.6	0.7	1.3	1.5

Source: BEST and World Bank statistics. All figures are in percentages.
*Data missing for these years.

During the period of the Primary Education Development Programme (PEDP) I (which fell under Mkapa's term) we can see that the number of primary school students enrolled increased rapidly, many classrooms and pit latrines where built, many teachers were hired and the number of desks increased. The number of children per book and pit latrine pupil ratios decreased, the class pupil ratio slightly decreased, the pupil per desk ratio remained roughly constant, though the number of students increased. The teacher pupil ratio slightly increased (see Table 11).

Table 11: Other Education Indicators During President Mkapa's Term

INDICATOR	2001	2005
Number of primary school students*	4,881,588	7,541,208
Class pupil ratio	80	78
Children per book	20	3
Available desks	1,198,400	1,750,239
Pupils per desk	4	4
Available pit latrines	74,251	113,820
Pit latrine pupil ratio	65	66
Available teachers	105,921	135,013
Teacher pupil ratio	46	56

Source: BEST.
*In public and private schools.

Health

Health indicators also improved during President Mkapa's term. However, they still remained at unacceptably high levels. The National Health Policy (1990 and 2003) was the major health policy initiatives during this period (URT, 1990; 2003). These policies aimed at improving public health and also increasing community and private sector participation in the health sector (Table 12).

Table 12: Health Indicators During President Mkapa's Term

INDICATOR	1991	1995	1996	1999	2004	2005	2009
Stunting rate (under 5 years)	49.7	*	49.7	48.3	44.4	*	43
Wasting rate	7.9	*	8.5	5.6	3.5	*	2.7
Malnutrition rate	25.1	*	26.9	25.3	16.7	*	15.9
Maternal mortality ratio (per 100,000 live births)	*	*	612	*	*	605	*
HIV prevalence rate	5.8	7.7	7.9	8	7.2	7	6.2

Source: World Bank statistics. All figures are in percentages, except for maternal mortality ratio which is per 100,000 live births.
*Data missing for these years.

There was a significant decline in the under-five mortality rate followed by infant mortality rate and neonatal mortality rate during Mkapa's term. The under-five mortality rate declined from 157.6 (1995) to 92.4 (2005), infant mortality rate declined from 95.8 (1995) to 58.7 (2005) and the neonatal mortality rate declined from 36.2 (1995) to 26.2 (2005), (all per 1,000 live births). However, these indicators remained high. The success of anti-malaria programmes is one of the reasons for the decline in these child mortality rates (RAWG, 2005). On average child mortality rates were lower during Mkapa's term (Table 13).

Table 13: Average Child Mortality Rates

INDICATOR	MWINYI (1986–1995)	MKAPA (1996–2005)
Under-five mortality rate	165.4	125.3
Infant mortality rate	100.4	77.4
Neo-natal mortality rate	37.8*	31.2

Source: World Bank statistics. All per 1,000 live births.
*(1990–1995)

Life expectancy during Mkapa's term improved from 48.7 years (1995) to 55.6 years (2005). This improvement can be attributed to a number of factors including anti-malaria and anti-HIV and AIDS programmes, as well as improvement of social services such as health facilities and water facilities.

During Mkapa's term the government also invested in the water sector. Whereas the population slightly increased over 31% the percentage of population with access to improved water sources remained the same (54.2% to 54.7%) (see Table 14a). The National Water Policy (1991 and 2002) were the major water policy initiative during this period (URT, 1991; URT, 2002). The main aim of these policies was to increase household access to clean and safe water and to encourage community and private sector participation in the water sector. Mkapa's regime put great effort in road construction and road repair. The Tanzania National Roads Agency (TANROADS) was created in July 2000 to supervise and manage roads. From 2002 to 2005 total roads network (trunk and regional roads)[1] increased from 28,510 km to 28,892 km and paved (tarmac) roads network increased from 14.4% to 14.7% (see Table 14b).

Table 14a: Indicators of Access to Water

INDICATOR	1990	1995	2000	2003	2005
Improved water source (% of population with access)	53.9	54.2	54.4	54.5	54.7
Improved water source, urban (% of urban population with access)	91.6	88.7	85.9	84.1	83
Improved water source, rural (% of rural population with access)	45.2	45.2	45.3	45.4	45.4

Source: World Bank statistics

Table 14b: Indicators on Roads Network

YEAR	TRUNK ROADS			REGIONAL ROADS			TOTAL NETWORK			PAVED (%)
	PAVED (KM)	UNPAVED (KM)	TOTAL (KM)	PAVED (KM)	UNPAVED (KM)	TOTAL (KM)	PAVED (KM)	UNPAVED (KM)	TOTAL (KM)	
2002	3,856	6,078	9,934	245	18,331	18,576	4,101	24,409	28,510	14.4
2005	3,919	6,016	9,934	327	18,630	18,957	4,246	24,646	28,892	14.7

Source: TANROAD Data, 2018

---

[1] Trunk roads are roads the main roads connecting one region to another. For example, a road connecting Dar es Salaam to Morogoro, Iringa, Mbeya regions is a trunk road. Regional roads are the roads within a particular region.

Governance and the Rule of Law

The Afrobarometer[2] results show that the Tanzanian public had positive views on the way President Mkapa governed. About 90% (2001) and 94% (2005) of the Afrobarometer respondents said that they trusted the president (see Table 15). While 90% (2001) and 94% (2005) said that they were satisfied with his performance. The formation of the Presidential Commission Against Corruption ('the Warioba Commission' 1996), the launching of the National Anti-Corruption Strategy and Action Plan (NACSAP I, 1999), the strengthening of the Prevention of Corruption Bureau, and the strengthening of public procurement regulations were the important anti-corruption initiatives during this period.

However, satisfaction with the way democracy was working in Tanzania declined from 63% (2001) to 37% (2005); while support for democracy as a form of governing in Tanzania also declined from 84% (2001) to 38% (2005), and support for multiple political parties also declined. However, respondents recognised an increase in political freedom, the percentage of respondents saying they had never, or rarely, had to be careful of what they said about politics increased. The majority of the respondents were satisfied with the government's social policy performance as far as handling crime was concerned. However, satisfaction with the government economic policy performance in creating jobs remained low at 29% (2001) and 35% (2005). Satisfaction with macroeconomic conditions was similarly low. The number of respondents satisfied with their present personal living conditions was also low, though a higher percentage agreed that it was necessary for people to experience hardships now so as to enjoy a better economy in the future (economic patience in the table below). This showed that there was public support for the economic reforms being undertaken by Mkapa's government, despite the hardships that such policies caused (Afrobarometer Network, 2006).

---

2   A pan-African series of national public attitude surveys on democracy, governance, and society. www.afrobarometer.org

Table 15: Governance Indicators during President Mkapa's Term

INDICATOR	2001	2003	2005
Trust in the president	90	79	94
Satisfied with the performance of the president	90	85	94
Perceived corruption among national government officials	69	23	9
Satisfaction with democracy	63	63	37
Support for democracy	84	65	38
Support for multiple political parties		67	52
Political freedom (never/rarely being careful of what you say about politics)	9	39	22
Satisfied with Government economic policy performance (creating jobs)	29	39	35
Satisfied with Government social policy performance (handling crime)	64	57	69
Satisfied with present macroeconomic conditions	22	33	30
Satisfied with present personal living conditions	29	25	22
Economic patience	53	58	53

Source: Afrobarometer Network. All figures are in percentages.

CONCLUSION

President Mkapa's term undertook deeper economic reforms and improved economic regulation. There was sustained improvement in economic growth as well as macroeconomic stability. During this period Tanzania experienced growth acceleration. Health and education indicators also improved. Public trust in President Mkapa's term was high. However, there was a small decline in basic needs poverty rate. This led to the introduction of the National Strategy for Growth and Reduction of Poverty (NSGRP I) in 2005 so as to make growth more pro-poor. President Mkapa's term had many positive social economic achievements and it was during this period that the country started to experience the benefits of many of the post 1986 economic policy reforms.

REFERENCES

Afrobarometer Network (2006). Where is Africa going? Views From Below: A Compendium of Trends in Public Opinion in 12 African Countries, 1999-2006. Working Paper No. 60, Afrobarometer Network, South Africa.

Li, Y., and Rowe, F. (2007). Aid Inflows and the Real Effective Exchange Rate in Tanzania. Policy Research Working Paper No. 4456, World Bank, Washington, DC.

Muganda, A. (2004). Tanzania's Economic Reforms - and Lessons Learned. World Bank, Washington, DC.

Mwase, N., and Ndulu, B. J. (2008). Tanzania: explaining four decades of episodic growth. In Ndulu, B.J., O'Connell, S.A., Azam, J., Bates, R.H., Fosu, A.K., Gunning J.W., and Njinkeu, D. (Editors) (2008), The Political Economy of Economic Growth in Africa, 1960-2000, volume 2 (Case Studies) (pp. 426–471). Cambridge University Press, Cambridge. Nord, R., Sobolev, Y., Dunn, D., Hajdenberg, A., Hobdari, N., Maziad, S., and Roudet, S. (2009). Tanzania: The Story of an African Transition. IMF, Washington, D.C.

Nyerere, J.K. (1973). Freedom and Development. Dar es Salaam: Oxford University Press.

StataCorp (2009). Stata Statistical Software: Release 11.2. College Station, TX: StataCorp LP.

URT, Bank of Tanzania (2011). Tanzania Mainland's 50 Years of Independence: A Review of the Role and Functions of the Bank of Tanzania (1961–2011). Dar Es Salaam: Bank of Tanzania.

URT, Ministry of Education and Culture (2001). Education Sector Development Programme: Primary Education Development Plan (2002-2006). Basic Education Development Committee (BEDC), Dar Es Salaam: MoEC.

URT, Ministry of Education and Vocational Training (various years). Basic Education Statistics in Tanzania (BEST), National data. Dar Es Salaam: MoEVT.

URT, Ministry of Health (1990). National Health Policy. Dar Es Salaam: MoH.

URT, Ministry of Health (2003). National Health Policy. Dar Es Salaam: MoH.

URT, Ministry of Water, Energy and Minerals (1991). National Water Policy. Dar Es Salaam: MoWEM.

URT, Ministry of Water and Livestock Development (2002). National Water Policy. Dar Es Salaam: MoWLD.

URT, NBS (2009). Tanzania Household Budget Survey (2007). Dar Es Salaam.

URT, National Bureau of Statistics (2018). National Population Projections, National Bureau of Statistics Ministry of Finance and Planning Dar es Salaam and Office of the Chief Government Statistician, Ministry of Finance and Planning, Zanzibar, February 2018.

URT, RAWG (2005). Poverty and Human Development Report 2005. Dar es Salaam: Mkuki na Nyota Publishers.

URT, RAWG (2007). Poverty and Human Development Report 2007. Dar es Salaam: Total Identity Ltd.

URT, RAWG (2009). Poverty and Human Development Report 2009. Dar es Salaam: Mkuki na Nyota Publishers.

URT, (1973). The Economic Survey 1972–1973. Dar es Salaam.

URT (2005). The National Strategy for Growth and Reduction of Poverty (NSGRP/MKUKUTA). Vice President's Office, Dar Es Salaam.

Utz, R. J. (2008). A Decade of Reforms, Macroeconomic Stability, and Economic Growth. In Utz, R. J. (Ed.) (2008), Sustaining and Sharing Economic Growth in Tanzania (pp. 17–40). Washington D.C.: The World Bank.

World Bank Group, (2018). Official exchange rate (LCU per USD, period average). https://data.worldbank.org/indicator/PA.NUS.FCRF?locations=TZ

Photograph Credits

Cover Photo: Osse Greca Sinare

Photo 1–5: Property of author, photographer unknown

Photo 6: Original source unknown

Photo 7 and 8: Property of author, photographer unknown

Photo 9: William Janssens

Photo 10 and 11: Property of author, photographer unknown

Photo 12: William Janssens

Photo 13: Macocha Tembele

Photo 14: Property of author, photographer unknown

Photo 15: Tanzania Information Services (MAELEZO)

Photo 16: From 'The Nationalist', written by author

Photo 17: Original source unknown

Photo 18: Amin Mohamed/Camerapix/Getty Images

Photo 19: Tanzania Information Services (MAELEZO)

Photo 20: Original source unknown

Photo 21: Tanzania Information Services (MAELEZO)

Photo 22 and 23: Property of author, photographer unknown

Photo 24: William Janssens

Photo 25 and 26: Tanzania Information Services (MAELEZO)

Photo 27–29: Ombeni Sefue

Photo 30: Tim Sloan/AFP/Getty Images

Photo 31: Martti Kainulainen/Lehtikuva

Photo 32: Alexander Joe/AFP/Getty Images

Photo 33: Tim Sloan/AFP/Getty Images

Photo 34–38: Ombeni Sefue

Photo 39: Alexander Joe/AFP/Getty Images

Photo 40: Peter Macdiarmid/AFP/Getty Images

Photo 41: Stephen Chemin/Getty Images.

Photo 42: Eric Draper

Photo 43: STR/AFP/Getty Images

Photo 44: Vincenzo Pinto/AFP/Getty Images

Photo 45: Ombeni Sefue
Photo 46: STR/AFP/Getty Images
Photo 47: Mwanzo Milinga/AFP/Getty Images
Photo 48: Ombeni Sefue
Photo 49 and 50: William Janssens
Photo 51: Muhidin Issa Michuzi
Photo 52: Reuters/Emmanuel Kwitema
Photo 53: Simon Maina/AFP/Getty Images

Index

A

Accident, 125, 197
Accountability, 49, 135, 147–148, 172, 198
Achebe, Chinua, 31
Adams, Jim, 123
Aesop's Fables, 11
African-American, 37, 38, 75, 77
African Chiefs, 25
African middle class, 36
Africans, 14, 17, 21, 23, 24, 27, 31, 38, 41, 43, 122, 147, 170, 190, 192, 222, 225, 229, 233
African Union, 89, 186, 225, 226, 228, 238, 238
African Wildlife Foundation (AWF), 221
Aga Khan, The, 32, 43, 183, 184, 234
Agatha Christie, 30, 220
Ahtisaari, Martti, 125, 238, 254
Alfred Tennyson, 42
Algeria, 74, 89
Allegations, 171, 201, 212, 232
Andrew Marvell, 42
Anglican Church, 183
Anglican Missionaries, 20
Anglican school, 8, 9
Anglophone Africa, 47
Angola, 45, 66, 73, 89
Apologetics and Catholic Doctrine, 16
Arabs, 51
Armed forces, 51, 90, 95
Arusha Declaration, 50, 56, 59–62, 65, 155, 180, 289, 291
Asian community, 23
ASP (Afro-Shirazi Party), 72, 80
Atlanta, 37
Australia, 11, 66, 186

B

Babu, Abdulrahman Mohamed, 52, 58
BAE (British Aerospace plc), 211
Ballali, Daudi, 116, 120, 207
Bank of Tanzania (BOT), 120, 207, 296, 297, 298, 306
Baraza, 30
Bellevue Hospital, 44
Benedictine Fathers,
Benedictine Priests, 10
Benedictine Sisters, 10
Bérenger, Paul, 188
Bgoya, Walter, 106, 255
Blair, Tony, 124, 192, 211, 225
Blomjous, Bishop Joseph, 18,
Bouteflika, Abdelaziz, 74
British, 10, 11, 14, 18, 19, 21, 24, 31, 33, 38, 39, 40, 42, 51, 52, 75, 76, 79, 80, 89, 95, 124, 158, 176, 186, 189, 192, 211, 212, 215
British Council, 76
British Empire, 10, 87, 245
Buganda Kingdom, 36
Burundi, iv, 93, 190, 193, 251

Butiama, 70, 102, 103
Butiku, Joseph, 71
Byrne, Father Cyril, 22

C

Cambridge School Certificate Examination, 20, 26, 27, 29
Campaigns, 248
Canada, viii, 11, 82, 83, 84, 128, 237
Capital Markets and Securities Authority (CMSA), 296
Carrington, Peter, 80
Carnegie Institute, 44
Catholic Church, 1, 16, 17, 183, 214
Catholic Diocese of Arusha, 44
Catholic missionaries, 1
Catholic secondary schools, 20
Central Bank of Kenya, 34
Chagula, Wilbert, 32, 58
Chalker, Baroness Lynda, 121
Chama Cha Mapinduzi (CCM), vii, 72, 103
Chanji, Ambrose, 32
Charlotte Brontë, 42
Charles Dickens, 11
Chief Justice, 32, 50
China, 47, 52, 64, 76, 85, 123, 185, 202, 234, 242, 294
Chissano, Joaquim, vii, 74, 98, 125, 184, 185, 217, 225, 230, 254
Chitepo, Herbert, 243
Chokungokela, Damien, 55
Christians, 5, 6, 183
Chungu, Aloyce, 10

Clinic, The, 53, 72
Clinton, Bill, 124, 225, 236
Club de Madrid, 222, 230
Colonial Office List, The, 20, 21, 27, 28, 29
Columbia University, 43, 87
Commission for Africa, 192, 222, 233
Confirmation, 16
Constitution, 78, 79, 94, 99, 169, 170, 173, 199, 206, 215, 217, 235, 289
Corruption, 49, 105, 115, 121, 130, 131, 132, 137, 179, 202, 203, 204, 223, 290, 292, 304, 305
Crash, 111, 197
CRDB bank, 13
Cuba, 76, 187
Cuban Missile Crisis, The, 45
Cyprus, 44, 45

D

Daily News, The, viii, 24, 57, 67, 68
Dar es Salaam, 19, 21, 22, 26, 29, 32, 33, 43, 46, 48, 51, 53, 58, 62, 72, 79, 82, 85, 88, 91, 94, 95, 100, 111, 117, 125n105, 137, 138, 139, 141, 143, 144, 147, 159, 166, 171, 172, 177, 179, 181, 183, 189, 190, 193, 197, 209, 210, 211, 216, 220, 234, 237, 243, 245, 303, 306, 307
Dar es Salaam International Airport
Dar es Salaam Stock Exchange, 296
Davos, 170, 192, 193
de Guiringaud, Louis, 76, 77
Democratic Republic of Congo (DRC), 74, 190, 229

Index

Denmark, 123
de Soto, Hernando, 156, 215, 230, 231
Detention, 199
Development Vision 2025, 294
Director of Education, 32, 33
Dodoma, 41, 43, 80, 100, 103, 182, 183, 197, 211
Durning, Bishop Dennis Vincent, 44

E
East Africa, 28, 31, 34n11, 43, 95, 104, 183, 234
East African Community (EAC), 58, 66, 71, 189, 190, 225, 245
East African Development Bank (EADB), 202
Edna St Vincent Millay, 42
Emergencies, 197
Emily Dickinson, 42
Equal Opportunities for All Trust Fund (EOTF), 215
Europeans, 19, 21, 23, 24, 51
External Payments Account (EPA), 206

F
Facing A Volcano, 28, 34, 35
Federation of Malaya, 37
Finland, 123, 156, 238
Foley, Father Cornelius (Con), 22
Food and Agriculture Organization of the United Nations (FAO), 204
Foreign Service, 42, 43, 44, 45, 46, 49, 52, 84, 137, 149
Francophone Africa, 47

FRELIMO (Front for the Liberation of Mozambique), vii, viii, 48
Frontline States (for the liberation of Southern Africa), ix, 71, 73, 74, 89

G
Gambari, Ibrahim, 74
Garba, Joseph, 74
G8 Summit, Gleneagles, 192
Geldof, Bob, 192
Georges, Justice Philip Telford, 50
Germany, 10, 73, 123, 149, 238, 240
Ghana, 52, 238
Gilbert and Sullivan's '*The Mikado*', 18
Ginwala, Frene, 67
Globalisation, 144, 156, 157

H
Halonen, Tarja, 156
Heavily Indebted Poor Country Initiative (HIPC), 299
Herfkens, Eveline, 149
Hertz, Noreena, 215
Hindi, 23
HIV/AIDS, 164, 193, 236, 303
Holy Communion, 16
Holy Ghost Fathers, 21
Hoseah, Edward, 204
Hussein, Saddam, 77, 78

I
ICF (Investment Climate Facility for Africa), 222, 223, 224
Ifakara, 38, 110

Immigration, 203
Independence, iv, 8, 22–25, 31, 38–42, 49, 51–53, 64, 78, 79, 80, 103, 104, 135, 149, 162, 163, 181, 186, 187, 190, 201, 220, 222, 224, 226, 228, 229, 234, 238, 241, 244, 245, 249, 290–293, 306
India, 9, 22, 34, 125, 202, 204, 246, 294
Indians, 14, 19, 23, 24, 40, 51, 132, 203
Integrity, 2, 22, 25, 50, 201, 206, 214, 242, 246, 248, 249, 253, 253
International Conference of the Great Lakes Region (ICGLR), 190, 229
International House, 44
International Monetary Fund (IMF), ix, 105, 120–124, 141, 142, 152, 190, 191, 208, 238, 293–295, 299, 306
International Union of Students, 37
IPP Media Group, 206
Iraq, 77, 78
Iringa, 10, 21, 26, 183

J
Jamal, Amir Habib, 71
Japan, 34, 66
Joan Wicken, 54, 63, 71, 199
Jones, Dr., 32, 33
Johnson, Hilde Farfjord, 149
Judges, 174, 201
Judicial integrity
Judiciary, 50, 199, 201
Julius Caesar, 23

K
Kaduma, Ibrahim, 72
Kamazima, Anatory, 204

Kambona, John, 13, 23, 29
Kambona, Oscar, 46, 55, 62
Kampala, 28, 29, 36, 40, 91, 92, 182, 183
Kampala City Council, 40
Kawawa, Rashidi Mfaume, 41, 104
Kasindi, Mary Josephine (Jo), 25
Kassum, Al Noor, 71, 132
Kaunda, Kenneth (KK), 49, 225, 235
Kennedy, President John F., 45
Kenya, iv, 28, 31, 34, 51, 77, 93, 94, 125, 180, 193, 225, 245, 251
Kigonsera, 17
Kikwete, Jakaya Mrisho, 107, 117, 197, 205, 217, 218, 219, 222
Kilombero, 38
Kilosa, 38
Kiongozi, 55
Kitine, Hassy, 119
Kiula, Nalaila, 203
Kiwanuka, Benedicto, 31
Kiwira Coal Mine, 201
KLM, 210
Korogwe, 143
Köhler, Horst, 123, 191, 238, 254
Kufuor, John, 225, 238
Kumalija, Costa, 55, 255
Kunambi, Chief Patrick George, 24, 5

L
Lady Macbeth, 22, 23
Lake Victoria, 29, 167, 197
Lancaster House Agreement, 78
Leadership Code, 59, 69, 249
Legislative Council of Tanganyika (LEGCO), 24–25

Liberation, vii-viii, xi, 41, 46-48, 56, 57,66, 71, 72, 73-75, 79, 81, 89-91, 93-94, 184, 186, 187, 189, 191, 213, 228, 229, 238, 243, 244, 249, 254, 290
Live8 concerts, 192
Lord Byron, 42
Lubega, Matias, 44, 87, 93
Lupaso, 1, 2, 6-9, 15, 100, 101, 215, 220
Lushoto, 183, 215, 220
Lynch, Father James (Jamie), 22, 254
Lyons, Father Bartholomew (Bertie), 22

M
Macbeth, 195, 207
Machel, Samora, x, 97, 184, 184
Magani, Philip, 13, 29, 50
Mahalu, Costa, 204-206
Makame, Rashid, 67
Makarios III, President, 45
Makerere Freshman's Ball, 29
Makerere University College, 20, 23, 27, 28, 40, 50, 51, 58
Makua, 1, 4, 13, 15, 162, 175
Makwaia, Chief David Kidaha, 25
Malawi, iv, 28, 66, 67, 92, 160
Malecela, John Samwel, 116
Malinyi, 39
Mandela, Nelson, 47, 80, 194, 216
Mangula, Philip, 214
Mapunda, Gisler, 38
Mark Antony, 23
Martin, David, 213
Mataka, Gray Likungu, 5
Maruma, Chief John, 32, 50
Masasi, 1, 25, 26, 48, 82, 101

Masasi African Democratic Union, 25
Matwani, William, 1
Mau Mau, 31
May Day, 136, 144
Mazrui, Professor Ali, 31
Mbarali, 198
Mbilinyi, Prof Simon, 119, 120
Mbita, Hashim, 56, 172, 186
Mboya, Tom, 31, 32
McHenry, Donald, 75
McTiernan, Father Michael, 22, 23
Media, 11, 33, 53, 61, 67, 79, 98, 152, 153, 155, 158, 177, 183, 184, 193, 200, 209, 210, 211, 217, 227, 232, 242, 243, 250
Members of Parliament, 16, 106, 132, 155, 162, 163, 179, 200, 213, 215, 244, 250
Mengi, Reginald, 206
Mgonja, Gray, 120
Mining, 144, 145, 235, 295
Minister of Labour, 39, 60, 109, 146
Minister of Science, Technology and Higher Education, 33, 100
Ministry of Education, 19, 33, 306
Mkapa, Anna, 50, 56, 73, 82, 83, 84, 85, 100, 102, 111, 175, 184, 209, 214, 215, 216, 219, 220, 233, 238, 240, 255, 261-263, 265
Mkapa, Benjamin William, vii-ix, 164, 236, 292, 293-295, 297-305
    Surgery, 214
Mkapa, Bernard, 3, 5-9, 13, 19, 25
Mkapa, Blasius, 3, 7, 25, 102
Mkapa, Marcella, 3, 102
Mkapa, Nicholas, 68, 85, 184, 216, 240
Mkapa, Stephan, 68, 84, 216, 240

Mkatte, Bernard, 44
MKURABITA, 154, 156
Mogae, Festus, 235, 238, 254
Mogwe, Archibald (Archie), 74
Mondlane, Eduardo, vii, 48
Monks of St Ottilien, 9
Montgomery, 37
Morogoro, 26, 39, 62, 110, 132, 151, 197, 220, 303
Mozambique, iv, ix, x, 1, 45, 48, 66, 73, 74, 89–91, 97, 125, 151, 184, 225, 251
Mponji, Vincent, 10
Mramba, Basil, 152
Msekwa, Pius, 69, 218
Msuya, Cleopa David, 71, 107, 116
Mugabe, Robert Gabriel, 75, 78, 79, 80, 125, 186, 188, 191, 243
Mulokozi, Bernard, 149
Multilateral Debt Relief Initiative (MDRI), 299
Museveni, Yoweri, 33, 58, 88, 93–95, 125, 141, 190, 194, 225
Muslims, 5, 21, 67
M V Bukoba, 21, 103, 197
M V Mombasa, 26
Mwang'onda, Cornel Apson, 120, 182, 255
Mwinyi, Ali Hassan, 83, 98, 99, 100, 113, 115, 127, 138, 140, 219, 291, 293, 297

N
Nachingwea, 18, 48
Nagenda, John, 33, 254
Nairobi, 28, 43, 52, 93, 245

Nambanga, Stephania, 2, 4
Nambanga, Cyriaca, 4
Nambanga, Benjamin, 4, 5
Nambanga, Agnes, 4
Namibia, 75, 90, 125, 189, 238
Nation, The, 43
National Anti-Corruption Strategy and Action Plan, 304
National Agricultural and Food Corporation (NAFCO), 13, 139
National Housing Corporation, 151
National interest, 200, 237,
Nationalist, The, viii, 53, 55–59, 61, 63–65, 67–68, 123
National Ranching Company (NARCO), 13, 140
National Strategy for Growth and Reduction of Poverty, 154, 294, 305, 307
NBC Bank, 208, 209
Ndanda, 1, 2, 7–9, 11–13, 16–19, 21, 22, 26, 27, 29, 30, 101
Ndegwa, Philip, 34, 41
Neogy, Rajat, 30
NETGroup Solutions Ltd., 146, 147, 202
New Delhi, 204
New York, 33, 43, 44, 45, 84, 85
Ngombale-Mwiru, Kingunge, 119
Ngũgĩ wa Thiong'o, James, 31
Nigeria, viii, 11, 44, 71–74, 83, 125, 239
Njombe, 26
Nkane, Benno, 14, 29
Nkomo, Joshua, 75, 79
Nkrumah, Kwame, 52, 53

Nnauye, Moses, 119
Non-Aligned Movement, 85
Norway, 37, 123, 149, 236
Nsa-Kaisi, Kabenga, 55, 57, 59, 65, 120, 165, 255
Nyalali, Francis, 32
Nyerere, Mwalimu Julius Kambarage, vii, x, 125n105, 255
    President, vii, 20, 23, 46
    Resignation, 23

O

OAU Liberation Committee, 47
Obasanjo, Olusegun, 71, 72, 125, 229, 230, 239
Obote, Milton, 31, 88, 89, 94, 95
O'Connor, Father Liam (William), 22
Odinga, Jaramogi, 31
Ole Saibul, Solomon, 51
Ora et Labora, 7, 9, 16, 19, 121
Organisation of African Unity (OAU), ix, 46, 47, 52, 56, 85, 186n154
O'Sullivan, Father Liam, 22
Owen, David, 75
Oxford University Press, 43

P

Paris Club, 123, 124
Parliament, viii, 13, 16, 23, 36, 60, 67, 69, 82, 100, 101, 106, 113, 126, 130, 132, 150, 155, 158, 179, 200, 201, 211, 217, 235, 246, 249
Pastoralists, 39, 198
Peasants, 4, 103, 104, 135, 198

Penpoint, 31
Peramiho, 7, 17
Percy Shelley's 'Ozymandias', 42
PF-ZAPU, 79
P.G. Wodehouse's *'Jeeves and Wooster'*, 30
Phares, Mutibwa, 34
Political parties, 72, 79, 155, 174, 175, 180, 186, 206, 214, 229, 249, 251, 290, 304
    Opposition political parties, 47, 109, 110, 113, 120, 158, 168, 170–176, 201, 246, 248
Political Science, 31
Political Union for Keen Africans, 23
Port Bell, 29
Prerogative of Mercy, 198
President, ix, 13, 20, 23, 31–33, 39, 44, 45, 47, 49, 50, 53, 56, 57, 62–68, 72, 74, 77, 78, 80, 82, 85, 87–91, 93, 95, 96, 97, 99, 100, 102, 107, 108, 112, 115, 116, 118, 119, 122, 126, 127, 131, 141, 143, 148, 151, 152, 161, 165, 169–171, 173, 181–185, 189, 193–196, 198–201, 205, 206, 209, 210, 212–220, 226, 227, 232, 234, 235, 237, 239, 241, 242, 245, 246
Presidential Commission of Enquiry Against Corruption, 202, 304
Presidential powers
Presidential Salaries Review Commission, 150
Presidential term limits
Preventing and Combating of Corruption Bureau, (PCCB), 131n110, 204, 205

Prevention of Corruption Bureau (PCB), 204
Primary Education Development Programme, 165, 300, 301
Privatisation, 138–145, 147, 166, 201, 209, 291, 295, 296, 298
Property and Business Formalisation Programme (MKURABITA), 154, 156
Public Finance Management Reform Program, 297
Public Works Department, 14
Pukka, 23

Q
Q.E.D. *quod erat demostrandum*, 22
Qorro, Patrick, 106

R
Radar, 210–212
Radio Tanzania, 51, 53
Rhodesia, 28, 45, 53, 66
Rodgers and Hammerstein's 'The King and I', 18
Royal Technical College, 28
Ruhinda, Ferdinand, 57, 65, 70, 106, 111, 116, 255
Russia, 39, 47
Ruvuma, x, 1, 17, 184
Rwanda, iv, 93, 224, 251

S
Sadleir, Randal, 33
Saidi, Augustine, 50
Sanare, Melkizedeck, 120
Sanga, Charles, 141, 185
Schramm, Father Gereon, 19, 254
Sea View, 94, 209, 210, 218
Secrecy/Secret, 172, 199, 200
Semboja, Prof. Joseph, xi
Separation of Powers, 199
Sese Seko, Mobutu, 74
Shakespeare, 11, 22, 42, 195, 207
Shangali, Chief Abdiel, 25
Sheehan, Archbishop Michael, 16
Short, Clare, 149, 211
Simba wa Vita, 41
Sims, Hilary, 41, 44
Songea, 7, 26
South Africa, 45, 47, 66, 67, 74–76, 80, 90, 125, 146, 147, 177, 189, 197, 202, 238, 246
Southern African Development Community (SADC), ix, 152, 186, 188
Southern African Development Coordination Conference (SADCC), ix
Southern Rhodesia, 75, 78, 79, 90
Soviets, 76
Soviet Union, 52
Sozigwa, Paul, 56
STAMICO (State Mining Corporation), 202
St Andrew's College, Minaki, 20
State House, 55, 70, 114, 118, 136m 147, 172, 193, 201, 208, 209, 212, 215, 218, 234
Statutory powers, 201
St Francis College Pugu, 18–20
St Thomas hospital, 124
Student Representative Council, 32
Students' Guild, 32

Sub-Saharan Africa, 175, 201, 225
Sukuma, 39
Sweden, 123
Switzerland, 10, 214

T
Tabora Boys' Senior Secondary School, 20
TANESCO (Tanzania Electric Supply Company Limited), 140, 145, 146, 166, 183, 202
Tanganyika, 1, 10, 13, 17, 19, 20, 23–26, 28, 29, 31, 32, 34, 36–40, 43, 44, 45, 48, 51, 52, 104, 170, 213, 220
Tanganyika African Association (TAA), 23, 132
Tanganyika African National Union (TANU), vii, viii, 23, 25, 31, 32, 38, 39, 41, 55, 58–60, 6, 65, 75, 80, 289, 290
Tanganyikan Mission to the United Nations in New York, 44
Tanganyika Standard Newspapers
Tanganyika Students' Body, 32
TANU Youth League, 64
Tanzania, vii, ix, x, xi, xii, 1, 5, 13, 15, 32, 44, 47, 48, 50, 52, 56, 58, 60–62, 72–74, 77, 80, 82–84, 87–92, 94–96, 99, 100, 109, 113, 117, 122–128, 132, 141–143, 145, 147, 152, 154, 156, 159, 160, 164, 169, 171, 174, 176, 180, 182, 184, 185, 187, 188, 191–193, 197, 199, 201, 204, 205, 211, 212, 216, 220, 222, 223, 224, 227, 233–235, 238, 241, 243–247, 249, 250, 291, 292, 294, 299, 304, 305

Tanzania Buildings Agency, 151
Tanzania Constitutional Review Commission, 206
Tanzania Investment Centre, 296
Tanzania Mini Tiger Plan, 155, 294
Tanzania News Agency, viii
Tanzania Revenue Authority, 120, 130, 297
Tanzania Road Agency (TANROADS), 134, 303
Tanzania Zambia Railway Authority (TAZARA), 51
Tembele, Macocha, xii
Territorial Standard Ten National Exams, 19
Texas, 37
Thailand, 34
Thatcher, Margaret, 79
Thomas Hardy, 42
Tiscenko, Sonja, xii
TISS (Tanzania Intelligence and Security Service), 120, 182
TPDF (Tanzania Peoples Defence Forces), 181
Transition, 30, 31
Transparency, 109, 120, 123, 130, 132, 143, 201
Tunduru, 26

U
Uganda, iv, 20, 27–29, 31, 34, 36, 51, 85, 88, 89–95, 123, 125, 141, 183, 245, 251, 291
Uganda Argus, 30
Uhuru, viii, 55, 57, 59, 61, 64, 65, 67, 226

Ujamaa, 59, 133, 139, 291
Ukweli na Uwazi, 109, 120
Uluguru, 25
UNICEF, 56, 73, 82, 83, 142, 193
Unilateral Declaration of Independence (UDI), 53
Union of Soviet Socialist Republics (USSR), 75
Unitarian, 42
United Kingdom (UK), iv, 7, 10, 40, 50, 74, 75, 121, 123, 125, 149, 211, 212, 245, 248, 250
United Nations General Assembly, 74, 85, 124
United Nations Millennium Development Goals, 155, 294
United States of Africa, 53
United States of America (USA), 22, 37, 74, 82, 188
United States Information Agency, 33
United States Information Services, 76
University Students' African Revolutionary Front, 58
University of London, 28, 79
University of Zimbabwe, 79
Uongozi Institute, xi, xii

V
Value Added Tax (VAT), 130, 297
Vance, Cyrus, 75
Vietnam, 57, 64, 67

W
Warioba, Joseph Sinde, 103, 202
Wicken, Joan, 54, 63, 71, 199
Wielzorek-Zeul, Heidemarie, 149
Wolfensohn, James (Jim), 122, 141, 142, 191, 254
World Bank, ix, 105, 120–124, 126, 134, 141–143, 152, 160, 166, 190, 191, 208, 246, 292–303
World Commission of the Social Dimension of Globalisation, 156
World Economic Forum (WEF), 170, 192
World Health Organisation (WHO), 230
World War I, 11
World War II, 10, 11, 18

Y
Young, Andrew, 75

Z
Zaire, 71, 194
Zambia, 71, 73, 151, 234, 235
Zanzibar, 28, 33, 40, 51, 52, 81, 91, 100, 107, 108, 162, 168–170, 172, 173, 211, 216, 227, 235, 236, 251
ZANU-PF, 79–80
Zimbabwe African National Union (ZANU), 75
Zimbabwe African Peoples' Union (ZAPU), 75
Zimbabwe, 79, 80, 91, 125, 186, 213